The Future of
United Kingdom

Related Titles from Brassey's

CHANT
Air Defence Systems and Weapons: World AAA & SAM Systems in the 1980s

MASON
War in the Third Dimension: Essays in Contemporary Air Power

MYLES
Jump Jet: The Revolutionary V/STOL Fighter

Brassey's Aircraft, Weapons Systems and Technology Series

Volume 1
MASON
Air Power: An Overview of Roles

Volume 2
WALKER
Air-to-Ground Operations

Volume 3
ARMITAGE
Unmanned Aircraft

Volume 5
WALKER
Air Superiority Operations

Volume 6
CHAPMAN
Transport Operations

The forthcoming European Fighter Aircraft. The operational support version is shown here, flanked by two air defence variants. *(From a painting by Brian Finch, Air Clues Magazine.)*

The Future of United Kingdom Air Power

Edited by

PHILIP SABIN

BRASSEY'S DEFENCE PUBLISHERS

(a member of the Maxwell Pergamon Publishing Corporation plc)

LONDON · OXFORD · WASHINGTON · NEW YORK
BEIJING · FRANKFURT · SÃO PAULO · SYDNEY · TOKYO · TORONTO

U.K. (Editorial)	Brassey's Defence Publishers Ltd., 24 Gray's Inn Road, London WC1X 8HR
(Orders)	Brassey's Defence Publishers Ltd., Headington Hill Hall, Oxford OX3 0BW, England
U.S.A. (Editorial)	Pergamon-Brassey's International Defense Publishers, Inc., 8000 Westpark Drive, Fourth Floor, McLean, Virginia 22102, U.S.A.
(Orders)	Pergamon Press, Inc., Maxwell House, Fairview Park, Elmsford, New York 10523, U.S.A.
PEOPLE'S REPUBLIC OF CHINA	Pergamon Press, Room 4037, Qianmen Hotel, Beijing, People's Republic of China
FEDERAL REPUBLIC OF GERMANY	Pergamon Press GmbH, Hammerweg 6, D-6242 Kronberg, Federal Republic of Germany
BRAZIL	Pergamon Editora Ltda, Rua Eça de Queiros, 346, CEP 04011, Paraiso, São Paulo, Brazil
AUSTRALIA	Pergamon-Brassey's Defence Publishers Pty. Ltd., P.O. Box 544, Potts Point, N.S.W. 2011, Australia
JAPAN	Pergamon Press, 5th Floor, Matsuoka Central Building, 1-7-1 Nishishinjuku, Shinjuku-ku, Tokyo 160, Japan
CANADA	Pergamon Press Canada Ltd., Suite No. 271, 253 College Street, Toronto, Ontario, Canada M5T 1R5

First edition 1988

Library of Congress Cataloging in Publication Data

The Future of United Kingdom air power /
edited by Philip Sabin.
p. cm.
Includes index.
1. Aeronautics, Military — Great Britain. 2. Great Britain. Royal
Air Force. 3. Air power. I. Sabin. Philip A. G.
UG635.G7F88 1988
358.4'03'0941--dc19   88-2220

British Library Cataloguing in Publication Data

The Future of United Kingdom air power —
1. Great Britain. Air-power
I. Sabin, Philip A.G., *1959*–
358.4'00941

ISBN 0-08-035825-X Hardcover
ISBN 0-08-036256-7 Flexicover

COVER: A Tornado F3 interceptor of 29 Squadron RAF. *(Photo: John Upsall, Department of Public Relations RAF. Crown copyright.)*

Printed in Great Britain by A. Wheaton & Co. Ltd., Exeter

Contents

v

Acknowledgements

In addition to the authors who have contributed papers to this book, special thanks must go to Air Chief Marshal Sir Michael Armitage, who provided the initial inspiration for the conference upon which it is based, and to Professor Lawrence Freedman and Group Captain Marten van der Veen, the conference organisers. Professor Peter Nailor and Air Chief Marshal Sir Alasdair Steedman performed admirably as conference chairmen and invaluable assistance was given by Olivia Bosch, Wendy Everett, Jean Taylor and Iris Lacey.

For the provision of the photographs used as illustrations, I am particularly grateful to the Editor of *Air Clues Magazine*, British Aerospace and the Director of Public Relations RAF. Crown copyright material is published by kind permission of the Controller of Her Majesty's Stationery Office. Finally, thanks are due to the Royal Air Force, King's College London and Brassey's Defence Publishers and the many individuals and organisations who combined to make the conference a success and this book a reality.

P.S.

List of Plates

List of Abbreviations

AAA:	Anti-Aircraft Artillery
ACE:	Allied Command Europe
AD:	Air Defence
ADV:	Air Defence Version
AEW:	Airborne Early Warning
AIMSA:	Advanced International Military STOL Airlifter
ALARM:	Air Launched Anti-Radiation Missile
ALCM:	Air Launched Cruise Missile
AMRAAM:	Advanced Medium-range Air-to-Air Missile
AOC-in-C:	Air Officer Commanding-in-Chief
ASRAAM:	Advanced Short-range Air-to-Air Missile
AST:	Air Staff Target
ASTOVL:	Advanced Short Take-Off and Vertical Landing
ASW:	Anti-Submarine Warfare
ASUW:	Anti-Surface Warfare
ATAF:	Allied Tactical Air Force
AWACS:	Airborne Warning and Control System
BAOR:	British Army of the Rhine
BEF:	British Expeditionary Force
BVR:	Beyond Visual Range
C^3I:	Command, Control, Communications and Intelligence
CA:	Controller Aircraft
CAP:	Combat Air Patrol
CBI:	Confederation of British Industry
CDP:	Chief of Defence Procurement
CINCHAN:	Commander-in-Chief, Channel
CINCFLEET:	Commander-in-Chief, Fleet
CINCUKAIR:	Commander-in-Chief, United Kingdom Air Forces
CTOL:	Conventional Take-Off and Landing
CVSA:	Anti-submarine and Attack Aircraft Carrier
DCA:	Defensive Counter-Air
DMZ:	De-militarised Zone

x

DTI:	Department of Trade and Industry
ECM:	Electronic Counter-Measures
EEC:	European Economic Community
EFA:	European Fighter Aircraft
EW:	Electronic Warfare
FEBA:	Forward Edge of the Battle Area
FIMA:	Future International Military/Civil Airlifter
FLA:	Future Large Aircraft
FOFA:	Follow-on Forces Attack
GLCM:	Ground Launched Cruise Missile
HARM:	High-speed Anti-Radiation Missile
HAS:	Hardened Aircraft Shelter
HMSO:	Her Majesty's Stationery Office
ICBM:	Intercontinental Ballistic Missile
IDF:	Israeli Defence Forces
IFF:	Identification Friend or Foe
IISS:	International Institute for Strategic Studies
IR:	Infra-Red
IUKADGE:	Improved United Kingdom Air Defence Ground Environment
LRINF:	Long-Range Intermediate Nuclear Forces
LTM:	Laser Target Marking
MBB:	Messerschmitt Bolkow Blohm
MBFR:	Mutual and Balanced Force Reduction talks
MINIS:	Management Information System for Ministers
MLRS:	Multiple Launch Rocket System
MoD:	Ministry of Defence
MPA:	Maritime Patrol Aircraft
MSC:	Manpower Services Commission
NADGE:	NATO Air Defence Ground Environment
NAEW:	NATO Airborne Early Warning
NATO:	North Atlantic Treaty Organisation
NBC:	Nuclear, Biological and Chemical
NORTHAG:	Northern Army Group
OCA:	Offensive Counter-Air
PDMS:	Point Defence Missile System
PLO:	Palestine Liberation Organisation
R & D:	Research and Development
RAP:	Recognised Air Picture
RPV:	Remotely Piloted Vehicle
RUSI:	Royal United Services Institute for defence studies

RWR: Radar Warning Receiver
SAC: Strategic Air Command
SACEUR: Supreme Allied Commander Europe
SAM: Surface-to-Air Missile
SDI: Strategic Defence Initiative
SLCM: Sea Launched Cruise Missile
SRINF: Short-Range Intermediate Nuclear Forces
SSBN: Nuclear-powered Ballistic Missile Submarine
SSGN: Nuclear-powered Cruise Missile Submarine
SSN: Nuclear-powered Attack Submarine
STOL: Short Take-Off and Landing
STOVL: Short Take-Off and Vertical Landing
TA: Territorial Army
TBM: Tactical Ballistic Missile
TTW: Transition to War
TVD: Theatre of Operations
UKADR: United Kingdom Air Defence Region
UKAIR: United Kingdom Air Forces
USAFE: United States Air Force Europe
USN: United States Navy
V/STOL: Vertical/Short Take-Off and Landing
WP: Warsaw Pact

List of Contributors

Air Chief Marshal Sir Michael Armitage, KCB, CBE, RAF is now Commandant of the Royal College of Defence Studies. He became Air Member for Supply and Organisation in 1986, having previously been Deputy Chief of the Defence staff (Intelligence) in 1983 and the first Chief of Defence Intelligence in 1984. He is the co-author of *Air Power in the Nuclear Age, 1945–84,* and author of a volume in the Brassey's Air Power Series.

Vice Admiral Sir Benjamin Bathurst, KCB is Chief of Fleet Support, having been Director of Naval Air Warfare in 1982, Flag Officer Second Flotilla in 1983 and Director General of Naval Manpower and Training in 1985.

Air Chief Marshal Sir David Craig, GCB, OBE, ADC, MA, FRAeS, RAF took up his present appointment as Chief of the Air Staff in 1985. In 1978 he became AOC No 1 Group, and in 1980, Vice Chief of the Air Staff. Prior to his present position he was Air Officer Commanding-in-Chief Strike Command, and Commander-in-Chief UK Air Forces from 1982.

Air Marshal Sir Barry Duxbury, KCB, CBE, RAF took up his present appointment as AOC No 18 Group in 1986; he also fills the NATO appointments of Commander Allied Maritime Air Force Channel (COMMAIRCHAN) and Commander Allied Maritime Air Eastern Atlantic Area (COMMAIREASTLANT). He was Director General of Personnel Management in 1982 and Air Secretary in 1983.

Professor Lawrence Freedman has been Head of the Department of War Studies, King's College London since 1982. His many publications include *The Evolution of Nuclear Strategy, The Price of Peace* and *Arms Control: Management or Reform?*

Professor Ted Greenwood is an Associate Professor at the Institute of War and Peace Studies, Columbia University, and is the author of *Making the MIRV: A Study of Defense Decision-Making.*

Major General Charles Guthrie, LVO, OBE is now Assistant Chief of the General Staff. He was appointed the General Officer Commanding 2nd Infantry Division and North East District in

1986, having previously been Chief of Staff of the 1st British Corps in Bielefeld.

Air Chief Marshal Sir David Harcourt-Smith, KCB, DFC, FRAeS, RAF was appointed Controller Aircraft in 1986, having been Assistant Chief of the Air Staff (Operational Requirements) in 1980 and Air Officer Commanding-in-Chief RAF Support Command in 1984.

Professor Keith Hartley has been the Director of the Institute for Research in the Social Sciences at the University of York since 1982. His publications include *NATO Arms Co-operation: A Study in Economics and Politics.*

Mr Peter Levene was appointed Chief of Defence Procurement in 1985, having been Personal Adviser to the Secretary of State for Defence in 1984 and a Council Member and Chairman of the Defence Manufacturers' Association (1982–85).

Lieutenant General Thomas McInerney, USAF is a command pilot with 3700 flying hours, who has served in Berlin, Cuba and Southeast Asia. In 1981 he became commander of the 313th Air Division in Japan. From there he was assigned as Deputy Chief of Staff (Operations and Intelligence) at the HQ Pacific Air Forces in Hawaii, and in 1985 became Commander of the 3rd Air Force based at RAF Mildenhall, before his appointment as Vice Commander-in-Chief of USAFE.

Professor Sir Ronald Mason, KCB, FRS has most recently held the post of Chairman of Hunting Engineering, but before that was Chief Scientific Adviser in the Ministry of Defence (1977–83). He became Professor of Chemistry at Sussex University in 1971, and Pro-Vice Chancellor in 1977.

Air Vice Marshal Roger Palin, RAF, currently AOC No 11 Group, was Assistant Chief of Defence Staff (Programmes). He has been on four tours on fighter squadrons (in the UK, Cyprus, and Germany), and commanded RAF Wildenrath (1981–82). He was also at the Woodrow Wilson Centre on an academic sabbatical, and contributed to a Brookings Institution publication.

Lieutenant General Sir Jeremy Reilly, KCB, DSO was appointed Commander Training and Arms Director in 1986; before that he was Director of Battle Development in 1983 and then Assistant Chief of Defence Staff (Concepts).

Dr John Roper is the Editor of *International Affairs,* and head of the International Security Programme at the Royal Institute of International Affairs, Chatham House. He was a Labour and later

SDP MP from 1970 to 1983, including a period as front bench spokesman on defence, and is the author of *The Future of British Defence Policy.*

Dr Philip Sabin is a Defence lecturer at King's College London, and is the author of *The Third World War Scare in Britain: A Critical Analysis.*

Major General Perry Smith, USAF (Retd) is a fighter pilot with more than 3400 flying hours, who commanded the F-15 wing at Bitburg, Germany, and served as Deputy Chief of Staff for Operations at the 2nd Allied Tactical Air Force. He was Director of Plans in the Air Staff in the Pentagon during the first two years of the Reagan Administration before becoming Commandant of the National War College (1983–86). His publications include *Taking Charge: A Practical Guide for Leaders* and (with others), *Creating Strategic Vision: Long Range Planning for National Security.*

Dr Philip Towle is a Defence Lecturer at Queens' College Cambridge, and is the author of *Estimating Foreign Military Power* and *Arms Control and East-West Relations.*

Group Captain Marten van der Veen, RAF is the Director of Defence Studies at the RAF Staff College, Bracknell. From 1982 he was the Engineering Inspector of Flight Safety, and before this spent two years with the French Air Force in Paris.

Air Vice Marshal John Walker, CBE, AFC, RAF assumed his present post as Deputy Chief of Staff (Operations) at the Headquarters of Allied Air Forces Central Europe in April 1987. Much of his early career focused on tactical development of ground attack weapons and systems, and he has commanded RAF Lossiemouth and RAF Bruggen, both Jaguar bases. He was Director of Forward Policy, MOD, before moving to HQ UK Air at High Wycombe in 1985 where he was Deputy Chief of Staff (Operations and Intelligence). In 1986, he edited the proceedings of a Slessor Commemorative Symposium on *The Future of Air Power,* and he is the author of two volumes in the Brassey's Air Power series..

The Right Honourable George Younger, TD, PC, DL, MP, Secretary of State for Defence since January 1986, has not only been a Minister of State for Defence in 1974, but has seen service in BAOR and Korea with the Argyll and Sutherland Highlanders, and is an honorary Colonel in the Territorial Army and a member of the Royal Company of Archers.

Introduction

Perhaps this book's most important quality is its authority. There has been continued speculation about such issues as the survivability of manned aircraft or the vulnerability of fixed airbases in the face of advances in offensive and defensive weapon systems, but because of our lack of practical experience of high-intensity combat, no clear consensus on such subjects has emerged. The authors of the various papers in this volume are in the best possible position to give authoritative judgements on these issues since they include top-ranking professional officers and scientific experts with 'hands on' experience and access to classified information. There is, of course, no guarantee that their judgements will be without fault but those judgements undoubtedly carry more weight than those of many of the pundits who have pronounced on matters relating to air power in recent years.

A second strength of these contributions is that they represent the collective views of a mix of civilians and military men. Thus they combined the insight and professional authority which only the practitioner can provide with the readiness of the academic to ask awkward questions and to challenge government policy in those areas in which service officers (whatever their private views) might feel obliged to tread more softly. Important contributions in defence of the official line come from the top political figures responsible for that policy — the Chief of Defence Procurement and the Secretary of State for Defence himself. Most interesting of all are the exchanges between the various contributors, making the value of the volume as a whole even greater than the sum of its individual parts.

A third feature is that the book concentrates on *British* air power, rather than trying to provide a necessarily less comprehensive discussion of air power in a broader East-West or even global framework. That having been said, the complete integration of United Kingdom air power within the whole complex of NATO defence is clearly recognised. Two sections by distinguished American officers map out for us this broader context within which British air power will have to operate. Nor, as is sometimes the case, is the discussion limited to the contribution made by the Royal Air Force alone. Not only are the roles of Naval and Army aviation included but senior representatives of these two Services give their own (sometimes rather different) perspectives of United Kingdom air power as a whole.

The book manages not only to cover the broader political, economic and strategic issues which will shape decisions specifically affecting air power, but also includes considerable detail on the 'nitty gritty' of particular technical issues. Many earlier works on the subject have adopted a rather narrowly operational viewpoint but this volume includes comprehensive discussion of such topics as East-West relations, arms control and defence budgeting. Although these issues have implications reaching far beyond the confines of air power *per se*, they may exert a decisive influence on future air policy — thus they have been included here to make the discussion complete. However, these wider issues have not been allowed to preclude analysis of such detailed matters as what new weapons are required to attack airfields or the parameters of the Hercules replacement. A host of such in-depth discussions will be found in the later chapters.

Finally, and perhaps most important of all, there is the forward-looking nature of the discussion. This is implicit in the title but deserves emphasis because air power is such a rapidly changing field as technology advances, bringing new implications for the whole field of defence. Since any descriptions of the current situation quickly become dated, the various papers, having incorporated the latest state of play as at mid-1987, focus less on the present and immediate future and more upon the issues facing United Kingdom air power in the year 2000 and beyond.

The papers presented in this book were produced for a conference run by the Department of War Studies at King's College London in July 1987. Some could not be presented at the conference because of a postponement from its planned date. However, they have been included here to ensure as comprehensive a coverage as possible of all aspects of the air power issue. Group Captain Marten van der Veen, Director of Defence Studies, Royal Air Force, has kindly contributed a paper on air defence which he has specially written for this volume. The other papers have been edited and re-arranged to turn them from a simple record of the conference proceedings into an orderly analysis of the future of United Kingdom Air Power.

The Chief of the Air Staff, Air Chief Marshal Sir David Craig, opens the volume with an appraisal of the contribution being made today to the defence of Britain by the Royal Air Force. Thereafter, the book divides into two parts. The first takes its inspiration from Professor Sir

Michael Howard's famous article on 'The Forgotten Dimensions of Strategy'[1] and addresses the political, technological, operational and logistic aspects which he rightly identifies as critical to any strategic issue. Part Two then gets down to a detailed discussion of specific roles such as air interdiction and maritime strike operations, focusing particularly on the type and mix of air forces which Britain should maintain to enable her to fulfil those roles in the future.

In Part One, Professor Lawrence Freedman discusses the political background and the likely impact upon United Kingdom air power of changes in nuclear strategy in the wake of an INF agreement, while the Right Honourable George Younger speculates upon Soviet motivations and the prospects for conventional arms control. Professor Ted Greenwood then assesses the likely course of the East-West air battle to which United Kingdom air power would contribute and Air Chief Marshal Sir Michael Armitage draws out lessons from past experience, ranging from the Normandy Campaign to the United States raid upon Libya. Two views then follow on likely developments in technology and the way in which they should be pursued — one from former Chief Scientific Adviser to the Ministry of Defence, Sir Ronald Mason, and the other from Major General Perry Smith, with his experience of the highly secret 'skunk works' in the United States. Finally, Professor Keith Hartley predicts the need for hard economic choices and offers some thoughts on radical ways of facing up to these, while Peter Levene, Chief of Defence Procurement, outlines the cost-cutting measures already in train; Air Vice-Marshal Roger Palin then contributes a short response from the military point of view.

Part Two opens with discussions by Major General Charles Guthrie and Lieutenant General Sir Jeremy Reilly of battlefield air support as seen by the Service being supported. These are followed by a section by Air Vice-Marshal John Walker defending the concept of deep attack, even if it does seem less immediately comforting to the Army. Air defence is then discussed with General Thomas McInerney of the United States Air Force giving the big picture and Group Captain Marten van der Veen assessing the specific implications for the Royal Air Force.

Two neglected but important tasks come next with an analysis of the theatre nuclear role (likely to become increasingly important after the INF deal) by Dr John Roper, and Dr Philip Towle's discussion on air transport and out-of-area operations (whose importance was so clearly demonstrated during the operations in the Falklands in 1982). Part Two concludes with naval and air force views on the various aspects of maritime air power from Air Marshal Sir Barry Duxbury and Vice

Admiral Sir Benjamin Bathurst, followed by some further thoughts by myself on air transport and maritime air issues. Finally, Air Chief Marshal Sir David Harcourt-Smith draws together the threads of the discussion into a series of general deductions embracing the whole subject of the conference, and offers some conclusions of his own.

PHILIP SABIN
King's College London
1988

Note

[1]Michael Howard. 'The Forgotten Dimensions of Strategy', *Foreign Affairs*, Summer 1979.

CHAPTER 1

The RAF's Contribution Today

AIR CHIEF MARSHAL SIR DAVID CRAIG, GCB, OBE, ADC,
MA, FRAeS, RAF

It may seem anomalous to discuss the United Kingdom's air power at a time when the East/West climate appears so much more favourable. We recently celebrated 42 years without a major war in Europe; a peace which has been sustained by the combination of a unique alliance and a collective determination to maintain an adequate level of defence security. The road of this security has been a long hard one for us all, with periods of doubt and uncertainty. Keeping peace has not come cheaply and has had to be underwritten by peacetime defence budgets of major proportions. Today, new hopes arise as prospects for reductions in superpower arsenals appear to strengthen; but in the crucial field of defence there is never any scope for complacency. Caution must be the watchword of the wise.

Policy changes and political intentions should never totally replace a sober assessment of the threat potential we face. Capabilities take years to develop — or redevelop once they are lost or given up. Intentions on the other hand, as Afghanistan and the Falklands affair showed only too clearly, can change rapidly — and they are always difficult to predict. You may recall Moltke the Elder's warning to a group of officers on a staff ride: 'Gentlemen, when you examine any situation, you will usually find that your enemy has three courses of action open to him — and invariably he will choose the fourth'. So Vegetius' sage dictum, '*Si vis Pacem, para bellum*', is no less valid today than it was in the fourth century. A sound, sober and widespread appreciation of the capabilities and limitations of today's military forces remains essential to understanding their contribution to the preservation of peace in the freedom which we all hold dear.

While all forms of military force have a place in protecting our security, I want to concentrate on the RAF's contribution to our defences and on the importance we should attach to modern forms of air power. Air power is still a young child — a fledgling alongside its older brothers of sea power and land power — but a child with growing muscle and great potential. Air power has developed very rapidly, and its operational and tactical concepts are changing constantly as technology evolves. The developments achieved in the 25 years between the start of World War One and World War Two were astounding, even if technology could not deliver all that the early protagonists of air power had prophesied. But since the end of World War Two, there has been an enormous evolution in the capabilities of aerial forces. It is no longer possible to dismiss their fighting and deterrent potential solely by reference to their failure to deliver what was promised half a century ago.

Major advances in airframe and weapon systems design have been complemented by equally significant developments in air-delivered weapon technology. New 'smart' weapons have brought about dramatic reductions in over-the-target requirements. They have greatly increased the feasibility of destroying with reasonable effort previously difficult target systems such as bridges, C^3 facilities and airfields. Developments in air-to-air refuelling add a new strategic dimension to this. Precision attacks can now be carried out over very long ranges. Today there are no safe havens totally immune from air attack. We saw this in the Vulcan raids on Port Stanley in 1982, and in the United States F-111 attack on Libya just over a year ago. We see it in the long range deployments and simulated attack missions being mounted by Soviet aircraft all round North America and elsewhere overseas. The over-the-horizon diplomacy of force potential and projection, so effectively refined in previous centuries — the so called gunboat diplomacy — is being superseded by the potential to reach out from distant airbases at home, or from a friendly, but still distant, airfield overseas.

Developments in other elements of air power have been no less significant. In air defence, air transport and maritime air, for example, we are seeing great increases in mission effectiveness over comparatively short timescales.

These advances in weapon and platform performance brought about by the onward march of technology, and the equally significant developments in tactics and techniques that have complemented them, have been magnified by improvements in data transmission and storage and in information technology. The quality of our command and control — our ability to use real time information and direction of forces, surely one of the great 'force multipliers' — has been enhanced dramatically. The history of warfare shows that larger forces and more advanced weapons are rarely deciding factors; success goes to those who are able to use what they have to best effect. And today, air forces can be controlled and directed far better even than 10 years ago. Improved aerospace reconnaissance systems and rapid all-sensor fusion capabilities can give essential early warning and do much to disperse the fog of war. Command staffs at all levels are better able to maintain an accurate real-time picture of the developing battle. All this has produced a meteoric development of air power, and presages profound consequences for operational concepts and defence strategies.

What role then should such air power play today in our own conventional and nuclear deterrent strategy? By way of an answer, let us identify the nature of contemporary air power capabilities and examine their application to our deterrent stance. Political intent and strength of will, no less than military combat capabilities, affect deterrent credibility. The very high readiness of nuclear strategic systems plays a key part in signalling will and intent, but the various elements of air power also have important contributions to make in underwriting deterrence.

The first of these elements is threat intelligence. We want to know all we can about adversary intentions and warlike preparations. Constant surveillance of potential adversaries is called for. This not only guards against the possibility of strategic surprise, but also aids the decision-making process by providing substantive information on which to base our responses and counter-moves. An enemy's in-place air forces may generate rapidly, quickly increasing the threat level. Our own air forces should be able to respond to this without recourse to provocative deployments or full-scale mobilisation. So, even in peacetime, we must maintain high readiness states. Our air defence sensor systems are continuously manned. Flight times between Eastern Europe and the United Kingdom are a couple of hours. Probing flights or attacks could suddenly threaten us, and so elements of the Royal Air Force's Quick Reaction Alert air defence units — fighters and their supporting tankers and AEW aircraft — are held at a few minutes notice to scramble throughout the year. This is no idle commitment. Year in, year out fighters are scrambled to investigate non-NATO aircraft over the North and Norwegian seas well out from our shores, and to close-escort them if they show signs of approaching our territorial airspace.

It is a NATO and a national requirement that the major part of our air forces should be capable of being generated for sustained action within a very few hours of the order being given, and this ability is regularly and thoroughly tested in Tactical Evaluation Exercises. Indeed, the high visibility of air power exercises — and the level of expertise that they demonstrate — is in itself an important factor in the deterrent equation. Thus, during peacetime or in tension, air power provides crisis managers with a flexible and responsive tool to signal intent, determination and capability. This high positive gearing, which allows modern air forces to switch rapidly from a peacetime to a wartime footing within hours of an alert message, is a cardinal feature of modern air power and its contribution to deterrence.

Should deterrence, nevertheless, fail, air power would play a key role in regulating the escalation process below and, if need be, beyond the nuclear threshold. Because of its inherent responsiveness and mobility, air power allows appropriate firepower to be concentrated rapidly at the point — or points — of greatest need, without the more time-consuming preparatory and deployment measures characteristic of other types of military force. In strategic terms air power may favour the defender provided he is not overwhelmingly outclassed in the air. It recognises no boundaries, and an aggressor is less able to limit the war to areas of his own choosing. The defender from the outset could, if he wished, carry the fight immediately into the enemy's homeland. Air power, adequately deployed and prepared, denies an aggressor a low-risk strategy. If he attacks he must face up to the consequences of a far from limited encounter.

At the operational and tactical levels air power also contributes to deterrent credibility and fighting capability — either on its own, when it can be used swiftly to replace or redress other force imbalances, or in support of land or naval forces engaged in battle. It was tactical air power which gave the Western Allies the decisive edge over the Wehrmacht in 1944 and 1945. Subsequent examples of the decisive impact of air power on land force operations include the siege of Khe Sanh in 1968, the battle of An Loc during the North Vietnamese offensive of 1972, and the Golan Heights battle of the Yom Kippur War during the following year. In each of these engagements, the ability to concentrate aerial firepower proved the decisive factor in defeating the enemy attacks. Air power was effectively used as a substitute for manpower when the requisite ground forces could not be made available at the time they were needed. This ability of air power to act as an ultra-mobile source of firepower, unconstrained by topography, can be used either to exploit or to redeem the situation on land and has, of course, become a very important factor in NATO's operational philosophy.

If air power exercises a considerable deterrent and restraining effect in the land battle, its role in maritime warfare could be as great. In World War Two, Taranto, Pearl Harbor, the loss of the *Prince of Wales* and the *Repulse*, the sinking of the *Tirpitz* and the whole Battle of the Atlantic underlined the unmistakable lesson that aircraft had become indispensable partners of surface warships and submarines in maritime warfare, a partnership which the Falklands Conflict of 1982 only served to re-affirm. Command of the sea has for many years now been impossible without command of the air.

This growth in the importance of air power has not gone unnoticed by the Warsaw Pact and is reflected in the present Soviet all-arms philosophy. The massive Warsaw Pact armoured forces have long been recognised as posing the most significant non-nuclear threat to Western Europe and, in the past, the other Warsaw Pact arms appeared to be designed solely to support an armoured land offensive. Air forces were structured to provide direct and indirect support for the armoured thrusts, while the main task of naval forces was to interdict the reinforcement routes so crucial to a sustained NATO defence. Warsaw Pact doctrine still envisages using massed armoured forces to carry the conflict into enemy territory at the outset. The high concentration of echeloned forces and the increasing use of night vision equipment are clearly intended to maintain the momentum of the advance under all circumstances. However, in recent years, the Soviet view of air power has undergone something of a metamorphosis.

The reorganisation of Soviet Air Forces over the past decade has created five offensively orientated strategic air armies, of which three have been equipped mainly with Fencer and two with longer range bombers. This development, linked as it was to the reorientation of Warsaw Pact tactical air forces to broader theatre objectives, increased significantly the Pact's military options. Soviet doctrine now emphasises operations in great depth using highly mobile systems. In his book *History Teaches Vigilance*, Marshal Ogarkov, the Commander-in-Chief of the Western TVD, explains that in view of recent increases in the range and power of highly mobile weapon systems, it is possible to decide military operations through their use. Any war in the near future, he says, 'will acquire unprecedented spatial scope and encompass entire continents and ocean expanses'. The Soviet Union's strategic and theatre capabilities are growing, and it is now capable of mounting flexible and highly effective power projection missions.

In assessing the significance of these developments, it is important to remember that NATO is a purely defensive alliance and must therefore be capable of reacting effectively to aggressor initiatives. The credibility of NATO's deterrent posture will depend on the potential aggressor's perceptions of our ability to withstand his initial attack, regain the initiative and if necessary exact retribution. NATO land forces are heavily outnumbered and short of some form of NATO-wide conscription or arms control agreement there is little prospect of redressing this imbalance in the foreseeable future. The quantitative imbalance in the air is little better. The current Warsaw Pact superiority over NATO in tactical aircraft in the Central Region of over two to one equals its superiority in main battle tanks. However, numerical superiority has never been the decisive factor in aerial warfare. Of far greater significance are the qualitative factors, and it is important to recognise that in this field the Soviets have also been making important gains. Technological advances have allowed the Soviets to produce highly capable aircraft such as Fulcrum, Flanker and Backfire, thereby eroding the West's qualitative edge. This process has been exacerbated by Soviet efforts to introduce more demanding and realistic training to enhance the operational standards of all Warsaw Pact aircrews. This growing capability in the air poses an increasingly formidable aspect of the total threat and one which, if left unmatched, could adversely affect the stability of the East/West conventional military balance.

What then is the RAF's contribution to ensuring this balance of forces is maintained and hence to preserving the security of the United Kingdom? The Royal Air Force, in terms of combat aircraft, is the largest of the Western European air forces, even though it ranks but third in personnel strength. Our capabilities span virtually the full extent of the air power spectrum, and we undertake more roles than any other European air force. We have a nuclear as well as a conventional capability. We have overland and maritime roles, we provide mobility and other support for our sister Services, and, of course, we have a major investment and capability in the offensive and defensive counter-air roles. As a Service, we contribute to all four pillars of British national defence policy and to the UK's out-of-area capability.

Our Tornado GR1s and Buccaneers contribute in both their nuclear and conventional roles to the deterrent stance of our defence policy. They bridge the gap between other conventional forces and our strategic nuclear submarines. They permit governments to threaten appropriate responses to varying degrees of aggression. A nuclear capability at this sub-strategic level enhances the credibility of our deterrent to any form of nuclear attack. The ability to be able to launch an aircraft with a nuclear weapon, against a theatre or tactical target, is an invaluable means of demonstrating resolve without immediately facing the prospects of surrender or escalation to a strategic exchange. However, it is beyond the scope of my subject to delve deep into nuclear philosophy. Suffice it to say that it will be very important to the credibility of Britain's deterrent strategy to ensure that our theatre nuclear forces remain viable.

Closer to home, the air defence of the United Kingdom base is a major and most important role for the RAF. The successful defence of the United Kingdom as our homeland is self-evidently close to the hearts of all Britons. But the defence of the United Kingdom as a base is also of paramount importance to NATO. Thanks to geography, the United Kingdom is strategically placed as a forward base for NATO forces operating in the Eastern Atlantic and North Sea, a main base for operations in the Channel and on the Northern Flank and a support base for British and trans-Atlantic forces operating on the mainland of Europe. Hundreds of NATO aircraft, including one third of the Central Region's offensive air assets, and a substantial portion of NATO's nuclear systems would be based here during wartime. We are the host country for large numbers of national and NATO communication facilities, and we accommodate a variety of headquarters for senior NATO commanders, such as CINCHAN and CINCUKAIR.

All this means that the United Kingdom would be an essential objective for enemy attack during wartime. Although we cannot rule out pinprick operations by enemy special forces and terrorists, the English Channel will dictate that major direct military action against our country must rely on air and sea power. A maritime blockade would face considerable odds and could not be sustained without air superiority and a significant victory on the continent of Europe. However, concentrated and accurate air attacks on key installations would have an immediate and devastating effect on our contribution to NATO. Hence, the crucial importance of the air defence of the United Kingdom to deny an aggressor this option.

Modern air defence is a complex and interactive chain with many separate but essential links. These links include early warning sensors, airborne missiles, fighter interceptor aircraft with their own radars, and surface-to-air missiles of varied range and capability. Activities like air-to-air refuelling to sustain the reach and endurance of fighter patrols, and linkage with neighbouring air defence systems to alert us to approaching air attacks are further requirements. Also vital is the protection of airfields, ground radars, control stations and other supporting facilities, by both passive and active means, to allow us to sustain our own efforts under actual attack. And to make it all work, we need the capability to store and pass vital information and command and control instructions between the many elements.

Air defence is a reactive business, so air defenders always start as Black on the chess board. In the 1960s and the era of NATO's tripwire strategy, the United Kingdom air defences were structured and operated to give no more than adequate warning to allow time (before the enemy attacks were pressed home) to launch nuclear strikes against the aggressor. Our peacetime capability was geared solely to policing the airspace around and over the United Kingdom. The adoption of the strategy of flexible response and the need to provide ourselves with defence against sustained air attacks without immediate recourse to nuclear weapons led to a whole new approach to United Kingdom air defence. Our concept has been to provide a layered defence in depth by using complementary systems to achieve the best overall capability. We are currently upgrading, substantially, every single link of our air defence system, with the prime emphasis being placed on increased firepower, sustainability and survivability.

Defence in depth should take us all the way from passive protection of the likely targets right out to attacking enemy bases from which their bombers mount their raids. However, let me leave to one side for the moment the offensive counter-air aspects of this defence in depth and concentrate on our approach to the purely air defence issues.

The main outer layer of our air defence (once enemy aircraft have penetrated or skirted around continental-based defences) is provided by the RAF's all-weather fighter force. For some years F4 Phantoms have provided the majority of this force. However, the Tornado F3 is now set to play an increasingly important role, and the seven squadrons planned will form the backbone of our all-weather fighter force well into the next century. We are augmenting this all-weather fighter force by using armed Hawk combat trainers in the day fighter role. In exercises the Hawks have shown themselves to be a valuable adjunct to their heavier all-weather cousins, particularly in countering mass air raids. We are also integrating available naval anti-air warfare vessels in our outer layers of defence. However, we still need a highly agile fighter in our force mix, hence the air staff requirement which the European Fighter Aircraft (EFA) is designed to meet.

Supporting our fighter forces, and providing the inner layers of defence, we have medium and short range surface-to-air missiles —

Bloodhounds and Rapiers — and an Auxiliary RAF Regiment squadron equipped with the 35 mm Oerlikon/Skyguard system captured during the Falklands War.

Developments in firepower are being matched by improvements in the resilience and capacity of our air defence control and reporting system. Of key importance to effective air defence in depth and against the threat of low level intruders is airborne early warning. Not only does it provide warning of attack well beyond the range of ground sensors, it can also fill gaps in coverage, particularly at low level, and give redundancy to the ground environment; it allows us to provide better support for naval forces at long range from our shores; and it also has a part to play in our out-of-area capability. In sum, it offers flexibility, mobility and reach, the key elements of air power.

We are acquiring a force of E-3s to replace our stalwart Shackletons in this role, and they will be fully integrated with the new Improved United Kingdom Air Defence Ground Environment (IUKADGE) which features greatly increased survivability, system redundancy, flexibility and interoperability. Consisting of a network of transportable radars, controlled from hardened and filtered sector operations centres, IUKADGE will be linked with adjacent air defence systems such as NADGE and the French system, STRIDA. Information from naval ships and civilian and military air traffic control radars will also provide inputs to ensure the most complete and comprehensive air picture.

Another essential task has been to enhance our sustainability. Weapons and other stocks have been increased, but sustainability is not merely a question of providing the maximum amount of consumable items that can be afforded. More important, it is the business of ensuring that the total resources in terms of aircraft, weapons, equipment, personnel and support are in proper balance to achieve the best effect with the resources available.

The effectiveness of fighters and AEW aircraft is greatly enhanced by air-to-air refuelling. In the last three years we have acquired VC10 and Tristar tankers which will add greatly to our fuel offload capability. Availability of aircrew to meet intensive rates of operation is another crucial factor. We have introduced systems to pull back quickly into the front-line aircrew officers holding ground staff appointments. Because of this, aircrew availability should not constrain the high rates of effort we must be prepared to mount. These are just a couple of examples of the many steps we are taking to 'fine-tune' our sustainability.

Then, there is survivability. An air defence system can hardly guarantee to destroy all of the attacking aircraft all of the time, so if it is to continue in operation, it must be capable of surviving attacks. Our main and forward operating fighter bases are being provided with a wide range of passive defence measures including hardened aircraft shelters, hardened and filtered personnel shelters and command centres, protected fuel supplies, rapid runway repair capabilities, decoys, visual tone-down and measures to reduce infra-red and radar signatures. Comparable passive defence measures are also being built into the key control centres, while off-base dispersal plans have been drawn up to improve the survivability of tanker and AEW aircraft.

But all of this would be unlikely to serve us well without the right arrangements for command and control. Over 10 years ago, as we perceived the need for closer integration of European air forces if we were to extract the maximum effort in the face of attack, we took steps to move more closely into NATO's command structure. The majority of United Kingdom-based RAF aircraft were assigned to NATO at an early stage in the formal alert process and the senior four-star operational RAF Commander (AOCinC Strike Command) became one of SACEUR's four major subordinate commanders as CINCUKAIR. Today, a major part of Strike Command's own assets would be transferred to SACEUR's operational command at an early stage in crisis (indeed the air defences I have been describing are under SACEUR's operational command in peacetime every day and hour of the year), and much of the rest of Strike Command's capability would be transferred in crisis and war to the other two major NATO Commanders. With its key responsibilities for air defence of the United Kingdom base, UKAIR plays a crucial role in our national contribution to deterrence and to security in the Northern and Central Regions of the European continent. The latest development (just recently approved by Parliament) has been the agreement to introduce an element of international staff into UKAIR. The contribution which officers from other NATO countries will make to refining our air power efforts in ACE will be most valuable, and the new arrangement helps to underline the solidarity of the Alliance and the key integrated role that air power has to play in its security.

While recognising the importance of the direct defence of the United Kingdom base, this alone will not lead to victory. In the final analysis, only offensive action can restore ground lost to an aggressor. As Napoleon was fond of telling his Marshals: 'He who remains in his trenches will be beaten!' In the Falklands conflict, the denial of Port Stanley airfield to high-performance combat aircraft, and the implied threat to Argentine mainland air bases compelling them to keep air defence fighters in reserve, were major factors in achieving a marginally favourable air situation for the subsequent land/air and sea/air battles, and hence to our success. A favourable air situation is of key importance to the prosecution of all forms of warfare against a sophisticated enemy, and never more so than when one is outnumbered on the ground.

Keeping the enemy air off the army's back is the first obligation that any air force has to its sister service. Operational evaluation studies and experience are at one in suggesting that the most effective way to achieve this would be through an offensive counter-air campaign. The RAF's Tornado GR1 force, armed with the new JP233 airfield denial weapon, would be particularly effective in this role and would play a crucial part in establishing a favourable air situation. The bulk of our Tornado GR1 force — two Wings — is based in Germany, forming the hard core of the RAF's contribution to the European pillar of British defence policy. But despite the overriding need to establish a favourable air situation, and the key importance that offensive counter-air would play in this task, it would be quite unrealistic to believe that the armies could be left to fend for themselves until the air forces had won the air battle. NATO land forces will need air support from the outset of any conflict, and this is the designated task of the RAF's Harrier and support helicopter forces — the second strand of our forward deployment on the Continent.

Given the dense mass of air defences in the Central Region, the utility of operating NATO fixed wing tactical aircraft in the close air support role has from time to time been questioned. Attrition inflicted on our aircraft by intact air defences could indeed be significant, although experience in recent Middle East wars suggests that effective defence suppression drastically limits aircraft losses. In any case, attrition in isolation means little; much more important is the exchange ratio of losses sustained versus damage inflicted. By this criterion fixed wing aircraft with their heavy weapon loads and superior mobility remain highly cost effective. They would be essential in helping to counter the gravest danger in the ground battle: the sustained breakthrough by enemy armoured forces.

Helicopters would also play an important part in this type of operation. However, we must not forget that the larger the support helicopter types (with greater conspicuousness and less tactical manoeuvrability), the less threatening the air environment they need if they are to be viable. Indeed, no helicopter operations of any kind could be mounted without thought being given to other elements of the air battle. Thus, although tasked for the support of ground forces, and therefore responsive to the needs of the land force commander, the effective operation of helicopters will depend on them being as closely linked to the air battle as they are to the land battle. Failure to recognise this fact could have disastrous consequences, particularly for those forces reliant on the largest types of support helicopters.

The role of tactical air power in creating a benign air environment is only one of several roles identified for air forces in the land/air battle. Interdiction, or NATO's Follow-on Forces Attack (FOFA) concept, is another most important contribution that air forces make. FOFA would be directed to break up the momentum of any future Warsaw Pact thrust into NATO territory by disrupting the forces echeloned in depth behind the front. Although the enunciation is new, the concept is in effect the classic air power role of interdiction by another name — a role in which air forces have long exercised primacy. The sealing of the approaches to the 1944 D-Day beachhead by allied air attack is one of many historical examples of this, and the combination of reach, flexibility and hitting power achieved in the intervening four decades have made today's tactical fighter bomber the FOFA instrument *par excellence*. Clearly we must exploit this advantage to the full, capitalising on the very significant investment in tactical air power that has already been made.

Turning to the maritime pillar of British defence policy, it is well known that, in war, a sustained defence by NATO would rely heavily on transatlantic resupply and reinforcement. Over a million men, many hundreds of aircraft and ships, nine million tons of equipment and a million tons of ammunition are earmarked for this, the lion's share of which must come by sea. As I have said, losing control of the airspace over the reinforcement routes would have disastrous consequences. However, even with a favourable air situation, Soviet submarines could pose a major potential threat. They must, therefore, be placed under counter-threat at the earliest possible opportunity and for this, a multi-layered forward maritime defence strategy is needed.

NATO submarines and surface ships with helicopters are important parts of the force mix needed to counter this menace, but they may not always be in the right place at the right time — hence the importance of maritime patrol aircraft. The RAF's Nimrods combine speed of response with long range and good endurance, extended when necessary by air-to-air refuelling. Equipped with very advanced avionics and armed with Stingray torpedoes, Nimrod is a flexible and highly effective anti-submarine warfare system. When fitted with Harpoon anti-ship missiles, it can also be used to attack surface vessels,

PLATE 1.1. The real future of the Royal Air Force: junior officers at RAF
Cranwell. *(Crown copyright.)*

supplementing our Buccaneers which are being fitted with more
advanced avionics and the new Sea Eagle anti-ship missile. Nimrod and
Buccaneer, together with assigned RAF air defence assets, form an
effective maritime air team whose operations are today fully integrated
with those of naval forces. The co-location of the Headquarters of the
RAF's No 18 Maritime Group with those of CINCFLEET ensures the

closest cooperation between air and naval forces — a factor essential for success in modern maritime warfare.

While NATO tasks must obviously have first call on our resources, we still retain other responsibilities outside the NATO area. This aspect of the United Kingdom's defence policy represents an important and demanding commitment for the Royal Air Force. We provide forces for the defence of the Falkland Islands and Belize, and we also retain units in Hong Kong and Cyprus. We have staging facilities in various parts of the world that enable us to discharge our wider out-of-area responsibilities.

Whether in or out of the NATO area, hallmarks of air power are range, payload and speed of reaction. VC10 and Tristar tankers are greatly increasing our fuel offload capability, and all the RAF's fixed wing operational aircraft will soon be capable of taking on fuel in the air. This is not only giving us greatly increased reach, but also enhances our ability to react speedily to events in remote areas. The collateral increase in our air transport capability — enhanced by the advent of Tristars with their large payloads — adds a further boost to our power projection capabilities. Exercise SAIF SAREEA, which took place in Oman in November 1986, demonstrated our growing ability to move ourselves and support our sister Services over great distances, a development underlined by the record breaking non-stop flight from the United Kingdom to Perth, Australia in April 1987 by a VC10 of 101 Squadron. It is a measure of this capability growth that we are now able to deploy non-stop a parachute brigade together with its ground support, as well as a fighter squadron, over strategic ranges, and to airdrop the leading battalion group.

Although I have dealt with each pillar of the United Kingdom's defence policy individually, it would be very wrong to give the impression that the RAF's contribution to each of the four pillars and to the out-of-area capability is separate and compartmentalised. The reach and speed of events in the air, and the interactions between air power and land or naval power mean that modern warfare must be treated in all respects as an integrated and joint undertaking. Similarly, the interaction between each of the pillars is considerable. For the Royal Air Force their boundaries merge and overlap, forming the 'seamless robe' referred to in successive Defence White Papers.

The modern United Kingdom defence equation resembles a matrix in which the horizontal and vertical factors are brought together to provide the optimum defence solution. The pillars of which I have spoken represent a vertical perspective of this defence matrix, but there is an equally relevant and important horizontal aspect. United Kingdom air power forms the major horizontal spar of our defence matrix, spanning as it does all roles and affecting virtually every type of capability. Consequently, the level of interaction and interdependency between the various air power roles is itself a factor of major importance which demands a sound understanding.

This form of flexibility comes in many guises. For example, our Tornados are dual-capable and with modern conventional weapons might best be used on interdiction or offensive counter-air (OCA) targets. However, we could switch them to close air support if the situation of our ground forces demanded it. Similarly, although the primary tasks of our Harriers are close air support and battlefield air interdiction, they can also be armed with Sidewinder missiles, and so could play a part in an air-to-air engagement, as indeed they did in the Falklands conflict. The Harrier GR5, which entered service earlier this month, will have double the range/payload capability of its predecessor, the Harrier GR3, and will have the potential to take part in interdiction and some OCA tasks.

Our United Kingdom Tornado F3 and Phantom all-weather fighter squadrons are assigned for United Kingdom and naval air defence, but they might be used also elsewhere to reinforce an area's air defences or to provide 'top cover' for attack force packages. If required, maritime Buccaneers could be targeted against land targets, Tornado GR1s with AIM9s could be used to supplement air defences, and Hercules transports could be employed as tankers or for maritime radar reconnaissance. Air forces based in the United Kingdom or Central Region could be used to support operations in one of NATO's geographic regions, and then be retasked on the same day for missions in another. The permutations for the employment of air power today are vast, and the ability to 'tailor' air operations rapidly to meet the prevailing operational or tactical needs is an asset of the highest value and importance in our defence against aggression.

The thrust of technological advance, favouring the development of multi-role aircraft such as EFA and the Future Large Aircraft, is likely to increase further this capability to switch direction and roles. The ubiquity, flexibility, speed of response and the hitting power of air forces compared with other forms of military force is set to grow even stronger in the years to come. However, in recognising this tremendous potential and the increasing opportunities that it creates, two cautionary factors must be borne in mind.

First, while being ready and able to respond to prevailing conditions, we must avoid being seduced into operational opportunism. A myriad of employment options may be on offer, and we will need to have a clear understanding of our own operational priorities and limitations and have a mature air power doctrine on which to base our decisions. At the top of this doctrinal priority list must be the need to fight to establish a favourable air situation at the earliest opportunity, for failure to do this will lead inevitably to defeat not only in the air but ultimately on land and at sea as well.

Secondly, it will be essential to keep firmly at the front of our minds the reality that although air power is an amalgam of roles, these are by their very nature interactive and interdependent. Air power in the round is far greater than the sum of its constituent parts. Air power can only be properly understood and effectively employed if it is treated as a single integer. Thus, although it is quite valid to conceptualise in specific capability areas — anti-armour warfare, air defence, anti-submarine warfare and so on — we must never, whilst doing this, lose sight of the overall air power perspective.

It should be a concern to us all that although air power issues have been much in the news recently, the general level of the debate has often been disappointing. Air power is an elusive concept to grasp, and many of the current contributions to the air power debate show a lack of understanding of its precepts and characteristics. Yet, because air power *is* exercising an increasingly dominant influence over all types of operations, it must play a role of growing importance in our national security in future years. It is most important, therefore, that every effort is made to foster a sound and widespread appreciation of its uses and abuses and of its strengths and limitations.

PART ONE

Air Power in Context

CHAPTER 2

The Political Dimension

THE STRATEGIC CONTEXT
Professor Lawrence Freedman

With the notable exception of the nuclear area, where traditional forms of air power may be enjoying a revival, air power is now essentially a critical element of military power in general rather than something quite separate. This point is only worth making by way of introduction because of the approach of the early air power theorists. Their arguments were distinguished by overstatement of the bomber's potential to 'get through', plus an exaggerated expectation of the political consequences should it do so. This was part of an effort to demonstrate that air power could be decisive on its own and so, in turn, to justify the development of a new, autonomous military service.

The old arguments about autonomy and decisiveness have now been fought and won and there is no need to return to them here. The theories associated with nuclear deterrence remain one of the most important legacies of that early thinking and that is one reason why I shall spend some time with them. Before moving on to the nuclear area, I will attempt to put the discussion in an even broader political context. I will conclude by considering the implications of the continuing mismatch between British defence commitments and British defence resources.

We were reminded during the 1987 election campaign that the period of peace enjoyed by Britain, and Western Europe in general, since the last world war is unprecedented, and is now comparable to the best decades of the Victorian and Edwardian eras. This remarkable regional stability was attributed during the campaign to the magnificent caution that the prospect of nuclear war induces in our statesmen. However, without neglecting the contribution played by nuclear deterrence, we can add the division of Europe into two ideologically-opposed armed camps. The establishment of this rigid alliance system had much to do with the fear of nuclear war, especially during the first decade and a half. It was also the product of the skilful application of American largesse that helped prevent Europe's liberal democracies from succumbing to post-war economic and political chaos. Since then it has become institutionalised.

This curious equilibrium created the conditions for economic revival followed by a period of sustained prosperity. It would have been amazing if the economic growth of the fifties and sixties could have continued indefinitely. What is surprising and important is that, despite the various shocks of the seventies and eighties, there has been no sign of the sort of calamitous slump that would threaten the internal cohesion of our societies.

Everything that follows in this paper presumes that the political stability and vitality demonstrated by the Western democracies over the past few decades has not been merely the fortuitous result of an aberrant period of economic good fortune, but rather reflects deep-seated strengths that can be expected to endure. Whatever the individual upsets that must occasionally afflict individual countries, the overall political stability of the main Western countries is, at least in a negative sense, the dominant feature of this stage in our continent's long search for security.

One can add that one of the most significant shifts since the late 1940s has been the decline of Marxism in its many variants as an alternative philosophy for the organisation of modern industrial societies, and the movement of liberal capitalism on to the ideological offensive. The improvement in our security has been further reinforced by the successful reconciliation of traditional enemies within the Western sphere — most successfully with France and Germany; though less successfully with Greece and Turkey.

To complete this optimistic picture, there has been the simplification of the continent's security problems as a result of the dismantling of the Empires and all that they entailed in terms of overseas bases and colonial campaigns. The quarrels of the post-colonial world still affect Europe, especially when they threaten oil supplies or intensify the conflict between the United States and the Soviet Union. So we are not free of external security problems. Nonetheless, the most important problems are internal to Europe. They can really be narrowed down to the dangers inherent in sharing a continent with a militarily powerful but economically suspect totalitarian state.

The current approach to regional security can be traced directly to traditional British concerns with regard to a European 'balance of power' — the prevention of a single European state being able to exercise hegemonic control over the continent. The wars of this century made it clear that Britain herself, even with her natural (and sometimes unnatural) allies, was incapable of regulating continental politics and maintaining a balance without the help of the United States. The great achievement of post-war diplomacy was to convince the United States that she had continuing responsibilities for European security.

Europe's post-war stability has depended on bringing in the power of the United States to balance the indigenous power of the Soviet Union. This has been so successful that war itself seems unthinkable in the foreseeable future and many can even wonder whether the exceptional measures of the forties and fifties were really needed to stabilise the situation in the first place. If the mechanisms held to be so essential to European security were quietly dismantled, would anyone notice the difference?

While few might go that far, in many ways the critical themes in the security debate that is already underway, and can be expected to develop over the coming years, revolve around whether we still require those once exceptional measures that have since become institutionalised — a large-scale American military presence in Europe, backed by nuclear threats.

The answer from the current set of governments in Western Europe has been orthodox and unambiguous. These measures are as necessary as ever. They wish to sustain an essentially satisfactory status quo, characterised by the close connection between American military might and the defence of Europe and by the doctrine of nuclear deterrence. If it works, don't fix it.

Their opponents are found on both sides of the Atlantic. They include conservative American geopoliticians, who view the American subsidy to NATO as an extension of welfarism, with the same deleterious effects on the self-regard of the recipients, and who believe that if only the Europeans were obliged to look after themselves, they would soon learn to appreciate the good things in life such as SDI, aid to the Contras and intervention in the Persian Gulf. Then there are left-wing Europeans who see the American bases as a means for dragging us into a global confrontation with the Soviet Union against our better judgement. American strategists complain that NATO has failed to do any of the things necessary to meet the defence requirements we have set for ourselves. European protesters fear that, at the first sign of trouble, the American President would rush for the nuclear trigger.

NATO governments may feel that they have successfully resisted these challenges up to now but they have hardly been defeated; nor can it be precluded that the champions of these challenges will come to hold high office in member countires. Their future will depend not only on the vagaries of the political process but also upon the evaluation of the costs of the current system. These costs are:

1. A divided Germany, at the heart of a divided continent.
2. The persistence of Soviet hegemony and political repression in the East.
3. The continuing dependence on the United States of proud European states, with their long traditions (of varying degrees of honour) and now comparable economic prosperity.
4. Dependence on nuclear deterrence, despite the many strategic, political and ethical objections to this policy.

The extent to which these costs are acceptable and will continue to be so is the stuff of political controversy. From an historical perspective it would be surprising if they were to be found acceptable in perpetuity. We are obliged to question the durability of security arrangements based on the domination of the continent's affairs by two superpowers – so named largely because of this domination — when their relative power, vis-a-vis those in their notional spheres of influence, has declined.

For how long can we expect the United States to expend substantial resources on the defence of a group of countries of equivalent wealth and, at least for the moment, rather more balanced budgets? In particular, for how long can we expect the United States to accept a degree of exposure to nuclear risk that would otherwise be absent because of the commitments made by an earlier generation of statesmen at a time when the United States enjoyed a comfortable margin of strategic superiority?

If a continuing American commitment along established lines cannot be taken for granted, for how long can the leading West European states continue to follow policies that only make sense if that commitment remains? Their dilemma is that the more they work on the assumption that they cannot rely on the United States the more they risk this becoming a self-fulfilling prophecy. Washington might welcome, with relief, evidence that the Europeans had at last grown up and were capable of looking after themselves. But have the Europeans developed a capacity for independence in their security arrangements until they are sure that this will be more than mere posturing?

In Eastern Europe, the restructuring according to the Soviet model of those societies taken by the Red Army at the end of the last war has failed to take root. One-party state socialism has proved to be neither authentic nor efficient. The lack of authenticity has led to a series of national challenges to Soviet hegemony over the years — East Germany, Hungary, Czechoslovakia, Poland — that have been contained through the application or threat of brute force. It is doubtful whether the application of brute force will be as straightforward for the Soviet leadership in the future as it was in the past. Nor will it be as easy to buy off dissatisfied populations with economic inducements. The system cannot deliver. The cumulative inefficiencies of the Soviet system have begun to tell — to the point where the new Soviet leadership is seized with the need for urgent and drastic remedial action.

It is hard to believe that economic reform within the Soviet Union can be pursued for long without considerable political upheaval. The Communist Party may be able to control these pressures at home but will find it more difficult to control the more explosive pressures within the Warsaw Pact, where there is the added ingredient of frustrated nationalism. Few scenarios for a breakdown in European order find it necessary to look much beyond Eastern Europe for a flashpoint.

If they do look beyond Eastern Europe, they tend to look to the Gulf, where Western interests must be protected in circumstances of high political turbulence. It is no longer as easy to assume, as it once was, that most trouble in the world can be traced to Moscow. Recent events in the Gulf, where the rationale for American intervention appears to be to offer help to a country that would otherwise look to the Soviet Union, hardly fit the conventional pattern. In the Iran/Iraq war, the superpowers' sympathies are with the same side, and we now have other examples where the Soviet Union finds itself as much a victim of the perplexing political currents that swirl around the Third World as are Western countries.

There remain areas where Soviet activism is hostile to Western interests but the fears of the 1970s of a steady build-up of Soviet power in the Third World can now be seen to be exaggerated. Our most pressing problems in these regions, and in particular in the Middle East, is how to cope with political leaders and movements who see the world through completely different eyes and refuse to accept the views of industrialised countries with regard to the proper rules of the international game.

As a result of all of this, the current political situation is fluid, without tending clearly in any particular direction. There is probably more uncertainty at the moment than there has been at any time since the 1940s, but while such uncertainty might be expected in principle to argue for new policy thinking, in practice there is little to be done but wait for a greater clarity. The key states are beginning to hedge, to explore alternatives and to canvass new political relationships. This is all very tentative; however, there is always the possibility that the process could acquire a dynamic all of its own and force the premature revision of policies, before the position becomes much clearer.

So there is no vivid sense of what an alternative security system might look like, nor any criteria by which we might judge whether an alternative was in some ways 'better', and certainly no compelling strategies for managing the transition from the status quo to something better. Drift rather than design seems the more likely route. The next decades will therefore require some feats of political adjustment as we begin to map out the lines of a new security system.

In the absence of clear political indicators for the future, it is natural that we should concentrate on the military indicators, especially those that are the most politically sensitive. This is most evident with nuclear policies, the twists and turns of which are often held to reveal more fundamental political intentions which might otherwise remain unstated.

Before considering the 'hidden agenda' of nuclear policy, let us examine the problem of nuclear deterrence on its own terms. At the centre of the debate is the explicit threat to initiate nuclear war by way of compensation for conventional weaknesses. This is a pressing problem in strategic logic because of the incredibility of such a threat in the face of equivalent nuclear strength. It is less pressing in practice, for there is no evidence that in contemporary international affairs the deterrent effect is anything other than robust.

There are very good reasons why one nuclear power faced with another will hesitate. However, even though the two nuclear arsenals might be expected to neutralise each other, so that any conflict could proceed uninhibited at the conventional level, it would be hard to be confident that hostilities could be so confined. Once war has begun, no matter what the promises of peacetime with regard to 'no-first-use' or the evident irrationality of 'first-use', first-use there could well be. Even with substantial disarmament, the residual arsenals will be at levels sufficient to cause horrific devastation should they be unleashed, even if 'civilisation as we know it' survived in some form and we were not condemned to a perpetual winter. In this way, nuclear deterrence will continue to exercise a powerful and important restraint on international behaviour for some time to come.

Moreover, even if we moved away from the presumption of 'first-use' we should not underestimate the importance of the 'second-use' threat.

The debate on 'extended deterrence' has been to some extent distorted by the apparent European requirement for the United States to threaten first-use in the face of the Warsaw Pact's conventional superiority. However, non-nuclear countries also rely on the United States to provide a *retaliatory* threat on their behalf. While this does not raise the issue of having to prepare to initiate nuclear war, it still raises the issue of having to be prepared to deter such a war on behalf of a third party.

This is an example of the sort of political issue that lies behind decisions on nuclear capabilities, doctrines, dispositions and arms control proposals. The peacetime commitments made through nuclear policies, and upon which non-nuclear countries aligned to the West rely, come to be challenged in the attempt to resolve the inherent contradictions of strategic doctrine.

It is one thing to draw attention to the possibility that one might do irrational things in circumstances conducive to irrationality; it is another to plan irrationality. The story of strategic thought of the past two decades — 1987 marks the anniversary of MC14/3 (the flexible response document) — is one of an attempt to inject some credibility into a patently incredible commitment. So long as war was considered (as it should be) a reasonably remote possibility, this need not have mattered. References to a capability for mutual assured destruction made the relevant point in an unequivocal fashion. So long as that was recognised as a possible, even if not likely, outcome of war there was little incentive to start one. A vague, instinctive sense that any future war would be catastrophic for all concerned sufficed. It was not necessary to enter into a detailed analysis of the mechanisms whereby this sound instinct might be ignored.

However, a nuclear stalemate might favour the bold and ruthless. What would happen with an attack organised on wholly conventional lines that could not be stopped without resort to nuclear weapons? Even worse, what would happen if the adversary devised forms of nuclear attack that would not in themselves bring about massive destruction but would nonetheless leave the victim shocked, militarily paralysed and politically submissive? Those who took such questions seriously argued the need to develop nuclear options that would mean that should deterrence fail, there would be responses available to Western leaders which enabled them to avoid the fateful choice between suicide or surrender. If that choice could not be avoided, the argument continued, then deterrence must fail as our enemies exploited our fear of utter destruction, gaining their political objectives without the need to escalate to all-out nuclear war, or possibly to fight at all.

This sort of argument gathered in strength during the 1970s. It was fortified by evidence of ambitious nuclear thinking and capabilities to match in the Soviet Union, awareness of the potential of the new technologies of precision guidance, surveillance and command and control, and the political anxiety brought about by the steady deterioration in East-West relations, despite the early hopes of the détente years.

The start of the Reagan Presidency represented the high point of influence for those of this way of thinking. It was claimed that relations with the Soviet Union were irredeemably conflictual, and that military policy had no choice but to follow this pattern, rather than hope for something to turn up in arms control. But help was at hand. Nuclear options could be developed to ease the risk calculus of this and future Presidents.

One of the most profound strategic developments of the 1980s has been the consummate failure of this approach. It has failed for two reasons that could have been, and were, anticipated beforehand. First, whatever the private assumptions of political leaders, their public stance cannot be one of unqualified hostility to the Soviet Union without any prospect of remission, and with an attendant prescription for intensive arms racing. It is necessary to hold open the prospect of better relations, obtained through diplomacy and negotiation. Moreover, if the rationales for policy depend on an adversary conforming to a demonic image then it may start to unravel should the adversary start to take on a warmer, more conciliatory, appearance.

Secondly, the effort to develop credible nuclear options floundered. There were technical problems, especially with such areas as command and control; political problems in convincing Congress to purchase sufficient quantities of the M-X missile, which was to have been the workhorse of the new strategy; intellectual problems in demonstrating how selective nuclear strikes could actually be implemented without uncontrolled escalation, or how an approach so dependent on *mutual* control of nuclear operations could fit in with a targeting policy designed to undermine the enemy's capacity to exercise control to the point where the political authorities might not survive to agree a cease-fire or call a halt should one be agreed. From the Nixon years onwards, the moves away from mutual assured destruction have been least controversial when presented in terms of denying the Soviet Union the means of initiating nuclear war rather than developing such means for the United States — in terms of *countervailing* rather than *prevailing*.

By the spring of 1983 this failure had become apparent. This led to what became the second stage of the Reagan strategic policy — the Strategic Defence Initiative (SDI). It has been suggested that a lot of time could be saved by conducting the debate on SDI through a simple reference system. Every conceivable argument for and against has by now found its way into print and become extremely familiar. Simply by shouting out a number, one might be able to avoid dreary repetition of well-rehearsed points. I propose here to avoid even coded references to the arguments. SDI has told us a considerable amount about the strategic philosophy of those who thought it up and promote it, but it tells us absolutely nothing with regard to the future strategic balance. The grandiose schemes currently being explored at such great expense will die with the Reagan Presidency, though no doubt research will linger on. However else we deal with our nuclear dilemmas, we will not be dealing with them through large-scale active defences. At most, such defences will provide *additional* protection for key military assets: it is doubtful whether much will happen even in this direction.

This brings us on to the third and current stage in the Reagan Presidency, which received its most dramatic manifestation at the Reykjavik summit of October 1986. This is more likely to have lasting effects. This stage has involved the rediscovery of arms control and its promotion in a radical form. Unlike SDI, where the President was unable to convince either adversary or ally that he was talking much sense, arms control reflects principles which are widely accepted, though not always more clearly thought through, and are now being pursued with a Soviet leadership just as radically disposed. While SDI itself may impose a blockage on strategic offensive arms control until 1989, the work already done means that the next President could well be able to move to a 'deep cuts' regime within months of taking office. Before then there is reason to expect a 'double zero' agreement, which will see the removal of all land-based missiles with a range between 500 and 5500 kilometres, and which will make a profound change to the European strategic landscape.

Before discussing the larger strategic issues raised by the move towards arms control, it might be useful to consider some of the more specific implications of the prospective agreements. The logical extension of a double zero agreement, should it actually be concluded over the coming months, is a treble zero — that is to remove all shells for nuclear artillery and Lance missiles on the NATO side, and the artillery, Frogs and SS-21s on the Soviet side. Given the disparity in numbers, the West would not be the loser in such a deal. The problems would be in verification.

The official view is that we should oppose such a development as another stage on the slippery slope of 'denuclearisation'. My view is that we would be unwise to cling on to every bit of nuclear kit, however uncertain we are about its military utility or the cost and likelihood of modernisation, in the belief that this was the last stand for nuclear deterrence. The argument that we should make no moves towards the treble zero until such time as we have agreed conventional and chemical disarmament seems to me to have no merit whatsoever. I will argue presently that the problems with nuclear deterrence can be viewed quite separately from those of conventional forces. If we stay with the double zero then the risk is that the whole burden of 'coupling' the United States strategic capabilities with the defence of Europe will be expected to fall on the battlefield systems which are really not suited for this role. One of the reasons why some commentators who might have been expected to enthuse over the first zero option, were wary about it from the start was because they saw an opportunity with the introduction of the longer-range cruise missiles to reduce dependence on the short-range battlefield systems, which were seen to carry much higher risks of premature nuclear escalation and to give too much encouragement to some of the wilder concepts of limited nuclear war.

A more promising approach is to stress what is known as the 'vertical firebreak'. Essentially, this means that while all the ballistic nuclear systems are being rolled up in the Geneva negotiations, the dual capable air systems are to be protected and even improved. There is no doubt that there is a sufficiency of nuclear capability bound up with these aircraft to ease concerns over denuclearisation. It may be ironic that the manned aircraft has the last laugh over the ballistic missile simply because it is less susceptible to arms control!

Greater reliance on nuclear-capable aircraft will involve difficulties. The INF modernisation was prompted in the first place by concerns over the expected life span of the longer range F-111s and Vulcans (the latter having now, of course, been removed). The question of the replacement of the F-111s by a system of equivalent range could become controversial, presuming that such a system was available. (It is most likely to be achieved by using the F-15 with a stand-off missile.) Supplementing the F-111s with B-52s will be more controversial still. Then, there are the long-standing questions arising from dual capability, born of the fact that it will be difficult to hold aircraft back as a nuclear reserve when they will be desperately needed in the conventional battle.

The offence-defence duel will also become much more critical. The conventional wisdom, to which I still subscribe, used to be that defences had more chance against aircraft and cruise missiles than against ballistic missiles. There have been some suggestions that this is changing in that the SDI technologies will make ballistic missiles increasingly vulnerable to interception while stealth technology is going to do wonders for aircraft penetration. I find it easier to believe the second of these propositions than the first. Moreover, substantial investments in air defences have been made and, if only for the conventional battle, further investment in air defence can be expected by both sides in the future. It might also be worth noting the advantages of geography enjoyed by the Soviet Union when it comes to protecting key civilian targets from air attack — at least when compared with the vulnerable eastern seaboard of the United States.

The risk, therefore, is that if the vertical firebreak is taken too far — as envisaged in current American proposals to abolish *all* ballistic missiles — then we have created the conditions for a qualitative arms race in which we would no longer have the certainties of the missile age. The risk is greater with strategic weapons than intermediate systems and in the end the vertical firebreak is likely to stop with F-111s and Backfire. However, this indicates the need to think through the implications of some of the more radical arms control ideas before rushing to put them on the negotiating table.

Events since October 1986 have generated a certain amount of alarm in Western Europe, precisely because they have been interpreted in terms of the absolutist inclinations of the Reagan Administration, and are therefore seen as representing a challenge to the fundamentals of nuclear deterrence. Without the previous exposure of a philosophy so clearly sceptical of the durability and morality of nuclear deterrence, during the course of the SDI debate and then at Reykjavik, the pressures towards double zero would not have been received with the same sort of alarm in Western Europe.

The most important point to emerge thus far from the concern expressed by European governments with regard to the double zero is that their concerns are not reflected in their domestic constituencies. Popular sentiment does not seem to be that different on the two sides of the Atlantic and does not lend much support to efforts to protect nuclear deterrence from the ravages of arms control. Mrs Thatcher's cautious welcome for the double zero was dictated in part by the imminence of a general election and the recognition that foot-dragging on arms control was not a popular cause. Chancellor Kohl's awkward about-turn was prompted by the clear messages from voters in State elections.

While the protest movements who made so much noise in the first half of the 1980s have now faded from view, their legacy is not only a heightened rhetoric in favour of 'peace' but also a place for the inadequacies of flexible response on the political agenda. As with the sentiment in favour of arms control, there has been a convergence across the Atlantic; the doubts of the hawkish American strategists have been echoed by the European protesters. The stereophonic effect makes it difficult for those who believe that there is no crisis in deterrence to play the issue down. Governments find that they must address the issue of the failure of deterrence as a real strategic problem rather than a remote hypothesis.

The reason why governments feel uncomfortable with this issue is that there is no good answer to the question of 'what do we do if deterrence fails?' Whether one sees the answer in guerrilla resistance, substantial conventional battles being fought all over European soil or a tentative entrance into nuclear war, the implications are horrendous. It is not necessary to go as far as nuclear release to make the prospect of war in Europe awful. The prospect is particularly awful for Germany but there is no need to allow our German allies to believe that the misery will be theirs' alone; it will be widely shared.

For the moment, the preferred method of easing concerns with regard to the over-reliance on nuclear deterrence is to seek improvements in conventional forces. Some well-known generals have recently argued that compensation in the conventional sphere is vital if politicians are now prepared to tolerate the diminution in nuclear deterrence being planned at Geneva.

Before considering what might be done in the conventional area, let us first consider the argument that there is a straightforward relationship between provisions for nuclear deterrence and those for conventional deterrence, to the extent that one must come up if the other goes down. This seems to me to be too mechanical. One is not a straight substitute for the other. For example, if nuclear use is only going to be authorized in the course of a fierce land battle, then weak conventional forces will mean that the conflict never reaches sufficient intensity to carry a conflict through the nuclear threshold.

SACEUR is tasked to develop options for nuclear use in the event of reverses in the conventional battle — to the point where the cohesion of the Alliance is threatened — and might therefore be forgiven some irritation when the means by which he might meet his requirements are denied him through arms control. However, as anyone familiar with the series of NATO studies and exercises will be aware, the likelihood that nuclear use could turn the tide of battle in war is not great, and the political inhibitions on nuclear release would be formidable, given that the most plausible consequences would be to make the situation far, far worse.

The source of these inhibitions is not to be found in the detail of the nuclear relationship but in the fact that the enemy will always have some means of retaliation. The problems with implementing nuclear threats are not made much better or worse by the proposed Geneva agreement and reflect long-standing concerns: there is an unavoidable degree of doubt that any state would initiate nuclear war as a deliberate act of policy, and the degree of doubt grows when the state in question is thousands of miles away from the territory under dispute.

This problem has been central to all NATO's strategic thought over the past three decades. These decades have seen the steady exhaustion of the answers to the point where we are obliged to recognize that there are no good answers except that, in the fury and chaos of war, any nuclear weapons, even loosely linked to the armed forces of the opposing sides, could well be used. The loss of confidence in the full-blown theory of nuclear deterrence pre-dates the current negotiations, although the debate generated by the Cruise/Pershing deployment and the associated negotiations accelerated this decline in confidence. If arms control was rejected it would be foolish to pretend that the old version of nuclear deterrence could reassert itself. The United States can be expected to continue to wish to reduce its nuclear exposure in Europe, while the Europeans will be unwilling to accept the additional systems and battle plans that would be necessary to inject extra credibility into the nuclear posture.

The shift in the balance away from the nuclear side has been and will be a gradual process. I doubt whether there will be an MC14/4 two decades after the adoption of flexible response. After all, flexible response has the undoubted virtue of flexibility. All it precludes is a formal renunciation of the nuclear option. However, in the near universal acceptance that it would be desirable to raise the nuclear threshold or move to a 'no early first-use' posture, the tendency is clear.

The general agreement that we should now attend to the conventional balance has not been followed by any noticeable increase in allocations to defence. Indeed the political rhetoric with regard to the balance suggests that the situation is all but hopeless. Words like 'massive', 'huge' and 'overwhelming' are habitually used to describe Warsaw Pact superiority. This phraseology tends to be used to warn against any further diminution in nuclear deterrence.

Is the balance *that* bad? Anyone who has studied the figures knows that they allow for a multitude of interpretations; there are lies, damn lies and analyses of the conventional military balance in Central Europe. If all the forces of NATO countries are included, then one soon wonders what all the fuss is about. By confining the analysis to the forces arrayed against each other along the Central Front, a discernible pattern of Warsaw Pact superiority emerges but not one that would warrant taking great risks. However, the real problem with interpreting these facts and figures is that they tell us absolutely nothing about the likely outcome of a confrontation. This is partly a question of the military factors that they cannot include — quality, morale, training, leadership, tactics, dispositions, supply lines and stocks. But it is also because of the impossibility of taking account of the two key political factors that would, in practice, determine the impact of the military relationship at times of crisis.

It might be that a future war would start with a set-piece confrontation along all fronts and on all flanks, so that nobody would feel left out. In peacetime exercises it is a political slight to suggest that any member of the Alliance could be safely ignored by the adversary. But the opening stages of a war are highly political affairs, with each side seeking to undermine his opponent's alliance as much as his armed forces, while shoring up his own. The sort of crisis that would make war at all possible in Europe would be one that would see the existing Alliance structure under enormous strain. Few countries will beg to be allowed to join in the fun; a number can be expected to renege on their obligations. Statecraft in these circumstances will be about the balance of the alliances as much as the balance of military power.

A second and related point is that the balance of military power will itself be transformed through the processes of mobilisation and preparation for war. It is not that either side (and certainly not the West) could prepare for war without warning. It is a question of whether the available indicators that something is up are recognized and acted upon by the Allies. It is not hard to imagine the arguments within and between Alliance countries over the meaning of these indicators and what should be the appropriate response.

Our leaders will take a lot of convincing before they put their countries on to a war footing. Even if a few accept the necessity, objections will still be raised by those who find the process too provocative. And if the response is made and the threat subsides, will the doubters be convinced that there ever was a threat and will those who were prepared to respond this time, be prepared to do the same a second time, given all the expense and bother entailed? This problem cannot be judged in the abstract, separate from the factors making for the crisis in the first place.

In terms of force levels, the main issue for the next few years at least, and probably over the long term, is not going to be how best to expand our conventional forces but how best to manage steady contraction. Whatever the arguments of the generals, it is unlikely that the climate created by a successful arms control deal on nuclear systems, backed up by Warsaw Pact proposals for dramatic reductions in the conventional sphere, will seem the time for major increases in defence spending. In Britain, the social priorities that the government now appears to accept as having a central place in its programme for the next four years leave little scope for anything more than that level of increase necessary to avoid a full defence review — and we may not even get that. In the United States, the budget deficit is going to loom larger as existing political mechanisms fail to grapple with it. While a future Administration may feel that there is sufficient fat in nuclear and maritime programmes to avoid attacking land and air forces devoted to Europe, the Congressional opinion may be different.

These are not pressures that the Soviet Union can easily avoid, so, in relative terms, the position may not alter so much. However, at issue is not simply the East-West balance but the structure of armed forces. For example, below a certain level, individual units cease to be viable. We have, of course, become aware of this problem with aircraft in that the high costs of individual items could eventually produce the situation where, to use the caricature, the whole of the defence budget must be allocated to a single aircraft.

This leads on to the question of a defence review in Britain. At the moment, the options would appear to be the extraction of extra funds from the Treasury, a full-scale defence review, or (most likely) what has come to be called a defence review by stealth — or perhaps more accurately, a defence review by drift. The latter is politically the least controversial. It involves managing the defence budget in such a way that no fundamental decisions are being taken with regard to roles and commitments, and ways are sought to find savings within the established framework. If such decisions are taken, they are taken in isolation from a broad view of priorities and therefore, in all probability, in response to short-term factors rather than a longer-term perspective.

My own view is that we should move to a system where we have a defence review as a matter of course, every five years, in which there is an opportunity to form judgments on key changes in the strategic environment and the implications of these for the balance of our defence effort. It would be helpful if such a review could be stripped of the connotations of political defeat and financial pressure. The management of defence in the absence of such a review, without regular increases in resources, can be expected to involve the familiar pressures on stores and training — that is the preference will be to sustain peacetime appearances rather than high levels of combat readiness.

Another issue raised by the pressures on the defence budget will be whether there should be more off-the-shelf purchases. One interesting aspect of this question is the extent to which there will be funds to support co-operative projects other than those with a very compelling industrial logic. While the political situation of a Europe hedging its bets against the possibility of future American withdrawal may argue for a greater demonstration of solidarity in armament development and production, the financial pressures may push in the opposite direction. Nonetheless, the European label may prove to be of value in securing some of the more expensive projects — EFA is a likely beneficiary. Treasuries may be expected to continue to argue that their governments should find less expensive forms of political symbolism.

To the extent that definitive choices are required, I think we should recognise that these are still unlikely to be so fundamental as to emasculate a single service in order to protect the others in some way. Britain's room for manoeuvre in terms of a shift from a maritime to a continental bias, for example, is limited. I would expect a steady tendency towards the continental commitment largely because of the political need to maintain strong links with the Federal Republic at a time when, for the reasons discussed earlier, it may be feeling uneasy with regard to the quality and durability of its alliances. With Trident now moving into its period of peak expenditure, the option of boosting conventional forces by abandoning the nuclear role is declining fast. After the next general election, Britain could still abandon Trident but this would have to be justified on grounds of principle rather than economy.

The major pressure therefore may not be so much on reducing our commitments to do a few things properly, rather than a lot of things not very well at all, but on finding new ways to meet our existing commitments in the most cost-effective manner. This will require ingenuity and new thinking.

The point can be illustrated by considering the problem of new equipment costs, which is the cause of so much strain on the budget. We can expect the steady movement towards two or even three tier force structures. By this I mean that distinctions will develop between units — squadrons, divisions, naval groups — fully equipped with the most sophisticated equipment and those that are 'making do' with older and/ or less capable equipment. This need not be a bad thing, if linked with new concepts of operations that do not rely on advanced technology systems for every task — for example, the use of light as against heavy divisions. However, there is obviously a risk that there will be a simple hierarchy — a first and a second eleven. Without going into these particular issues now, it is not too hard to see how the debate could develop with regard to airmobility, organic naval airpower and long-range interdiction.

These issues will be influenced by a general Alliance debate on conventional strategy. Two sets of questions appear to be of particular importance. The first revolves around the question of mobility versus attrition. Military reformers on both sides on the Atlantic have been rediscovering the virtues of manoeuvre warfare. They see this as involving more of the 'operational art' than the crude trading of casualties involved in attrition warfare. However, they are also rediscovering the political difficulties involved in not committing forces in peacetime to the forward defence of West Germany, as well as the command and control and logistic problems involved in managing manoeuvre warfare. However, if the future battlefield can be expected to be much more fluid, then this has important implications for the mobility of troops and equipment in and around the combat zone.

The second and related area concerns the extent to which NATO forces will be expected to attack targets behind the enemy lines rather than being confined to engagements on the forward edge of the battle area. This question is raised by those who are concerned that preparations for *any* military operations into the enemy rear are inherently provocative and destabilising. It is raised in a different form by those who have no objections in principle but are concerned that it could mean a diversion of resources from the primary task of holding onto NATO's own territory. This issue has come to the fore with such schemes as Follow-on Forces Attack (FOFA) which has been criticised by some as being of marginal value if NATO's front-line has insufficient resources to cope with the first wave of the Warsaw Pact attack.

In both sets of questions, the implications for air power are self-evident and need not be elaborated. I would however conclude with one observation. The contribution made by air power must be set against those of land and sea power. One of the reasons why it is possible to argue that a continued emphasis on interdiction by air is important and need not be provocative is that the ability to strike deep into territory cannot by itself constitute a true offensive capability — that requires the follow-up of land forces that can seize and secure the enemies' political centres. In a curious way, the lack of a capacity for follow-through makes this classic exercise of air power acceptable. Outside Europe this is not necessarily the case. The lack of follow-through is an important disadvantage. One of the temptations of air power is that its range allows you to attack enemies that would otherwise be inaccessible. This was obviously one of the virtues of the great bomber offensives of the early 1940s. There was no other way of hitting back at Germany. We discovered then that this was not a means of forcing an enemy to surrender. One of the risks of the current situation, all the more evident as the United States embarks on another trial of strength in the Middle East, is that the ease with which it is possible to launch air strikes against unsavoury régimes is not necessarily matched by the political consequences. You can punish an adversary but not necessarily force him to change his behaviour. That requires a more substantial commitment of land power and if the West is not prepared to follow through with that sort of commitment then it must recognise the limits of solitary air strikes — however dramatic their immediate impact.

There is obviously a tension between the demands of force planning, where our normal time horizon is a decade, and the strategic context of the moment which may suggest priorities and requirements that can soon seem hopelessly inappropriate. As I have indicated, we lack a clear picture of how the strategic context is likely to develop in the future and it would therefore be unwise to insist that force planning begins to adjust to a new set of political circumstances that we can only dimly perceive. However I suspect that, in a fluid political situation, the pressure will be to keep up appearances so as to extract the maximum political influence from the armed forces. If this happens then one has to hope that the influence is used wisely and that the adjustments towards a new security system are not too fraught. Armed forces designed to make a political point are not necessarily so well placed to fight wars.

ARMS CONTROL AND SOVIET INTERESTS
The Right Honourable George Younger, TD, PC, DL, MP

I should like to concentrate on two issues that affect not just British defence policy but the NATO Alliance as a whole. One is Arms Control; the other is Defence Expenditure. With regard to the latter, let me say hastily that I do not intend to discuss the difficulties of matching resources to commitments. That is a perennial problem that all governments have faced. Whatever the impression given by the news media, it is not a particularly new one at the present time. Instead, I should like to discuss the linkage between the two subjects. After all, especially since the Harmel Report, which has its 20th anniversary this year, Alliance policies have recognised that arms control and defence capabilities are both constituent parts of security. And, of course, many people's expectations are that success in one *should* lead to a reduced need for the other.

These expectations have been considerably raised by the prospects that are currently being held out for real and significant arms reductions and by recent changes within the Soviet Union. I shall touch upon both these developments later.

First, I think it would be useful to look a little at the background. Since the Second World War, the Soviet Union has seen military strength as the major constituent of its claim to be recognised as a world power. Its status, its external relations generally, all lean heavily on its military power. And the Soviet concept of security is substantially different from our own. The Soviet Union seems — or has seemed — to believe that it must have a military capability at least equal to the sum of the strengths of all its possible adversaries. The massive military potential that the Soviet Union has developed and chosen to deploy facing the West is indisputable; and it is at the service of an adversarial ideology.

One result of this is the conventional imbalance that we see today in Europe, an imbalance which means that the Soviet Union's offers of proportionate reductions — based upon the presumption of overall equality of force strengths — cannot be the basis of an increase in stability and security. Reductions in the West's forces cannot be so readily envisaged.

There are a number of detailed reasons for this. For example, we in the West do not enjoy the luxury of being able to choose where to concentrate our forces. As a defensive alliance we have to be prepared to defend along the entire length of our frontier with the East. The general layout of the West's defence, therefore, looks uncomfortably like a thin blue line and one which is dependent on long and vulnerable lines of communication for reinforcement. The West's defensive posture is also dependent, to a considerable degree, upon the quality of its forces; their ability to capitalise on superior technology, for example, to compensate for some of the differences in size and firepower between the Warsaw Pact armies and our own.

This imbalance has bedevilled our attempts in the past to persuade the Soviet Union to move to a more stable relationship of conventional forces at lower levels. The currency of arms reduction talks is *quantitative* whereas the thrust of our military response in the West has been qualitative. We have little with which to bargain and the Soviet Union has had little real interest in conventional arms control proposals that reduce its own consciously acquired superiority. We will seek, as we have sought, to move to lower force levels but the journey is likely to be a long one, to be pursued with caution and with a continuing requirement, along the way, for the West to preserve the structure of its forces, the broad range of its equipment and the need to update its weaponry.

Such a basis for the maintenance of our strength will remain one of the prerequisites for successful arms control. But when the West responded to the Soviet build-up by deliberate and sustained increases of defence expenditure, as we did in particular following the NATO Summit decision in 1978, this was not in the expectation of extracting arms control concessions from the East. I don't think we can think in terms of impelling the Soviet Union towards cuts in its conventional armoury by increasing our expenditure in that way — or not at a price we would want or be able to afford. Nor would we want to become the mirror image of the Soviet Union. Our policy has been, rather, to try to narrow the increasing gap in capabilities before it became too dangerous. In this country, at least, our efforts have mainly taken the form of increases in *quality* and *effectiveness* within our existing force levels. We have expanded the reserves, true; and we have put into effect a substantial shift of resources, *within* the Services, towards the 'Teeth'.

But most of the £16 billion, in real terms, that we have spent on our conventional forces since 1979 has gone on a substantial re-equipment programme: in real terms, we now spend over a quarter as much again on equipment for every trained regular serviceman as was spent in the late 1970s.

This has been, and remains, our predicament. The time still seems a long way off when the twin policies, of the pursuit of conventional arms control and the provision of defence forces, are likely to converge in the sense that we could pursue one in the hopes of early relief from the need for the other. Removal of the conventional imbalance remains a priority aim; but that is something we could not hope to barter away by offering equivalent reductions in our own forces. It would require a fundamental change in the attitude of the Soviet Union towards European security and to the use of military power.

But has this rather depressing position now changed? Here I move into defence review territory — not, I hasten to add a *British* defence review. The review to which I refer is the one that must, I think, have been conducted in the Soviet Union shortly after Mr Gorbachev's accession to power. We have already seen some of the results of this review. A recent count showed that there had been 27 arms control initiatives from Mr Gorbachev over the past 14 months (although many of these were actually Soviet responses to Western initiatives).

Are we, in fact, seeing a fundamental Soviet reappraisal of policy towards the West? Are there other pressures on the Soviet Union to reduce the burden of its conventional defence expenditure? If the answer to both these questions were 'No', I think that our answer to recent Warsaw Pact overtures on conventional arms reductions would be a very clear rejection. We have had proposals for troop reductions on the table in Vienna for some years now. If the Soviet Union were serious, it should respond positively to *those*.

If there is just a possibility that there might be a real change taking place within the Soviet Union, then it is incumbent upon us to explore the scope for real progress in East-West relations, including the arms control field. That is why, in the past year, the West has announced new initiatives in the field of conventional arms control in the Halifax Communiqué and the Brussels Declaration — although, of course, the opportunity still exists for the Soviet Union to show, in a practical way, what it is prepared to do in the MBFR talks in Vienna.

Since his arrival, Mr Gorbachev has concentrated his attention on internal problems. His first and obvious priority is the revitalisation of an economy racked by inefficiencies. But we are not seeing the abandonment of socialism. We shall, I am sure, be disappointed if we think that Mr Gorbachev is a 'closet capitalist'. So what do his attempts to restructure the Soviet economy mean for Soviet foreign policy?

In the first place, Mr Gorbachev has indicated his belief that military power is no longer a sufficient, or even a desirable, means of pursuing the traditional struggle between Communism and Capitalism. Crudely translated, this might be characterised as a recognition of the limitations of relying solely upon a suit of heavy armour in which to court world opinion. He even seems to be saying, on occasion, that in a world of great interdependence, the struggle can never be won. This 'new thinking' appears to go some way beyond the old idea of peaceful coexistence, but it has to be said that Mr Gorbachev's own pronouncements on the subject are rather contradictory. The idea of a struggle between the systems has not completely gone away.

Secondly, and perhaps more substantially, it may be that the suit of armour is becoming too heavy for the Soviet Union to bear, and the corporate body within it too flabby to sustain the weight. But whether Mr Gorbachev has decided that it is necessary to reduce military expenditure *now*, in order to provide a breathing space for the economy to expand, we do not know. What we do know is that most of the resources for the major re-equipment programme that we have seen in the 1980s have already been committed. Indeed, the momentum of the programme seems likely to continue over the next few years. As for manpower, a reduction here would be of marginal benefit to the Soviet economy. The problem which the economy faces at present is the productivity of labour and capital, not manpower shortages *per se*.

What is more likely is that the Soviet Union will need to restrain investment in defence research and development and equipment procurement *in the future*, and that in the longer term it will face something like the demographic squeeze that we in the West are predicting for ourselves. If the Soviet economy expands, as Mr Gorbachev intends, there may be an increased penalty to be paid in having so many fit young men tied up in the military machine. If so, the demographic squeeze *may* be felt more actuely. However, the Soviet Union would certainly see an advantage in constraining the West's ability both to effect improvements in technology, and to reverse the steady progress that Soviet scientists have made in narrowing the qualitative gap between East and West.

Thus, I think that we have to enter an open verdict upon Soviet intentions in the conventional arms control talks now starting. The evidence suggests that the Soviet Union may be faced with resource problems over the next few years. It does not suggest that these are going to be so critical as to determine Soviet attitudes towards arms control. But we shall see.

Turning to the nuclear field, there is clear evidence of Soviet interest in an INF agreement. Unfortunately, I know of no serious commentator who suggests that we would be able to cut our own defence budgets if, as we hope. we see the back of some 1,000 Soviet nuclear missile systems, in return for rather fewer of our own. The Soviet Union would retain many thousands of nuclear warheads, of all ranges, targeted on Europe. The Millenium will not have come and the West will still be faced with the need to preserve its ability to sustain its strategy. Indeed, the other areas of our nuclear and conventional capabilities — none of them cheap — would be even more crucial in this respect. In short, we will still be faced with the need to maintain effective *nuclear* deterrence; and we are looking now to see how this should be done. The removal of one category of Soviet and American nuclear weapons does not alter this. We are not primarily in the arms control business because we hope to save money. We are in it, as we have always been, to reduce the level of tension between East and West, to minimise the scope for misunderstanding; and to increase our security. We can hope that, in the long term, the success that we achieve now makes it possible to save scarce resources, and devote them to other things. There are plenty of good candidates for alternative use. But prosperity cannot be enjoyed if peace is not secure; and arms control negotiations do not realistically pose any prospect of a change to our need to spend enough to maintain deterrence, flexible response and forward defence.

I see a very real danger in the climate of expectation that has been raised by the prospect of the first nuclear arms reductions. The danger is that it will give rise to a reduced willingness among the democratic nations of the West to support the expenditures necessary for our nuclear and conventional posture. That may, of course, be what the Soviet Union hopes will happen.

What then are the implications of all this for air power? For an Alliance faced with the problem of deterring a great land power like the Soviet Union, air power is bound to acquire additional importance. This, indeed, is what we have seen happening, over the last decade and more, in Central Europe.

In Britain we have traditionally maintained a balanced air force which supports each of the pillars of our defence policy. Since 1979, we have set in hand the largest and most ambitious re-equipment programme undertaken for some 30 years. The key elements have included the much needed regeneration and expansion of Britain's air defences as part of the improvement of the defence of the Home Base, confirmed in Cmnd 8288, and the build-up of the Tornado Strike/ Attack force. We are also introducing the new Harrier GR5 offensive support aircraft, which will transform the battlefield, and we are enhancing the reach and flexibility of air power, through purchases of Tristar and VC10 air-to-air refuelling aircraft. Our task now is to complete this modernisation and ensure that we maintain a proper balance between aircraft and weapon systems by pressing ahead with plans for the weapons needed to counter the growing Soviet threat.

Deterrence requires that our defensive posture should be credible. To achieve that credibility, the forward defence of European territory places high demands on surveillance, tactical flexibility and the rapid movement of reinforcements. If we are interested in maintaining deterrence and in lowering tensions in Europe, then we are bound to place a high priority on the sort of qualities that air power possesses. And, on the nuclear side, as I have mentioned, the prospect of the removal of land-based missiles will place increased importance on other means of delivery, including, of course, dual-capable aircraft.

Thus it is no accident that the Soviet leadership has placed a particular emphasis on tactical aircraft in framing its recent proposals on conventional forces. Cuts in our holdings of tactical aircraft would do much to increase the effectiveness of other Soviet weapon systems and weaken Western defence. I think we can take it as read that it will be the intention of the Soviet Union, in pursuing its interest in arms control, to constrain those parts of our capability which (like the famous lager!) they, otherwise, cannot reach.

Let me conclude by drawing together some threads.

There is the possibility, no more, that the Soviet Union's own internal difficulties and new management may be having an impact upon its attitudes to its military forces. We need to ensure that the chance of achieving security at lower force levels is tested patiently and constructively.

At the same time, we need to recognise that these internal difficulties are not such as to drive the Soviet Union to disarm overnight and if they are going to reduce their forces at all, Soviet leaders will be determined to extract as high a price for their reductions as they can.

There are therefore dangers, as well as opportunities, for the West in this new climate. The danger is that the Soviet Union will achieve, by smiling upon the West, what it has never been able to do by bluster — to weaken fatally our conventional and nuclear deterrent posture.

In all of this, air power is assuming even greater importance.

CHAPTER 3

The Operational Dimension

THE ROLE OF AIR POWER IN A NATO-WARSAW PACT CONVENTIONAL CONFLICT
Professor Ted Greenwood

The objective of this paper is to perform a functional analysis and evaluation of the role of air power in a potential NATO-Warsaw Pact conventional war in Europe. First it identifies the functions that air power would be called upon to perform in the event of war. It then assesses qualitatively the ability of each side's air power to perform these functions, given the size and composition of forces, their strategy and their level of technology and training. Based on this assessment, it reaches conclusions about the role of air power in the conflict. Finally some implications will be suggested for NATO's air power force structures and investment strategy.

In doing the analysis, a distinction will be drawn between three phases of military activity in the European theatre: the period prior to the outbreak of hostilities on the ground; the early stages of ground combat; and the duration of the conflict. This distinction is useful because the functions that air power would be called upon to perform are significantly different in each phase.

The task of assessing relative military capabilities between NATO and the Warsaw Pact is always difficult and is no less so for air power than for other military forces. The usual methodology of force comparison, namely static numerical comparison of budgets, combat units, manpower or weapons, is grossly inadequate and often misleading. Every student of the subject knows, for example, that Warsaw Pact and NATO economies are not equally efficient and that NATO and Warsaw Pact divisions are very different in size, firepower, readiness, and modes of operation on the battlefield. Yet even serious analysts persist in employing numerical comparisons of expenditure, divisions, or other similar quantities, such as the number of combat aircraft, as if they conveyed real insight into the European force balance. The trouble is that comparisons of the number of squadrons or combat aircraft possessed by each side, or of air force budgets or manpower, do not take account of significant differences in aircraft technology, training levels, maintenance capability, munitions, anti-aircraft capability, electronic warfare, or the missions that each side's aircraft would be called upon to perform in war. More sophisticated aggregate metrics, such as armoured division equivalents, exist for heterogeneous ground forces.[1] Although at best they only measure inputs, not performance of military forces, they are sometimes useful if their biases are recognised. No such aggregate metric exists for heterogeneous air power, however. Although numbers of aircraft or other forces are important and must be taken into account, force evaluations based upon numbers alone are better eschewed.

A more useful approach, at least in principle, is to use mathematical models that capture the most salient features of how forces perform in combat. However, appropriate models often do not exist. Even when they do, their use often requires more precise numbers and knowledge of weapon system performance characteristics than are reliably available. Their realism and applicability to a particular situation are often uncertain and in dispute. In addition, many potential consumers of comparative assessments of military forces are either insufficiently schooled in quantitative techniques or are so sceptical of the whole approach that it is rendered valueless for them. Moreover, the use of elaborate quantitative analysis is notorious in the policy analysis community for obscuring both important qualitative aspects of a problem and value-based assumptions and for permitting, if not fostering, an often misleading impression that numerical results of the analysis have unequivocal policy relevance. Despite these limitations, models can be useful in force evaluation if they are carefully employed and their results not taken too seriously.

The analysis of this paper will not rely on mathematical models, although it is informed to some degree by such analyses performed by the author and by others employing such models.[2] Nor will it rely exclusively on numerical comparisons of air forces on the two sides, although such numbers will be considered and taken into account when appropriate. Rather, the analysis here will be based upon the judgements of the author, taking into account numerical comparisons, strategy, geography, and differences in technology, training levels, and maintenance capability on the two sides. The judgements presented can certainly be challenged, but at least they will be made explicit and their rationale will be provided.

Functions of Air Power

The functions or missions of conventional air power in Europe or elsewhere are usually divided into six categories: airlift, counter-air, air interdiction, close air support, reconnaissance, maritime air operations, and special operations.[3] Each of these will be considered briefly in turn. Because this is a discussion of the role of air power in conventional warfare, nuclear missions will be omitted, except to note that NATO's plan to hold perhaps 10–15 per cent of its combat aircraft in reserve for such missions significantly reduces its conventional capability.[4]

Airlift

There are two categories of airlift. The first is strategic airlift, moving men, equipment and supplies between theatres, such as from the United States to Europe. The second is tactical or theatre airlift, moving men, equipment and supplies into forward areas from rear areas within a theatre. The latter includes insertion of airborne and airmobile ground forces behind enemy lines.

Strategic airlift would transport the United States personnel needed to employ United States prepositioned ground force equipment and the support structure for United States reinforcement squadrons across the Atlantic in the early days of mobilization. By far the largest part of the equipment going to Europe for ground units without prepositioned equipment and most of the supplies and equipment to support and sustain both initial and subsequently arriving ground and air units would come by sea. However, critical items needed before sealift could deliver them would move by air. Moreover, even after sea links were established, airlift would still move some reinforcement personnel and some high priority cargo.

Tactical airlift is important to both sides. Although much of the manpower, supplies and equipment moving to the front from rear areas in the theatre would go by rail or by road, high priority items would go by air. If the ground transportation system were badly degraded as a result of enemy interdiction bombing, theatre transportation would have to depend more heavily on airlift, perhaps using transport aircraft, like the C-130, that do not require runways to land. Insertion of airborne and airmobile ground forces behind enemy lines is a tactical airlift activity that would be conducted primarily by the Warsaw Pact.

Counter-Air

There are three categories of counter-air, all of which share the objective of achieving air supremacy. The first is offensive counter-air, which seeks to decrease the sortie rate of an opponent's aircraft. The second is suppression of enemy air defences: the effort to destroy, neutralise, or degrade temporarily enemy air defence systems so that friendly ground attack aircraft can perform their missions. Defensive counter-air detects, identifies, and attacks enemy aircraft that are attempting to penetrate friendly airspace or attack friendly forces.

Offensive counter-air primarily involves attacks against enemy airfields, rather than enemy aircraft. However, both ground attack aircraft and accompanying fighters would engage in self-protective air-to-air combat if necessary. One objective for attacks against enemy airfields is to prevent the use of runways. This is accomplished by cratering and by sowing area denial munitions. A second objective is to destroy specific targets such as aircraft on the ground, fuel supplies, flight control centres, maintenance facilities and other structures. Attacking airfields is a high priority function because it can be more effective than ground-based air defences or air interception in preventing an opponent's airpower from accomplishing its missions. Preparing for offensive counter-air also forces an opponent to invest scarce resources in defending its airfields. At least initially, approximately 15–20 per cent of NATO fighter/attack aircraft are likely to be allocated to airfield attack.

Suppression of enemy air defence, or defence suppression, employs physical attack against enemy air defences or electronic disruption of their sensors to assist friendly aircraft to carry out their missions without interference. It can take place over or near the battlefield in support of close air support or battlefield air interdiction or over enemy territory in support of deep interdiction and offensive counter-air missions. Suppression of enemy air defence would be the primary mission of approximately 5 per cent of NATO fighter/attack aircraft.

Defensive counter-air seeks to prevent enemy aircraft from entering friendly airspace and attacking friendly forces and to ensure freedom of operation for one's own air assets over friendly territory. It involves air-to-air combat by fighter aircraft and ground-to-air attack by air defence guns and surface-to-air missiles. Although the primary objective of defensive counter-air is the destruction of enemy offensive aircraft, even forcing them to defend themselves while *en route* to targets might cause them to jettison their ground attack weapons and abort the mission. Approximately 25–30 per cent of NATO's aircraft are likely to be allocated to the defensive counter-air function initially, but substantially less later.

Air Interdiction

Air interdiction seeks to delay, disrupt, divert or destroy an enemy's military potential before it can be used effectively against friendly forces. Two categories of air interdiction can be identified, depending on where it occurs. *Battlefield air interdiction* is the name given to attacks on forces and supplies that can have a near-term effect on friendly ground forces. Long-range artillery and short-range missiles can be used for this purpose in addition to aircraft, if they have a suitable target acquisition capability. Approximately one third of NATO fighter/ attack aircraft might be employed for battlefield air interdiction, although the fraction would be lower in the early stages of conflict. The remainder of the air interdiction effort, to be called *interdiction* or *deep interdiction*, covers attacks against targets remote (perhaps many hundreds of miles) from the battle area. Aircraft or highly accurate missiles must be employed for this purpose.

Two types of targets can be attacked in air interdiction. The first is fixed targets. These include military headquarters and other command, control and communications centres; nuclear storage depots and nuclear delivery vehicles; tactical ballistic missile sites; storage areas for military supplies and equipment; and key transportation nodes such as ports, pipeline pumping stations, rail and road bridges and tunnels, and rail transfer points. Significant incentives exist for both sides to attack such targets as early as possible in the conflict, and repeatedly throughout its duration because successful destruction or even serious degradation of these targets would significantly impede the other side's ability to pursue the war. The second type of air interdiction targets are mobile, including tanks, armoured fighting vehicles, trucks, and trains.

Of special interest is NATO attack against Warsaw Pact follow-on forces, that is, second or subsequent echelon forces moving toward the battle area. By attacking these forces *en route*, NATO would hope to prevent their reaching the front or, at least, to ensure that their capability is degraded when they do so. Such attacks might also disrupt schedules that, in a war of manoeuvre and attempted breakthrough, it would be important for Soviet strategy to maintain. Soviet follow-on forces might be attacked as they approach the battlefield, at great distances from the battlefield, or anywhere in between, depending on NATO's choice and on how much forward movement the Warsaw Pact completes before the outbreak of hostilities.

Close Air Support

Close air support is the use of airpower in direct support of ground forces within the battle area, by attacking enemy forces that are in close proximity to friendly forces. In the case of war between NATO and the

Warsaw Pact in Europe, the primary targets for NATO close air support would be troops and vehicles, such as tanks, armoured personnel carriers, and self-propelled artillery. Approximately one quarter of NATO aircraft are specially designed for close air support.

Obviously, the line between close air support and battlefield air interdiction can not be drawn precisely. The execution of close air support missions requires close co-ordination with ground forces whereas battlefield air interdiction, being somewhat more remote from friendly forces, requires less co-ordination. Close air support and battlefield air interdiction, together with aspects of tactical reconnaissance, can be considered constituent parts of the combined mission, offensive air support.

Tactical Reconnaissance

Tactical reconnaissance is the collection of information about localised or specific targets using radar, visual observation, and visual or infra-red photography and imaging. It can provide information to ground commanders about the size, composition, disposition and movement of enemy forces. It can be employed in a pre-attack mode to help identify and locate targets of interest, including moving targets. It can also be employed in a post-attack mode to evaluate the effectiveness of an attack and determine how soon a target that can be repaired should be attacked again. Approximately 10 per cent of NATO's combat aircraft deployed in Europe are specially fitted to perform tactical reconnaissance.

Maritime Air Operations

Aircraft can be used to locate and attack enemy shipping and naval forces, including amphibious forces, and to protect friendly naval forces and shipping. Included would be counter-air operations at sea, minelaying, reconnaissance and surveillance, and interdiction of enemy surface and sub-surface forces and port facilities. Both sides would conduct maritime air operations in the North Atlantic, the Warsaw Pact to interdict shipping between North America and Europe and NATO to destroy Warsaw Pact maritime strike aircraft, conduct anti-submarine warfare and help NATO's naval forces attack whatever portion of the Soviet surface navy ventured into those waters. Any Warsaw Pact amphibious operations against north Norway, Turkey or in the Baltic would also be supported by Soviet aircraft and opposed by NATO aircraft.

Special Operations

Both sides in a European war would employ aircraft to deliver special operations forces behind enemy lines. On the NATO side, the relatively small number of Special Forces have intelligence collection and psychological warfare missions. The Warsaw Pact has a larger number of so-called *Spetsnaz* forces.

Prior to D-Day on the Ground

The use of air power does not wait until hostilities begin on the ground. Strategic and tactical airlift would be very active from the moment a decision is made to mobilise forces. Moreover, although the assumption is usually made that Warsaw pact air and naval attacks would not precede its ground attacks or would do so only slightly, the opposite is possible and must be considered.

Airlift

Strategic airlift is absolutely crucial to NATO's mobilisation plans. Approximately one half of the ground combat troops that the United States promises to have available in Central Europe within ten days of the start of mobilisation would have to come by air. This is the manpower for $5\frac{1}{3}$ divisions plus support elements that are not deployed in Europe but for which equipment is or will be prepositioned. The same is true for the United States Marine Corps brigade for which equipment is prepositioned in Norway. These troops would go in the approximately 300 commercial passenger airliners pledged by United States and European airlines to the United States Air Force for use in wartime. Equipment for any other elements of the United States Marine division that might go to Norway and for other divisions reinforcing Central Europe would move by sea, but their troops, too, would fly. On the southern flank, some elements of an American division (probably Marine Corps) might be airlifted with their equipment to Turkish Thrace. No equipment has been prepositioned there. Personnel as well as large amounts of supplies and equipment for the 30 reinforcement squadrons that the United States promises to send to Europe in the same time frame would also have to move by air.[5]

Once all the prepositioning currently underway or planned for American ground and air forces is complete, and assuming that arrangements to employ commercial aircraft function as intended, that there is no large diversion of airlift assets for contingencies elsewhere, and that NATO's airfields in rear areas are usable, the chances that American reinforcement units would actually be in position within the time promised after mobilisation began are good.[6] Prepositioned ground and air force equipment and supplies are critical, however, as is the preparation of bases in Europe to accept United States aircraft, the Co-located Operating Bases. There is no likelihood that NATO could be ready to meet a rapidly prepared Warsaw Pact attack in the Central Region if all the equipment for United States reinforcement units had to move by air or by sea. In the light of the shortage of strategic airlift assets to move heavy equipment, prepositioning in Thrace and additional prepositioning in Norway — at least to replace the Canadian brigade, soon to be reassigned to Germany — would be useful.

Both sides would rely on tactical airlift in this early period. Active duty British, Dutch and Belgian forces that are not deployed in Germany in peacetime but are dedicated to their corps sectors, as well as subsequently mobilised reserves, would have to move forward quickly to strengthen their sectors. United States supplies and materiel arriving at ports or main operating air bases in rear areas must also be moved forward. Most of this movement would be via road and rail, but some would be by air. Assuming that Soviet mobilisation did not occur faster than expected, that NATO did not postpone its own mobilisation longer than expected, and that NATO rear and forward airfields were usable, the more than 200 transport aircraft of Belgium, the Netherlands, Britain and Germany, mostly C-130s, together with a portion of the approximately 500 American C-130s, would provide an adequate tactical airlift contribution to NATO's mobilisation. Soviet forces moving toward the front from the Soviet Union would also rely in part on airlift, but not critically.

Just how much time NATO would have to conduct this initial airlift and for how long it could do so with impunity are unclear. NATO strategy is predicated on two relevant assumptions. First, it assumes that the Warsaw Pact could mount a large ground attack within two weeks of starting to mobilise and that therefore NATO would have only this long to prepare. If this were true, delay of more than a few days could be fatal for NATO. Second, NATO strategy assumes that during the period before hostilities begin on the ground, airlift operations and the breaking out of stored equipment could be conducted without fear of attack. There is reason to question both assumptions.

Of the 90 or so divisions that NATO usually assumes that the Warsaw Pact would employ in an attack in the Central Region, only some 28 per cent are Soviet forces deployed in Eastern Europe. Soviet forces deployed in the three western military districts, far from the Front, comprise 39 per cent; 33 per cent are East European. Similarly, from the perspective of readiness, 57 per cent of these forces are Category I, 27 per cent are Category II, and 16 per cent are Category III.[7] There is little doubt that the physical capability exists to move such forces forward fast enough to effect the short mobilisation that NATO planning envisions if everything worked according to plan. However, such flawless logistics are unlikely. More important, even if all these forces did arrive in place in time, the combat readiness of many of them would be so low that the Warsaw Pact would be unlikely to attack without further training and preparations. On the flanks, the Soviets' problems of mobilisation are even more difficult. It is more likely, therefore, that the Warsaw Pact would take at least thirty, and perhaps as much as ninety or 120 days, to make ready its forces before initiating hostilities on the ground.[8] In other words, much more time than is currently expected might be available for NATO to bring its ground and air forces forward and prepare its defence line. In that case, the demands on airlift capability would be significantly less.

Early Air War

The second assumption, that the initial airlift to Europe and breaking out of prepositioned equipment prior to the outbreak of hostilities on the ground would be unimpeded by the Warsaw Pact, might also be wrong. The Soviet Union would have a great incentive to disrupt NATO's preparations for the coming ground war by engaging in offensive counter-air, defence suppression and interdiction strikes soon after it began mobilisation. For this purpose the Soviet Union could use medium range bombers (Backfires, Badgers and Blinders), light and fighter bombers (Fencers, Floggers and Fitters), and tactical ballistic missiles. Unless successfully opposed, such a Soviet strategy could be devastating to NATO's ability to resist a Warsaw pact ground attack when it comes.

Airfields, air defence radars and missile sites, and equipment warehouses would not be the only highly valuable targets that the Soviet Union would have an incentive to attack with these assets prior to the outbreak of hostilities on the ground. Other high-value interdiction targets include nuclear weapon and delivery system storage sites, command and control centres, ports through which NATO sea-borne equipment and supplies would later come, and other key transportation nodes, such as bridges and railroad yards. Some of these targets could be attacked not only by aircraft or tactical ballistic missiles but also by submarine-launched cruise missiles.

The initiation of air attacks — and therefore of war in Europe — before its ground forces were ready to fight would of course carry risks for the Warsaw Pact. Unless incapacitated by early Warsaw Pact air attack, NATO would certainly retaliate with a massive air campaign against the Warsaw Pact that might seriously impair the latter's own ability to prepare for the ground war. Moreover, if the Warsaw Pact took time to make ready Category II and III units or if not all East European forces participated, NATO would actually be more ready to fight on the ground than the Pact in the early stages of mobilisation, unless NATO delayed excessively. Although NATO would be hesitant to initiate ground hostilities as long as the Warsaw Pact desisted from attack, this might not be true once air attacks were initiated.

Despite these disincentives for the Warsaw Pact to launch air attacks soon after commencing mobilisation, NATO must be prepared in case Warsaw Pact decision-makers are convinced that it would not respond with a ground attack or that air strikes against a still largely unprepared NATO would prove decisive. NATO's air defences, both ground-based and air superiority fighters, must be ready to function almost from the start of Warsaw Pact mobilisation, well ahead of NATO ground forces. NATO has this capability in the Central Region today and there is no reason to expect the situation to change. Hawk and Nike/Patriot ground-to-air missile sites in Germany and the air forces of West Germany, the United States and other allies are in a high state of readiness for the mission of defending Allied airspace from a surprise attack. The same is true of RAF Strike Command with respect to its mission of defending the United Kingdom Air Defence Region, through which most of the airlift from North America must pass. NATO's Airborne Warning and Control aircraft (AWACS) would be an important element in NATO's ability to blunt a surprise Warsaw Pact air attack and to extract a high price for whatever success it achieved.

The regions in which NATO's air defence system is least able to meet an early Pact air attack are the northern and southern flanks. Again, the availability of AWACS will help and certainly the small, but capable, Norwegian Air Force would respond quickly. But ground-based air defences are weaker on the flanks than in the Central Region and the augmentation of indigenous air superiority aircraft by Allied reinforcement squadrons might take too long. Measures to reduce the time required for such additional deployment should therefore be given high priority in NATO.

Even in the Central Region, if the Warsaw Pact initiated air attacks while NATO was still mobilising, important NATO assets would be lost. In addition to minimising such losses by providing adequate air defence early, NATO should also act to minimise the consequences of the losses that would occur. Equipment should be broken out of storage locations as quickly as possible. Preparations should be made to use back-up ports and airfields in the event that primary ones were damaged. Alternative command and control facilities should be prepared. Another possible course of action is to plan to disperse nuclear weapons and delivery systems early, but here the implications for crisis stability would have to be dealt with.

Warsaw Pact tactical ballistic missiles present a special threat against which NATO has no defence today. However, the number of such missiles is not large compared to the number of potential targets in Western Europe if they were used with conventional rather than nuclear warheads, if allowance is made for unreliability and inaccuracy, especially of the older missiles held by Soviet allies, and particularly if a significant portion is assumed to be reserved for possible nuclear use later.[9] Moreover, this number would be significantly reduced by an arms control agreement, such as the one now under discussion, that would ban ballistic missiles in Europe with ranges greater than 300 miles. Nonetheless, tactical ballistic missiles now pose a significant threat to airfields and other fixed, high-value targets and this threat is likely to increase over time. Armed with chemical warheads, rather than high explosives, they would be a very serious threat today. A NATO strategy for dealing with the tactical ballistic missile threat is clearly needed.

If the Warsaw Pact takes longer to mobilise for its ground attack than NATO planning assumes, military equipment and supplies might be moving by sea from North America to Europe in this period. In that case, the Warsaw Pact would have incentives to initiate early naval attacks no less than to launch early attacks from the air. A Soviet maritime interdiction campaign could involve submarines, perhaps surface ships, and long range bombers from the Northern, Baltic and perhaps Black Sea Fleets.

The Soviets have some 60 bombers in their Northern Fleet and 40 in their Baltic Fleet. On maritime air interdiction missions, these aircraft would be met by British and United States fighters, the latter operating from the United Kingdom, Iceland and aircraft carriers. Most of the relevant sea lanes are beyond the range of Soviet escort fighters. Consequently, the Backfires, Badgers and Blinders would be highly vulnerable. In the Mediterranean, if any of the hundred Backfires and Badgers in the Soviet Black Sea Fleet tried to conduct maritime air interdiction missions they would be met by Turkish and Greek fighters and whatever American fighters (including carrier-based) had been brought into the area. If they did not venture too far, Soviet naval attack aircraft in the Mediterranean could have fighter escort from Bulgaria. Of course, Soviet naval airfields would be subjected to direct attack by NATO aircraft and NATO's naval escort ships would also take a toll with their anti-air capability. Given its geographic and technical advantages, NATO seems assured of winning the maritime counter-air battle in the Atlantic, including the Norwegian Sea, although some very important cargoes might be lost to Soviet maritime air attacks. NATO's prospects in the Mediterranean are less favourable and could depend on the degree of co-operation between Greek, Turkish and American forces there.

Soviet submarines and surface ships attacking NATO shipping would certainly be opposed by Allied navies.[10] However, if Soviet vessels entered the shipping lanes before the initiation of hostilities, they would avoid running the gauntlet of NATO's maritime barriers (at the Turkish Straits, Gibraltar, the Baltic narrows, and the Greenland–Iceland–United Kingdom Gap, for example) until they had to return to port for weapons reloads or resupply. NATO's capable convoy escorts would certainly take a toll of Soviet surface ships and submarines attacking Allied shipping. However, the role of NATO maritime patrol and attack aircraft, armed with anti-ship and anti-submarine munitions, would also be very important. Britain has four squadrons of Nimrod maritime patrol aircraft and two squadrons of Buccaneer aircraft carrying Sea Eagle anti-shipping missiles. Norway has one squadron of P-3s and four squadrons of F-16s, carrying Penguin anti-ship missiles. The United States has 24 active and 13 reserve P-3 squadrons, although many of these have missions remote from Europe. Even United States B-52s might participate, not only through attacks on Soviet naval facilities ashore, but also by dropping mines and attacking naval combatants directly with Harpoon anti-ship missiles. The battle for control of the seas would not be resolved quickly, but through a gradual process of attrition. Air power would play a significant role in assisting NATO surface navies and (primarily United States) attack submarines in their efforts to protect Allied shipping and eventually to win command of the seas.

Early Stages of the Ground Conflict

During the early stages of ground conflict in Europe, both sides would employ air power for several quite different missions: airlift, maritime air operations, counter-air, deep interdiction, and offensive air support.

Airlift and Maritime Air Operations

Airlift of men, equipment and supplies would continue during this stage and as long as the necessary airfields remained available. Sealift, too, would become extremely important to NATO, as the vital link between North America and Europe. If the Soviet naval and maritime air operations against NATO shipping, previously discussed, had not begun well before the outbreak of hostilities on the ground, they would probably begin just before or simultaneously. NATO's countervailing maritime air operation would be as discussed above, unless the Soviet Union had managed to erode NATO capability through its offensive counter-air attacks. However, most of the relevant NATO airfields are well back, primarily in the United Kingdom, Norway and the United States, where they would not be likely to be affected by Soviet offensive counter-air.

NATO maritime air operations might have another role during the early stages of ground combat: preventing Soviet amphibious assaults on NATO coasts, especially in Norway, Denmark, north-eastern Germany, northern Turkey and near the Bosphorus, and perhaps Iceland. Air power could not and would not be expected to do this job alone, but it could provide powerful assistance to naval forces. P-3s, Nimrods and perhaps B-52s would be employed as well as ground attack aircraft deployed within range. Of particular importance in the Baltic would be the German Navy's two wings of Tornados equipped with Kormoran anti-ship missiles,[11] as would the Norwegian F-16s with Penguin missiles in defending the coast of Norway.

Warsaw Pact military strategy calls for the insertion of airborne, airmobile and Spetsnaz forces behind enemy lines early in the ground conflict. The first and last would parachute out of fixed-wing aircraft. Airmobile forces would move by helicopter. Both types of transport aircraft would presumably be escorted by fighters. The objective of these forces would be to seize key facilities and terrain (including river crossings) in the rear areas, to disrupt critical rear area activities including mobilisation, and to sow confusion. In Norway, key airfields and ports, road demolition sites, and centres for the mobilisation of reserve forces would be likely targets. In Western Turkey, shore defences along the Straits and critical points on the few roads from northern Thrace to Istanbul are likely targets.

If these forces succeeded in landing, they could cause severe problems for NATO, especially if the pre-hostilities mobilisation time had been brief and NATO had not had time to prepare fully. NATO airpower, including helicopters, and NATO's own mobile ground forces would be able to contain and eventually to eliminate any airborne or airmobile Warsaw Pact forces that managed to seize their objectives. However, serious damage to critical facilities would occur in the meantime and forces badly needed for other purposes would be diverted. NATO's preferred means of dealing with these forces, therefore, is to shoot the delivering aircraft out of the sky.

Adequate warning and the ability to concentrate superior air-to-air combat forces are the keys to the successful accomplishment of this task. Tactical warning would come from AWACS and ground-based radars, unless the latter were previously destroyed. Either should be adequate to permit NATO fighters to intercept and destroy the delivering aircraft. Insertion of airborne or airmobile troops would be a difficult mission for the Soviet air force. The transport aircraft themselves are very vulnerable. Unless the Soviets were willing to allocate very large numbers of fighter escorts at a time when these would be in high demand elsewhere, their prospects for success seem slim.

Counter-Air and Deep Interdiction

If the Warsaw Pact had not initiated offensive counter-air, defence suppression, and air interdiction attacks well in advance of beginning ground hostilities, it would surely do so simultaneously with, or just prior to, the start of its ground offensive.[12] NATO would do likewise as soon as hostilities began. On both sides, targets would have been determined and allocated to particular squadrons in advance. Each side's attack, of course, would be opposed by the defensive counter-air capability of the other, both airborne and ground-to-air. The result would be intense air-to-air, air-to-ground and ground-to-air battles throughout the Central Region and quite likely on the flanks as well. Losses would probably be high on both sides.

Although the outcome of these early air battles is uncertain, there is good reason to believe that NATO would get the upper hand both offensively and defensively, despite the Warsaw Pact's numerical advantage. Estimates of the numbers of aircraft in or relevant to the

Central Region differ widely, but there is no doubt that the Warsaw Pact has more than NATO, although not by an overwhelming margin. IISS data indicates that the Warsaw Pact has some 3140 fixed wing combat aircraft deployed in the entire Western TVD, not counting medium range bombers.[13] The British Government's figures are 2650 Warsaw Pact tactical aircraft in Poland, Czechoslvakia and the German Democratic Republic, close to the IISS's comparable figure of 2540.[14] The United States Department of Defense indicates that the Soviet Union has 2000 tactical aircraft in the Western TVD and the other Warsaw Pact states have 1600.[15] IISS data indicates that NATO has some 1800 combat aircraft deployed in the Central Region, not counting French forces and that France could add another 450. The British Government's number, excluding France is 1250. Isby and Kamps' total for NATO in the Central Region, excluding France, is approximately 1600 combat aircraft.[16]

Of course both sides could add to these assets by bringing aircraft from outside the area. The 30 American reinforcement squadrons, for example, represent some 700 aircraft, although not all would go to the Central Region. The British, too, would send several reinforcement squadrons into Germany. According to the IISS, the Soviet Union has some 390 combat aircraft in the regions of its Central Reserve forces. Alberts gives the number 3478 for Warsaw Pact aircraft in the Central Region, including 225 bombers and reinforcements, and 2441 for NATO, including French and Spanish assets and reinforcements from Britain and North America.[17] The United States Department of Defense indicates that with both sides fully reinforced, the Warsaw Pact would have 6550 combat aircraft to NATO's 5125, with the Warsaw Pact having an advantage in fighter/interceptors, reconnaissance aircraft and bombers, and NATO having an advantage in fighter/ ground attack aircraft.[18]

Against the Warsaw Pact's numerical advantages in aircraft, its much greater numerical advantage in deployed air defence missiles, and its recent technological improvements, however, must be weighed significant NATO qualitative advantages: AWACS; higher quality fighter aircraft, especially F-16s and F-15s, with superior look-down shoot-down capability; more capable air-to-air missiles; better trained NATO pilots; better maintenance capability and superior electronic countermeasures and counter-countermeasures.[19] In addition, NATO airfields are at least 100 miles, and usually further, back from the front, providing some strategic depth and warning time against Warsaw Pact attack. NATO has important deficiencies in its command and control systems and its capacity for distinguishing friendly from unfriendly aircraft. The latter limits the tactics that can be used by air defence missile crews and pilots, especially reducing the effectiveness of long-range ground-to-air and air-to-air missiles.[20] However, the Warsaw Pact is plagued by these problems at least as much as NATO and probably more. As already mentioned, Warsaw Pact tactical ballistic missiles pose a significant threat, against which NATO is currently protected only by their limited number.

NATO's defensive counter-air will take a heavy toll of Warsaw Pact attack aircraft and their escorts. There is no doubt that Warsaw Pact long-range fighter escorts, especially the new Su-27 Flanker, will exact a toll of NATO fighters in return and that many Warsaw Pact bombs will find their marks. Valuable NATO targets, including airfields, command and control centres, nuclear storage sites, air defence missile sites and transportation nodes, will doubtless be damaged and some destroyed. However, with air-to-air combat exchange rates expected to be favourable to NATO, the result is likely to be the rapid destruction of the Warsaw Pact's long-range airpower.[21] There is a good chance that NATO can emerge from the Warsaw Pact's air and tactical ballistic missile attack without having suffered irremediable damage to airfields or high-value interdiction targets. Either way, however, the matter is likely to be decided within a few days or, at most, a few weeks.

NATO's primary aircraft for offensive counter-air and deep interdiction are United States F-111Es using Durandel cratering munitions and cluster bombs, United States F-111Fs using accurate laser-guided munitions, and British Tornados using bombs and JP233 containers that release cratering and area denial munitions.[22] These will be opposed by the Warsaw Pact's large defensive counter-air capability, both ground-based and fighter aircraft. Although in short supply, the EF-111 electronic warfare aircraft and the F-4G and associated F-4E defence suppression aircraft, the latter two armed with anti-radiation munitions, would help these aircraft penetrate the dense air defence missile environment near the FEBA.[23] Operating at night, in all weather and with terrain-following capabilities and electronic counter-measures, the F-111s and Tornados should be highly survivable when escorted by fighters with better air-to-air capability or even on their own, as Tornados would tend to go. NATO's offensive aircraft would be outnumbered initially and losses are inevitable, especially from the new Soviet Fulcrum and Flanker fighters with their look-down shoot-down capability. Indeed, losses might be high. Nonetheless, NATO's advantages suggest favourable exchange ratios in the counter-air campaign and considerable success in destroying critical interdiction targets. Within a few days to weeks, NATO is likely either to have accomplished its offensive counter-air objectives or to have lost the ability to pursue them.

The outcome of these deep interdiction campaigns and the intensive counter-air battle in the Central Region would hold great importance for the overall conflict. The winner would have achieved command of the air over his own territory and eventually over the battlefield. After his own facilities were repaired, supplies and reinforcements could flow relatively unimpeded to his ground forces. He could provide offensive air support to his own ground forces and conduct air interdiction attacks against the opponent throughout the duration of the conflict. Moreover, the loser's ability to do any of these things would be greatly impaired.

The outcome of military engagements is notoriously difficult to forecast. Nonetheless, a balancing of NATO's advantages against those of the Warsaw Pact does suggest that, despite heavy losses, NATO would probably gain the edge in the air in the Central Region during the early air battle and then hold it thereafter.[24] The crippling of the Warsaw Pact's long-range air power would imply that NATO rear areas would become relatively safe from attack. (SLCMs might still be a problem, depending on how the anti-submarine warfare campaign was faring, but their numbers are modest.) NATO airfields could then be repaired and air operations continued at a relatively high sortie rate with remaining aircraft. Significant damage to Pact airfields, the degradation of Pact ground-based air defences, and significant attrition of Pact fighter aircraft would translate into a NATO ability to continue its offensive counter-air campaign and to prosecute interdiction attacks, including against Warsaw Pact follow-on forces.

The prognosis for NATO's northern flank is also favourable. If aircraft from American carrier battle groups and the United States Marine Corps wing programmed for Norway are included, as they should be, the numerical disparity favouring the Warsaw Pact is not great. Alberts estimates 900 Warsaw Pact combat aircraft available to NATO's 660, but the latter do not include carrier-based or Marine Corps aircraft.[25] Northern Norwegian airfields might well be put out of action early, but the cost to the Soviet Union in terms of aircraft lost is likely to be high. Norway's F-16s carry drogue parachutes that allow operations from the numerous short runways and both they and USAF aircraft could also operate from southern Norway. British and United States Marine Corps Harriers can operate free of runways and the task of eliminating American carriers operating in Vestfjord would be a

PLATE 3.1. The Boeing E-3A AWACS: a force multiplier for NATO and soon to be acquired by the United Kingdom. *(Crown copyright: by courtesy of Air Clues Magazine.)*

difficult one for the Soviet Union. Moreover, NATO strikes would probably be made against the airfields in the Kola Peninsula, using F-111s or B-52s operating out of the United Kingdom. Losses might be heavy, but the effect in degrading Soviet air operations on the northern flank would be likely to make the exchange worthwhile. In the end, NATO would probably achieve superiority in the air over Norway, particularly given the long distances between critical areas of the country and Soviet airfields.

Neither side has a clear advantage on the southern flank, in Thrace. The Warsaw Pact numerical advantage is not great. According to IISS data, the Warsaw Pact has some 1055 combat aircraft deployed in the Soviet military districts of the Southwestern TVD, Bulgaria and Romania. Greece and Turkey together have 700 combat aircraft. In addition, NATO forces would include United States reinforcements and carrier-based aircraft and perhaps all or part of a United States Marine Corps wing. NATO's technological edge is less here than elsewhere, but that will change as Turkey and Greece modernise their air forces. In contrast to the northern flank, the distance to targets for Soviet aircraft operating out of Bulgaria or Romania are short and carrier battle groups are quite vulnerable off Thrace. Of course, a Warsaw Pact victory would have serious consequences for the ability of Greece and Turkey to defend their territory and for Turkey's ability to seal the strategic Straits.

Offensive Air Support

Simultaneously with the counter-air and deep interdiction campaigns, both sides would engage in offensive air support, that is battlefield air interdiction, close air support and tactical reconnaissance. From the outset of the ground battle, both sides would attack the opponent's command and control, supplies, equipment and forces near the FEBA on all fronts. NATO would attack second echelon Warsaw Pact forces and operational manoeuvre groups as they position themselves to relieve embattled first echelon units or exploit whatever tactical successes the first echelon had achieved. The Warsaw Pact would try to impede NATO from deploying ground reinforcements to strengthen weak spots in its defensive line or to pinch off and destroy Warsaw Pact forces that had penetrated. On the NATO side, British Harriers and Jaguars, German Tornados, Canadian CF-18s, Belgian, Dutch and American F-16s, German F-104s and F-4s would all be eligible for this battlefield air interdiction mission.[26] However, not all would be available for it during the early stage because many would be diverted to defensive counter-air.[27]

Both NATO and the Warsaw Pact would also engage in close air support of the ground forces during the early stages of ground conflict and throughout its duration on all fronts. Close air support aircraft, both fixed wing and helicopters, would make an important contribution to the ground conflict, despite their vulnerability.[28] They can respond quickly to tactical needs and opportunities, delivering intense and accurate firepower against troops, tanks, fighting vehicles, artillery and defensive emplacements anywhere on a battlefield. Neither helicopers nor specialised fixed-wing close air support aircraft, such as the A-10s, Alpha Jets and the SU-25 Frogfoot, can be diverted to defensive counter-air and they would therefore engage in close air support from the earliest stages of ground combat. Later, once the defensive counter-air requirements recede, the winner of the counter-air battle might re-allocate some multipurpose aircraft to close air support, but probably not many. These would be employed primarily for battlefield air interdiction.

Tactical reconnaissance aircraft would also be engaged from the onset of the ground battle. On the NATO side, these include German and American F-4s, British Jaguars and Harriers, Dutch F-16s and Belgian Mirage 5BRs, a total of some 160 aircraft, according to Isby and Kamps. The Warsaw Pact has more reconnaissance aircraft than NATO, approximately 280 in the Western TVD, according to the IISS. This disparity, suggests, perhaps, that the Pact expects a higher attrition rate. Reconnaissance will play an important role in providing information to ground commanders and to those who allocate aircraft sorties.[29]

Offensive air support aircraft on both sides will come under attack from enemy air superiority fighters, but probably not many in the early stage, given the more urgent demands for these latter aircraft to defend against the opponent's offensive counter-air and deep interdiction strikes. Some Soviet helicopters, notably the new Hokum, have an air-to-air capability against other helicopters that is worrisome for NATO. German Alpha Jets also have some capability against Warsaw Pact helicopters. However, the most important tactical threat to offensive air support aircraft will be ground-based air defences, including anti-aircraft guns, short-range SAMs, and large numbers of hand-held anti-aircraft missiles.[30] Some protection against these systems would be available to NATO aircraft from EF-111s and F-4Gs and to Warsaw Pact aircraft from Brewer-E and Badger-H and -J electronic counter-measure aircraft. Indeed, the electronic warfare capabilities of these aircraft would be an important asset to both sides, although NATO's are generally more capable. Nonetheless, offensive air support aircraft, both helicopter and fixed wing, must depend primarily on their own characteristics to survive tactically in this period: on their offensive capabilities, and on their ability to fly low, hide in the terrain, and run away.

Of course, offensive counter-air operations are the greatest threat to offensive air support, including helicopters, just as they are to other air operations. Only helicopters and the small number of RAF V/STOL Harriers can operate independently of airfields. Moreover, as a practical matter, even these depend on some centralised facilities for maintenance.

It is difficult to judge whether offensive air support operations would favour NATO or the Warsaw Pact more in the early stage of the conflict. A much larger fraction of total Warsaw Pact aircraft are committed to and designed primarily for defensive counter-air than is the case for NATO air forces. As a result, the numerical balance for offensive air support aircraft would be approximately even.

Nonetheless, the Soviets are building an impressive capability. The quality and numbers of their attack helicopters are of particular concern to NATO and they do have more ground-based air defences that could engage offensive air support aircraft. But NATO offensive air support assets are also extensive and capable. NATO aircraft have better night and all-weather capability and superior electronic warfare capabilities and decoys to negate Warsaw Pact air defences. Moreover, success in battlefield air interdiction and close air support requires air crews who are able to exercise judgement quickly and to exploit tactical opportunities. Such characteristics are not usually attributed to Soviet airmen. On balance, the ground forces may expect to benefit from friendly offensive air support. However, they will also suffer attrition from the adversary's air power without a decisive advantage either way until the counter-air battle takes its toll on these aircraft. Ultimately, the winner of the counter-air war will have command of the sky over and near the battlefield and in the long run will get the most out of offensive air support as well.

Even before the counter-air battle is resolved, however, offensive air support would be of significant help in NATO's efforts to contain any breakthroughs achieved by Warsaw Pact ground forces. With the ability to concentrate and sustain large quantities of lethal firepower anywhere on the battlefield quickly, helicopters and fixed wing close air support aircraft could be decisive in disrupting and delaying breakthrough forces until NATO artillery could target them and ground forces could arrive to destroy them and pinch off salients.

The Duration of the Conflict

The role of air power for the duration of the conflict in Europe will be determined largely by the outcome of the early, intensive counter-air battle in each region. The prize for the winner will be command of the air over his own territory and the ability to operate with declining losses over the battlefield and enemy territory. It will probably be won within, at most, a few weeks of the initiation of air combat.

The small size of the Central Region means that there will probably be a single winner of the counter-air battle there. As indicated, this would most likely be NATO. Such an outcome is unlikely to be reversed later. All, or almost all, Soviet tactical ballistic missiles would presumably have been expended in the earlier phase. Although the Soviets might have large numbers of aircraft elsewhere, once the Warsaw Pact airfields in a theatre were destroyed or seriously degraded, only limited reinforcements could be accommodated whilst NATO would have enough ground attack aircraft remaining to continue regular airfield attacks. At this stage, too, NATO's continuing offensive counter-air campaign would include a larger number of secondary Warsaw Pact airfields on its target list. Although specialised anti-airfield munitions are likely to have been depleted or nearly so, ordinary ones would probably be sufficient, because the Warsaw Pact repair capability would be degraded. In the meantime, NATO could repair its own airfields on the continent and bring in any squadrons, such as United States Air National Guard and Reserve, still not committed.

A Warsaw Pact victory in the early Central Region counter-air battle might not be as decisive. Such a victory would probably be limited to the continent and not include the United Kingdom which is far from Warsaw Pact airfields and well defended by aircraft and missiles. Any NATO long-range aircraft that survived and any not yet committed to the battle could therefore continue the air war from Britain. The latter might include Strategic Air Command B-52 bombers allocated to conventional missions, and perhaps some re-allocated from nuclear missions, if confidence had developed that neither side intended to escalate to nuclear war.[31] United States carrier-based aircraft might also be allocated, operating out of the North Sea or eventually perhaps from the Baltic.

The winner of the early air battle on the Norwegian and Turkish flanks might conceivably be different from the winner in the Central Region. Again, a NATO victory would probably be achieved if attacks on Warsaw Pact airfields could be sustained. Such attacks might have to include Soviet naval airfields in the Kola Peninsula, the eastern Baltic and the Black Sea. Otherwise, reinforcements could be brought west from the Pacific Fleet, unless its aircraft too had been destroyed. However, NATO again has other sources of reinforcements that could be brought into the northern and southern flanks, including United States carrier and Marine Corps wings and possibly long-range SAC bombers. If NATO lost the first round of the counter-air battle on one or both flanks, a second round might follow some time later. NATO's prospects of success must be judged greater in this second round because the Pact's offensive and defensive counter-air would certainly have been degraded.

The winner of the early counter-air battle in each theatre could count on air power to make an important contribution to the prosecution of the continuing ground battle. Airfields relatively near the front would be available for delivery of replacement manpower and high priority supplies and equipment. The opponent's high-value deep interdiction targets not destroyed in the early stages, and those replaced or repaired subsequently, could be attacked or attacked again. The continuing offensive counter-air strikes against airfields and the re-allocation of fighters from defensive counter-air to air superiority over and near the battlefield would gradually degrade the opponent's offensive air support capability. Close air support and battlefield air interdiction would steadily become one-sided and an extremely important force multiplier for the winner's ground forces.

Air attacks against follow-on forces could proceed in earnest in this stage. The Warsaw Pact plans to commit its ground forces in echelons, with fresh forces periodically replacing units engaged earlier. If NATO could delay the arrival and degrade the effectiveness of these follow-on forces, their relief value and their capabilities in combat would be much reduced. The ability of NATO ground forces to hold their positions would be greatly enhanced as a result. NATO also has reserves that the Warsaw Pact could profitably attack as they move forward, if the Pact retains the ability to do so.

Under the assumption that NATO has emerged the victor from the early counter-air battle, it is worth examining the question of how NATO should allocate its existing assets and investment between battlefield air interdiction and interdiction more remote from the battlefield. There is little doubt that attacking and re-attacking the relatively small number of fixed, but remote, high-value interdiction targets, such as command and control centres and rail and road transportation nodes all along the Soviet supply routes, and even in the western Soviet Union itself, would be useful. Even after the early counter-air battle had essentially been won by NATO, however, such a campaign would result in some attrition of the attacking NATO aircraft. Nonetheless, these targets would only have to be re-attacked occasionally and the benefit would be worth the cost.

The same is not true for attacks against mobile interdiction targets remote from the battlefield. Certainly the destruction of supply trucks, tanks, artillery, and fighting vehicles in follow-on forces moving towards the front would be useful. But, given the modest value of each target, the intrinsic difficulties of finding and hitting remote, mobile targets, the likely shortage of NATO aircraft at this stage of the conflict, and the availability of other routes to the same end, the likely attrition inflicted by remaining ground-based Pact air defences would be too great for deep interdiction attacks to be worthwhile. Moreover, if the Soviet Union had taken weeks to months rather than days to prepare its ground offensive, many of its follow-on forces might be waiting their turn to fight near the front rather than in the rear or moving forward.

Therefore, interdiction against mobile targets, such as follow-on forces, would be most usefully focused on battlefield air interdiction, not deep strikes. Here, target acquisition, although still difficult, would be less so. With shorter distances from bases to target area, sortie rates would be higher and flying time per sortie would be less, important considerations in a period when attrition and high utilisation rates would have taken a heavy toll on NATO's aircraft, crews and maintenance capability.[32] In addition, scarce assets could then most easily be allocated as needed to different locations and, for multi-role fighters, between interdiction and air superiority. The implication of this is that NATO planners should allocate existing aircraft and investment resources more to battlefield air interdiction than to deep interdiction of mobile targets. Current efforts to improve NATO capability to attack follow-on forces would be most effective if directed toward aircraft, missiles, sensors and other systems designed for use against enemy forces near to rather than remote from the battlefield.

Implications and Future Prospects

This brief analysis of the role of air power in a NATO-Warsaw Pact conventional conflict suggests that, overall, the balance of air power would favour NATO in such a conflict today. Even if the ground war broke out only two weeks after Warsaw Pact mobilisation began, as NATO (unrealistically) assumes for planning purposes, if NATO does not delay long in reacting and if a Warsaw Pact air offensive is not launched after only a few days of preparation, currently planned prepositioning and NATO's existing airlift capabilities would be sufficient to move committed United States ground and air forces to their designated European locations in time and NATO's air defences would be ready to meet the expected large-scale Warsaw Pact air offensive.

Within days to weeks of the initiation of the air offensive, one side is likely to have emerged as victor. This would probably be NATO, at least in the Central Region and on the northern flank. This means NATO would probably be able to blunt the Warsaw Pact air offensive, including the prevention of the successful landing of most of their airborne or airmobile forces, and would largely cripple Warsaw Pact long-range air power without suffering irremediable damage in the process. NATO would probably also be able to carry out its own offensive counter-air campaign and interdiction strikes against fixed, high-value Warsaw Pact targets with an acceptable level of attrition of its own aircraft. The situation in Thrace is less favourable to NATO and the outcome at best uncertain.

Offensive air support, including close air support, battlefield air interdiction and tactical reconnaissance, will benefit both sides considerably in the early stage of the conflict, until the counter-air battle begins taking a toll on offensive air support aircraft. The winner of the counter-air war will dominate the sky over and near the battlefield and, in the long run, will get the most out of offensive air support as well. Even before the air battle is resolved, however, offensive air support would be a significant asset to NATO's efforts to contain any breakthrough by Warsaw Pact ground forces.

Although the overall assessment made here of the role of air power is favourable to NATO, several areas of weakness in NATO's current air power posture are clear and the analysis points to directions for possible improvement. First, several actions are necessary to hedge against the possibility of a Warsaw Pact air offensive soon after its forces begin mobilising. United States strategic airlift should be augmented and the planned prepositioning of United States Air Force equipment and supplies and the arrangements under Co-located Operating Base Agreements should be completed. In addition, the alerting procedures for NATO's ground-based air defences should ensure that they are ready faster than the rest of NATO's ground forces. These actions are especially important on the flanks, where NATO's peacetime deployments of airpower are relatively weak.

Second, some action is necessary in the face of the Warsaw Pact tactical ballistic missile threat. Several possibilities present themselves. One is to seek to contain the threat through arms control. Frog, SS-21, Scud, SS-23 and SS-12/22 missiles all have nuclear as well as conventional capability and at least the longer-range ones might be included in an agreement on elimination or reduction of nuclear missiles in Europe. Another possibility is to develop and deploy an anti-tactical ballistic missile capability around critical targets, such as airfields and ports. The development of such a system would be difficult and expensive. What is suggested here, however, is a capability to deal with conventionally-armed tactical ballistic missiles, a much less onerous challenge than one to deal with nuclear-armed missiles.[33] Finally, measures could be taken to reduce the consequences of a tactical ballistic missile attack against airfields. These might include further hardening of structures, preparing to clear and repair runways quickly, procurement of more aircraft able to operate from short runways and rough fields, and further preparations to disperse aircraft and their support structure. This latter approach might be especially fruitful because the threat is, after all, likely to be brief, with all or almost all tactical ballistic missiles expended quickly. Deciding the optimal mix of measures involves cost/effectiveness considerations and is beyond the scope of this paper.

Third, NATO must maintain its edge in training and in all aspects of air power technology. Of particular significance too would be a further increase in the realism of NATO's air crew training, improvements in command and control and in the ability of aircraft and ground-based air defence crews to distinguish friendly from hostile aircraft. NATO needs to enhance its advantages in night-time and all weather operations and in electronic warfare, so vital to the maintenance of command and control, accomplishing defence suppression and impairing the effectiveness of an opponent's air-based radars. The latter will take on a new dimension as the Soviet Union begins to deploy its own effective airborne early warning system. Continuing to improve the range, electronic counter-counter-measure characteristics, and lethality of air-to-air and air-to-ground munitions, including anti-radiation munitions, is also important. At the very least, existing night vision and electronic counter-measure systems should be more widely distributed among NATO's air forces and stockpiles of advanced munitions should be enlarged.

Fourth, NATO's air power allocation to the defence of Thrace should be strengthened. This implies moving forward as fast as possible with the modernisation of the Greek and Turkish aircraft and air defence systems and with the preparations for bringing Allied reinforcement aircraft into Turkey during mobilisation. If possible, the Greek Air Force should be more fully integrated into the NATO command structure. In addition, the permanent deployment of United States squadrons and the prepositioning of ground force equipment in Turkey should be considered.

Fifth, NATO should continue to maintain a mix of single-purpose and multi-purpose aircraft. The former are most cost-effective in performing critical missions. The latter are also important, however, because as air-to-air fighters, they can contribute initially to winning the critical early counter-air battle and then, as ground attack aircraft, they can be re-allocated to battlefield air interdiction.

Sixth, once the early air battle is won, only relatively few air assets should be allocated to deep penetration ground attacks because only airfields and high-value fixed interdiction targets are worth the risk which repeated attacks entail. Interdiction against mobile targets, including follow-on forces, should concentrate on the geographic region near the battlefield where target acquisition would be easier, sortie rates higher, attrition rates lower, and leverage on the ground conflict greater.

Finally, the argument for focusing on battlefield air interdiction for follow-on forces attack applies to all new systems now being developed for that mission, not just aircraft. Follow-on forces attack is worth pursuing so long as the hardware remains affordable. Whether they rely on tactical ballistic or cruise missiles or provide ways to make attack with manned aircraft more effective, new technologies should be developed and deployed only if they are more cost-effective than achieving the same results in other ways.

NOTES

1. For a description of the armoured division equivalents methodology and an application of it to analyse the Central European force balance, see William P. Mako, *U.S. Ground Forces and the Defense of Central Europe* (Washington DC: Brookings, 1983).
2. Of particular relevance are Epstein's work on Soviet interdiction campaigns, Joshua M. Epstein, *Measuring Military Power: The Soviet Air Threat to Europe* (Princeton, NJ: Princeton U. P., 1984), and Posen's attrition-FEBA expansion model which incorporates the effect of close air support into a model of a dynamic ground battle, Barry Posen, 'Measuring the European Conventional Balance,' *International Security,* Volume 9, Number 3 (Winter 1984/85) pp. 47–88. An alternative approach to modelling ground warfare and the effect of close air support on it is provided in Joshua M. Epstein, *The Calculus of Conventional War* (Washington DC: Brookings, 1985). Although these analyses should not be taken too seriously because the models employed have significant technical deficiencies, they are of considerable value if read with appropriate scepticism.
3. This discussion of missions follows standard United States Air Force definitions, as delineated in Department of the Air Force, *Basic Aerospace Doctrine of the United States Air Force,* AFM 1-1 March, 1984, Chapter 3. Readers familiar with these missions might wish to skip directly to the next section on page 51.
4. This and subsequent estimates of allocations of NATO aircraft to missions are the author's estimates, based on data provided in The International Institute for Strategic Studies, *The Military Balance 1986–87* (London: International Institute for Strategic Studies, 1987); P. J. Alberts, *Deterrence in the 1980s: Part II, The Role of Conventional Air Power,* Adelphi Paper Number 193 (London: International Institute for Strategic Studies, 1984) and David C. Isby and Charles Kamps Jr., *Armies of NATO's Central Front* (London: Jane's, 1985), and on discussions with government analysts.
5. These, plus the equal number of squadrons permanently deployed in Europe, would make up the 60 tactical fighter squadrons that the United States has committed to NATO.
6. The 253 United States long-range passenger aircraft committed to the United States Air Force have the capacity on their own to move all the manpower for five 1/3 divisions to Europe in two days.
7. Isby gives the following definitions of the readiness categories for Soviet ground forces: Category I units are at 75–100 per cent assault strength in both men and equipment. Category II units are manned at 50–75 per cent strength, the average being slightly more than 50 per cent. Equipment is close to full strength, but less than Category I divisions and most is in storage. These divisions are deployable within 30 days of mobilisation. Category III units are manned at 10–30 per cent personnel strength and usually have only 33–50 per cent of their required equipment, most of it in storage. They are deployable 90 to 120 days after mobilisation, although composite divisions could be fielded within 60 days by merging two Category III divisions. David C. Isby, *Weapons and Tactics of the Soviet Army* (London: Jane's, 1981) p. 28.
8. The evidence from Soviet mobilisations against Czechoslovakia in 1968, Afghanistan in 1979 and Poland in 1981 suggests that the Soviet Union prefers taking the time needed to prepare its forces fully rather than rushing into action

prematurely. See William W. Kaufmann, 'Nonnuclear Deterrence,' in John D. Steinbruner and Leon V. Sigal, *Alliance Security: NATO and the No-First-Use Question* (Washington: Brookings, 1983) p. 70.

9. The International Institute for Strategic Studies estimates approximately 565 Frogs and SS-21s, with ranges of 70 and 120 kilometres respectively, 520 Scuds and SS-23s, with ranges of 300 and 500 kilometres, and 77 SS-12s with a range of 900 kilometres facing NATO Europe, including both Soviet and other Warsaw Pact assets. International Institute for Strategic Studies, op. cit, p. 208. The United States Department of Defence uses the number 810 for Warsaw Pact tactical ballistic missiles in the Western TVD. United States Department of Defense, *Soviet Military Power 1987*, (Washington DC: United States Government Printing Office, 1987) p. 17.

10. It should be noted that there is considerable controversy among Western analysts concerning the fraction of its submarine force and surface navy that the Soviet Union would employ for attacks against NATO shipping and what fraction it would reserve for protecting its ballistic missile submarines and for denying the United States Navy access to the sea approaches to its coast. This paper does not enter into that controversy, but makes the assumption that is the worst case from the perspective of the current discussion, namely that a large fraction of these Soviet assets would be employed against NATO shipping

11. Alfred Price, *Air Battle Central Europe* (New York: Free Press, 1986) Chapter 14, provides a useful discussion of these forces.

12. For a discussion of the nature and the role of air operations, including airborne assaults, in Soviet theatre strategy, see Philip A. Petersen and John G. Hines, 'The Conventional Offensive in Soviet Theatre Strategy,' *Orbis*, Volume 27, Number 3 (Fall 1983) pp. 695–739.

13. International Institute for Strategic Studies, op. cit.

14. *Statement on the Defence Estimates 1987 1* (London: Her Majesty's Stationery Office, 1987) p. 62.

15. United States Department of Defense, op. cit., p. 17.

16. Isby and Kamps, op. cit.

17. Alberts, op. cit., p. 56.

18. United States Department of Defense, op. cit., p. 92.

19. For a discussion of the deficiencies of Soviet aircraft maintenance and pilots, see Epstein, *Measuring Military Power,* op. cit., Chapters 3 and 4.

20. On the problems of Identification Friend and Foe, see Price, op. cit., pp. 9–10, 39–40, and 161–163.

21. For useful discussions of the tactics of NATO fighters in the defensive counter-air role, see Price, op. cit. Chapter 3 and Michael Skinner, *USAFE: A Primer of Modern Air Combat in Europe* (Novato, CA: Presidio Press, 1985) Chapter 5.

22. See Price, op. cit., Chapters 3, 4, and 6 and Skinner, op. cit., Chapter 3.

23. See Price, op. cit., Chapters 12 and 13 for descriptions of the functions of EF-111s and F-4Gs. The ability to deal with a dense environment of Soviet air defense missiles was demonstrated by the Israelis in Lebanon and by the United States Navy in the spring 1986 attack on Libya.

24. This conclusion is consistent with that reached by Epstein in his analysis of the Soviet counter-air and interdiction campaign. See Epstein, *Measuring Military Power*, op. cit.

25. Alberts, op. cit., p. 56.

26. Price, op. cit., Chapters 7 and 8, provides useful descriptions of Tornados and Harriers in battlefield air interdiction missions.

27. CF-18s, F-4s, F-16s and perhaps Jaguars would probably be diverted.

28. See Price, op. cit., Chapters 9 and 11, for descriptions of A-10s and helicopters

engaging in close air support. The role of forward air controllers in guiding A-10s to their targets is well described in Skinner, op. cit., Chapter 4.

29. Price, op. cit., Chapter 10, provides a useful discussion of tactical reconnaissance by RF-4Cs.

30. This is truer for A-10s than for helicopters or Harriers because the former must climb to between 700 and 1,000 feet in order to use their weapons.

31. B-52s have participated in deep interdiction exercises in Europe. See Michael Feazel, 'NATO Deploys Boeing B-52s in Deep-Strike Attack Exercise, *Aviation Week and Space Technology* (September 9, 1985) pp. 28–29.

32. NATO would average about two crews per aircraft in wartime, and crew fatigue would be a matter of considerable concern.

33. The desirability of a capability to deal with nuclear-armed tactical ballistic missiles is beyond the scope of this paper.

THE LESSONS OF OPERATIONAL EXPERIENCE
Air Chief Marshal Sir Michael Armitage, KCB, CBE, RAF

A large variety of factors contribute to the way ahead in a complex topic such as air power, as may be seen from the accompanying chapters dealing with threats, with operational requirements, with industrial factors, with difficult questions of resource and so on. I should like to discuss some lessons from operational experience, in other words some lessons from history, which implies the selection of those particular events or circumstances in the past from which we should look forward to the future.

Because of limited space, my treatment of the subject will be highly selective, which makes very difficult an exercise that has never been easy, and one that abounds with traps for the unwary. Some very distinguished people have fallen into those traps in the past. One or two have done so in spectacular fashion, like for example Admiral Leahy who, when offering his views on the atom bomb to President Truman in 1945 said: 'That is the biggest fool thing we have ever done. The bomb will never go off, and I speak as an expert in explosives.'

Nor have we in aviation always managed to circumvent the pitfalls, and even in our own Service we have sometimes been seriously in error. One recalls for example the forecasts made in 1937 by the Air Ministry of likely casualty numbers in the expected war with Germany. The figures were based on the operational experience of World War One, refined, if that is the right word, by some of the results of the bombing of cities during the Spanish Civil War. The resulting figures on which the United Kingdom Civil Defence measures at the start of World War Two were planned, in order to meet the expected knock-out blow by the Luftwaffe, were that 66,000 civilians would be killed and another 134,000 injured each week. In fact, during the whole of the first year of the war, the total civilian casualties in this country amounted to only 257 killed and 441 hospitalised.

Or one could take as another example of the difficulties of projecting forward into the future from the experience of the past the statement by the Commander-in-Chief Bomber Command included in a long and detailed letter of May 1939 to the Air Ministry about the problems of a future war. He said that he was 'convinced that the idea that we shall be able to fight the next war with mass-produced pilots and crews as we did in the last war is fallacious.' As things turned out, the total number of RAF and Commonwealth aircrew trained during World War Two totalled no fewer than 326,552.

To be sure those two examples are more than 50 years old, and a great deal has happened since then. That lapse of time means that we have far more experience on which to draw, and experience *should* reduce our margins of error. But, in fact, experience can actually contribute to a misappreciation in some cases. I offer just one example, drawn from the Suez campaign of 1956.

Very briefly, the Anglo-French air operations at Suez were divided into three phases. One phase was offensive counter-air against the Egyptian Air Force, and a second was air support for Allied ground forces. But the third phase was what was called at the time 'Aero-psychological bombardment.'

This particular air mission seems to have come about because of the experience of World War Two just over a decade previously. The concept of using bombing to destroy the morale or the will of the enemy to resist had been carried forward into post-war thinking. We saw that concept in the Casablanca Directive of 1943 where we read of '. . . the progressive destruction of the German military, industrial and economic system, and the *undermining of the morale of the German people* to a point where their capacity for armed resistance is fatally weakened.' We then see it again in The Royal Air Force Manual of Operations of 1947, which stated that 'The primary role of the Royal Air Force is to attack the civil and military organisations of the enemy and by so doing *to disrupt and destroy his will and ability* to continue the war.' And finally we have the version in the 1956 directive for the Suez operation, whose air component was to 'consist of air attack against selected key points with a psychological warfare campaign designed to *reduce the Egyptian will to resist.'* [*Author's italics*]

But by the end of the first day of this air bombardment at Suez, and before the Allied landings had even taken place, the international outcry about the bombing attacks caused them to be halted. The fact was that the politico/military circumstances were entirely inappropriate to the air mission being attempted.

I have already suggested that experience should narrow the margin of error. But since the 1950s, and working against that factor, has been the increasing complexity of air warfare. There are now more technical factors to be considered; in terms of capabilities there are more options available; and because air power itself is sensitive to technological developments – particularly perhaps in electronic warfare – air warfare has, in one sense, become less stable.

Another difficulty that we face, as we try to distil the lessons of experience, is that some of the experience seems to have been ambiguous. One particularly striking field, in terms of ambiguous or even contradictory results, is to be found in a role of considerable current interest, that of air interdiction.

Take for example the Korean War, a campaign in which the United Nations Command held almost total air superiority, and in which very considerable Allied resources were eventually deployed and devoted to air interdiction. Based no doubt on the experience of World War Two only five years earlier, a subject to which I will return in a moment, great things were expected of air interdiction in Korea. Between August 1950 and June 1952, it is possible to distinguish no fewer than eight separate air interdiction campaigns that were launched against the Communist rail and road networks in the north of that country.

To be sure, these attacks had a direct military effect on the Communist forces, and an indirect effect in terms of the resources devoted by the Communists to defending and to maintaining the systems that were under attack. But contrary to most of the claims at the time and since, the fact was that – as the United States Navy Official History tells us in a notable euphemism — after June 1952, interdiction was 'de-emphasised'. In other words it was halted; and it was halted because it had failed.

Why had interdiction failed? Briefly, there were five reasons. First, the logistic needs of Asian-style massed armies had been wildly over-estimated. It turned out that a North Korean division could fight on as little as 50 tons of resupply per day. The average figure for a Western style division was at that time about 650 tons.

Second, the resilience of a coolie-maintained logistic system had been just as badly *under*-estimated. Third, outside logistic choke points the Communists dispersed their columns by day, and moved them forward by night. But the Allied air forces had no night capability, and thus no answer to this strategem. The supplies and the reinforcements continued to trickle forward in a kind of logistic osmosis.

Fourth, where choke-points did exist in the North Korean logistic system, the accuracy and the effectiveness of the air attacks were poor. But then when air attack did manage to hit features such as key bridges, the Communists turned out to be far better than had been thought at repair and improvisation. River bridges, for example, were often repaired or by-passed within hours of being brought down. A single rail

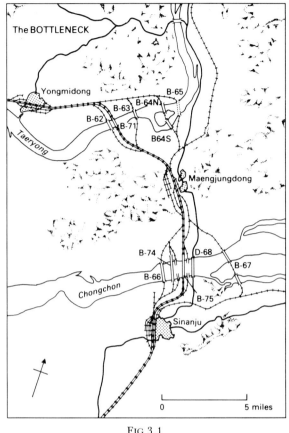

The BOTTLENECK

Yongmidong

B-65

B-64N

B-63

B-62

B-71

B64S

Taeryong

Maengjungdong

B-74

D-68

B-67

B-66

Chongchon

B-75

Sinanju

0   5 miles

FIG 3.1
The Bottleneck.

cut could be restored within two hours, and a really badly hit section of
railway line was working again within four to seven days.

Figure 3.1 illustrates the determination with which bridges were
rebuilt or replaced, and this was quite often at a faster rate than that at
which they could be brought down with the types of inaccurate air
weapons available at that time. It is clear from the scale of this
Communist effort that at least their commanders had no doubts about
the likely effects on their forces of a successful United Nations air
interdiction campaign.

Finally, those misappreciations by the United Nations Command
were compounded by a failure to appreciate that if the enemy is free to
decide the intensity of the combat at the front, as the Communists
usually were, then the enemy will adjust his combat activity to match
the logistic effort that is escaping the interdiction blockade. In Korea it

was not essential to the Communists that they should apply constant or urgent military pressure on the Allies, and they could therefore afford to build up their strength gradually before launching their various offensive initiatives. Successful interdiction always means that consumption outstrips supply.

This failure of interdiction in Korea was to be repeated in different circumstances in Vietnam over a decade later. Even when weapon effects, night attack capabilities and, particularly, weapons accuracy improved, as they did from about 1967 onwards, those improvements in operational effectiveness were more than offset by the very tight political restrictions imposed on the air forces operating over Vietnam.

The result was to constrain the selection of target types. Dams and dykes, for example, could not be attacked. There were numerous bombing halts. There were geographical restrictions. These excluded Laos and Cambodia, and also put a 25 nautical mile sterile zone around the capital Hanoi and the main port, Haiphong, until 1972. And this even though air reconnaissance clearly showed the masses of equipment parked in the streets of Hanoi and the unloading activity from ships in Haiphong.

These geographical restrictions were crucial, and they had a crippling effect on the interdiction offensive against the railway lines from China through Hanoi and down to the main distribution area about 150 miles north of the DMZ. That effect was made worse by the fact that on this vital route a buffer zone 20 miles deep had been applied outside the Chinese border to prevent accidental incursions by attacking aircraft into Chinese airspace. Finally, air attacks were prohibited against all the built-up areas of North Vietnam.

The Communists were able to take advantage of these comprehensive restrictions by moving trains up to the edge of the Chinese buffer-zone by day ready for a night run south. They then shuttled trains by night between residential areas on the way to the DMZ, lying up or unloading within these sanctuary areas by day. They could thus move gradually south, progressively and with a high degree of invulnerability, towards the war zone.

As a result of those factors, we saw in Vietnam a massive interdiction potential once more failing to bring the decisive results that were expected of it, but only because the one extensive target array suited to interdiction efforts was excluded by the political restrictions on air attack. Interdiction took on a quite different significance once the B52s were employed. When these aircraft launched their massive and concentrated attacks on key targets in Hanoi and Haiphong in

December 1972, the North Vietnamese opened negotiations only a month later that ended that phase of a war that had been fought on and off since 1946.

I am not suggesting that these important failures of interdiction in Korea and Vietnam necessarily caused the whole concept of interdiction to be called into question; but I do suggest that had these interdiction campaigns in the Far East succeeded, the proponents of air power would be in a stronger position when they emphasise the vital role of interdiction in modern land/air warfare.

As evidence of the real potential of interdiction, it would pay us to look at the most relevant experience we have, rather than the most recent. That should direct us to the campaign in Western Europe in 1944, when the Allied air forces attacked the French transportation system in North West France before the invasion of Normany.

I am not saying that the military factors in that air interdiction campaign were straightforward, or that we can simply read across to the circumstances of today in Europe. It is true, for example, that a massive air effort in terms of aircraft numbers was devoted to the campaign, numbers far beyond the inventories of today.

But against that we should note, first, that two-thirds of all the air effort before the invasion was directed to areas outside Normandy and its approaches, so as to conceal the site of the intended landings. Second, that our aircraft had virtually no night capability against targets such as bridges. Third, that although we had a high degree of air superiority by the time of the invasion itself, the interdiction attacks met fierce opposition from German air and ground defences. And fourth, we should remember the important fact that German supplies had been built up in their forward areas over a period of four years.

Yet despite all these important negative factors, the results of the interdiction campaign were very striking. *Figure 3.2* shows the position of the lines of interdiction along which all the bridges were attacked, and *Figure 3.3* gives an indication of the kind of result that was produced. The German view of those results is best illustrated in the statement by von Rundstedt after the war. He said it was 'all a question of air force, air force, and again air force,' adding that:

> The main difficulties which arose for us at the time of the invasion were the systematic preparations by your air force; the smashing of the main lines of communications, particularly the railway junctions. We had prepared for various eventualities . . . that all came to nothing or was rendered impossible by the destruction of railways, communications, railway stations and so on. The second thing was the attack on the roads, on marching columns and so on, so that it was impossible to move anyone at all by day, whether a column or an individual, that

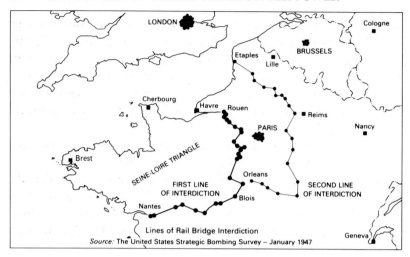

FIG 3.2
Lines of Rail Bridge Interdiction.

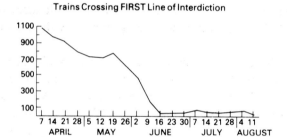

Trains Crossing FIRST Line of Interdiction

Source: The United States Strategic Bombing Survey – January 1947

FIG 3.3
Trains Crossing First Lines of Interdiction.

is to say to carry fuel or ammunition. That also meant the bringing up of the armoured divisions was out of the question — quite impossible.

Moving now away from interdiction, I have said that some of the operational experience of the 1950s and late 1960s was characterised by ambiguity. But there were also events in those decades that left a clear impact on the exercise of air power. I offer two of the more important ones.

First, there was the destruction in May 1960 of the U-2 strategic reconnaissance aircraft over Sverdlovsk by a Soviet SA-2 SAM. It is true that there were other factors involved at the time, including the cancellation of Skybolt in 1962, but there is no doubt that the loss of the

U-2 played a very significant part in changing the tactics of our own Air Force in 1962, from the very high-level penetration of hostile air defences — above the ceiling of most air defence systems — to a concept of very low-level penetration below the lobes of most air defence radars. It took the U-2 incident to accelerate the introduction of the counter-measures that would clearly have been essential had we been engaged in hostilities at that time.

A second formative event was the devastating pre-emptive attack by the Israelis on 25 Arab airfields on 5 June 1967. On that first day of the six-day Middle East war, the Israelis destroyed over 250 Arab aircraft on the ground. Just three hours into the war, 75 per cent of the combat strength of the Egyptian air force was wreckage on its own airfields. Similar treatment then immediately followed for the Syrian, the Jordanian and the Iraqi air forces.

It was this event that provided the impetus for the long overdue replacement of revetments on airfields throughout Europe. The Warsaw Pact began to build hardened aircraft shelters in the spring of the following year, and by May 1976 they had built 1,867 of them. In NATO we followed, rather belatedly perhaps, with the first ones in January 1974.

We should note that the threat had for long been obvious. Indeed the high vulnerability of aircraft standing virtually unprotected on their bases had been a feature of air warfare since World War 1. But again, it took a demonstration like that day in June 1967 to stimulate air forces to take the necessary counter-measures. One of the general lessons we therefore do need to note from past operational experience is that so far we have had time to react to obvious developments. We cannot assume that the luxury of time will be available to us in the future.

I would now like to bring us much closer to the present, by dealing briefly with just five other engagements in which air power was concerned. The first three occurred in the Falklands campaign of 1982, the others were the Israeli raids on Tunis and Baghdad.

The first thing to be said about the Falklands campaign is that it was *sui generis*. It is difficult to conceive of any other campaign that might be fought virtually unsupported over a distance of 8,000 miles, and we should be cautious when we try to draw general lessons from that particular experience.

To take the Argentinian side first: their most potent weapon was recognised by the Defence Intelligence Staff as early as 2 April — before our task force even sailed — to be the Super-Étendard armed with Exocets. The Argentine Navy had only five of these aircraft, and only four of these were serviceable. Yet they not only sank two major ships — they obliged our Carrier group to operate at ranges close to the maximum radius of action of the Harrier aircraft. That fact determined much of the character of the whole campaign.

As to our own air effort, one need mention only the effect of the long-range attacks by single Vulcans on Port Stanley airfield. Although the runway was not hit badly enough to close it, the realisation by the Argentines that such long-range attacks just might be directed against the mainland in general, and against Buenos Aires in particular, led to the deployment northward of their most important squadron of Mirage interceptors, thus depriving the Argentine commanders in the South Atlantic of any hope of securing air superiority over the Falklands or over the surrounding sea areas. So the experience of both sides in that campaign should remind us of the disproportionate leverage that relatively modest air resources can exert.

The Israeli air attacks on the nuclear facility at Tuwaitha near Baghdad on 7 June 1981, and on Tunis on 1 October 1985, also had some notable features. In the Baghdad attack, the Israelis employed a force of only eight F-16 attack aircraft with six F-15s flying top cover, to fly a round trip of about 1,400 miles, probably with post-attack refuelling. They flew across the Gulf of Akaba and Saudi Arabia to deliver a successful attack of great precision with 2,000 lb retarded iron bombs onto quite a small target. The precision of the attack need not surprise us from such a well-tried air force, but the reach of air power in making such a long-range attack, the audacious routing and, above all, the degree of surprise should not escape us.

The attack on the PLO headquarters in Tunis was another interesting demonstration of air power. As far as we can tell, four or five F-16s carried out this attack with two or three F-15s giving top cover. Three Boeing 707s (two refuellers and one ECM aircraft) were also in the attack package. Even greater accuracy was achieved here than at Tuwaitha, probably because laser-guided bombs were used. Once again, we should note the long range, this time a round flight of almost 3,000 miles, involving, by the way, the transit of four Flight Information Regions. Once more, we should particularly note the vital element of surprise in the time and the place of the attack.

To bring us even closer to the circumstances of the European theatre, at least in terms of the air warfare assets employed on both sides, I would like to mention, first, the United States raid on Libya in April 1986, and second, the Israeli assault on the Syrian air force over the Bekaa in June 1982.

In the raid on Libya in April 1986, about 100 American aircraft took part in precision raids lasting only twelve minutes on five targets in Tripoli and Benghazi, involving a round trip of 5,500 miles. Seventeen different aircraft types were engaged one way or the other, ranging from U-2 reconnaissance aircraft, through F-14s and F-111s, to KC-135 tankers. Here we had an attack on point targets by a highly capable force opposed by some of the latest Warsaw Pact equipment — as well as against some advanced Western air defence systems such as Crotale.

The raid was only a qualified success. I say qualified partly because collateral damage was caused to friendly embassies near the barracks. But far more important, the attack was not delivered with the full weight that had been intended. I am dealing now only with the United States Air Force element of the attack. Here the requirement was that eighteen F-111 aircraft should carry out the strikes, and that each aircraft was to identify and acquire its target with two fire control systems so as to ensure proper target selection.

Twenty-four F-111s took off, eighteen mission aircraft plus six spares. Two aircraft suffered systems failures before the first air-to-air refuelling, and were replaced by spares. After that refuelling, the other four spares returned to base, but one mission aircraft then aborted and landed in Spain. Of the seventeen aircraft that then flew on to the target, four found that they were unable to use both fire control systems and so could not release their weapons, and one aircraft was lost to the very considerable anti-aircraft defences. So in summary, of an available force of twenty-four aircraft, twelve struck the target area, seven suffered systems failures, and one was shot down.

The degree of success that was achieved was dependent not only on high technology, on very carefully co-ordinated planning, and on skilful crews, but again — once more — on the essential ingredient of surprise and even audacity. Most important of all, however, I suggest we need to note the high penalty exacted in terms of operational effectiveness by the simple factor of unreliable equipment. This is something to which — because of our limited numbers and our increasingly complex systems — we are going to have to pay far more attention in the future than we have in the past.

Finally, I want to say something about the engagement over the Bekaa. On the face of it, this was a clear demonstration of Western style equipment and training inflicting an overwhelming defeat on an air force trained and equipped by the Warsaw Pact. In particular, some observers attributed the Israeli success to the Shrike anti-radiation missiles used against the Syrian SAMs, or to drones, which somehow overcame the Syrian defence in a way that manned aircraft could not have done; or to both these things.

There is no time here to go into a detailed analysis of the Bekaa action, but I think it may be useful to mention a few of the other important factors in this engagement that we need to bear in mind, particularly if we are to extract lessons that may have any value in other theatres, including Europe.

For one thing, the Syrian SAM sites were so far forward that they could be taken under fire by Israeli artillery. Also, the Soviet advisers were nervous about exposing their latest air defence systems in forward areas, and various other systems were used as 'fillers'. The Syrians therefore did not have anything like a comprehensive Warsaw Pact SAM layout. For example, there were only two early warning radars in the Bekaa instead of the eight or ten that should have been there with the nineteen SAM batteries.

Another important factor was that the whole engagement took place in a relatively small area — only 30 miles across and 25 miles deep — in other words, an area about the size of Luxembourg. A great deal of intelligence gathering and surveillance could thus be focused by the Israelis on to the combat area long before a shot was fired. In addition, the terrain favoured the attack. The high ridges at the southern end of the Bekaa completely masked Israeli activity from the Syrian SAM sites, and the low hills in the area gave very good cover for Israeli low-flying aircraft. Finally, the Syrian SAMs had only recently arrived in the area. They were not properly dug-in, nor were they otherwise protected.

Taking advantage of all these factors, the Israelis launched a very carefully co-ordinated campaign against the Syrian SAM system. This included, first, a simultaneous commando raid on the Syrian command post controlling the air defences in the Lebanon, with the result that all co-ordination was lost. Second, the Israelis used E-2C AWACS aircraft to report the position of Syrian ground radars as they were switched on so that this intelligence could be transmitted to ground control stations. And third, the Israelis used RC-707 aircraft acting as stand-off jammers.

Then, in the second stage of the engagement, Syrian fighters rose to join the battle. The result was that very skilful Israeli pilots, flying the best American fighters with the most advanced missiles, well directed by controllers, were flying against less well trained Syrian pilots, flying mediocre Soviet aircraft armed with poor quality missiles, and with their control neutralised. The result was a score of 85:0. But we should also note in passing that this extraordinary result was not all that far removed from the success of 1967, when the Israelis shot down 60 for 3; or of 1973, when the ratio seems to have been something like 250:6.

So what were the key features of the engagement? Well, the significance of EW and C^3I is obvious, the importance of defence suppression cannot be over-emphasised, and the superior combat equipment of the Israelis clearly played a crucial part. But I suggest that behind all that there are three other important things to note.

First, as I pointed out, circumstances in the Bekaa were quite unique and the operation must be seen in that light. Second, yet again, surprise played a decisive part in almost every aspect of the whole engagement. But third, and this is essential to our understanding of the Bekaa, it was not merely the Israeli technical assets that accounted for the scale of the Syrian defeat; it was the fact that the IDF retained the operational initiative throughout, and that they displayed clear advantages in leadership, in organisation, in tactical ability and in adaptability. Their success lay not in their technology, but in how they used their technology. That is the real lesson of the Bekaa.

Finally, and as to lessons from air power experience as a whole, is it possible to draw together any conclusions or even any useful threads from so brief a survey? I offer just three threads and one conclusion. First, we must take care not to carry forward too readily into entirely new circumstances lessons from past air power experience, as Suez and Korea showed. But second, when proven concepts such as interdiction fail in new circumstances as they did in Korea and Vietnam, it does not necessarily follow that the basic concept was wrong. Third, in the past some very obvious air power lessons have been waiting for their moment. We may not always have the luxury of time on our side in the future.

As to a conclusion, it can only be a very broad one from a survey of the kind I have offered, and it is this: aviation is a dynamic business, but our quite proper concern with the extremes of technology leading us into the future must not lead us to ignore the lessons of the past. We need to analyse very carefully indeed air power operational experience if we are to avoid misjudgement or worse in shaping our plans for the future.

CHAPTER 4

The Technological Dimension

THE CONVENTIONAL AIR BATTLE IN THE YEAR 2000
Major General Perry Smith, USAF (Retd)

The purpose of this paper is to stretch the mind of the reader in two important but related areas. First, I wish to contemplate the rather distant future as regards air technology and the impact of this new technology on the conventional battle in Europe. Second, I would like to address other more general aspects of both technology and planning in hopes of encouraging the reader to think more deeply about the long-range future of the Alliance.

The potential for major improvements in NATO conventional capability over the next few years is quite high, particularly in the air environment. Much of that improvement relates directly to technological advances, but advances in doctrine, tactics, and training can and should also play an important role. It is most important that military leaders of all NATO nations keep abreast of the changing battlefield environments as well as actively pursuing improvements in technology, doctrine and tactics.

The close co-ordination of land and air will be even more important in the years ahead than it has been in the past, since technology is moving so fast and barriers to good co-ordination are actually becoming greater. In the past eight or nine years, compartmentalisation has become an important phenomenon in the research and development world. If present trends continue, the operational world could be significantly affected by compartmentalisation in the years ahead. While there are many advantages to controlling access to very sensitive programmes, there are some major disadvantages. Leaders from each of the NATO countries with major research and development programmes must weigh these factors carefully when developing and implementing weapons systems, programmes and policy. These issues relating to compartmentalisation are so important both to the air-land battle in the 21st century and to the future of the Alliance that they deserve a few paragraphs in this paper.

Innovation Through Compartmentalisation

One of the evolving truths of compartmentalisation is that innovation is considerably easier in a black programme than in an open, or white one. In my judgement, this fact is even more important than the advantages of hiding the technology from potential enemies, since doctrinal and conceptual innovation is so difficult in the white world. Another advantage of compartmentalisation is the rapidity with which a radical technological idea can turn into an operational system So many bureaucratic barriers are removed in compartmentalised programmes that a weapons system which normally would take a decade or more to develop can be fielded in five or six years.

These advantages must be weighed against a number of significant disadvantages. The Air Force of an individual nation in NATO may be developing a radically new system which may help solve a major problem the Army or Navy is facing, but if the leaders from the other services and from the other nations are not informed of this programme, they may waste money and effort on an inferior system to address the same problem. In addition, there is often a 'doctrinal lag' in incorporating into the mainstream of the operational world new operational systems which were developed very rapidly through compartmentalisation. This doctrinal lag can become particularly harmful when the officials responsible for developing doctrine are not cleared for the programme either during the research and development phase or after the system becomes operational.

This problem of doctrinal lag is further compounded when service lines are crossed, and the problem becomes particularly acute when national lines are crossed. For instance, getting an officer from the German Navy to share closely held secrets from a tightly compartmentalised research and development programme with an American Army officer (or vice versa) is just plain tough.

Autonomous Systems

Perhaps the most important technological development which will significantly affect the air-land battle in the early part of the next century will be the deployment of autonomous systems in large numbers. One example (among many) of these systems would be a very small pilotless aircraft with a very efficient small engine, an airframe made of plastic or composite material, a super-sensor in the nose and a very small warhead. The super-sensor, using one or more of a number of techniques, could be programmed to target a very specific type of enemy vehicle, aircraft, radar and so forth. This airborne vehicle would have a very long loiter time (many hours to a few days) and could provide a considerable capability in the realms of deterrence and war fighting.

The deterrent value of this vehicle could be its most important quality. Historically, the Soviets have had great respect for, and fear of, Western systems based on high technology. At times, they have overestimated the capability of such systems. This fear, admiration and overestimation could be very helpful in causing Soviet decision-makers to forego contemplated offensive operations, if they thought that the Alliance had large numbers of these autonomous vehicles deployed and on alert status in Europe. Sometime in the future it may be useful to lift, ever so slightly, the dark veil of compartmentalisation to enhance the deterrent value of some of these systems.

Autonomous systems which depend heavily on high technology sensors, engines, and airframes are likely to be better than similar Soviet systems, since the Soviets will probably continue to lag behind in these important technical areas. Hence, if Western civilian and military leaders are particularly prudent about how they manage compartmentalisation, they can have the best of both worlds. In other words, technological leakage to the Soviet Union can be restricted while defence and deterrence can be enhanced.

To develop the point about autonomous systems further, let me speculate about how they may change the face of the air-land battle. An enemy land force, facing a myriad of autonomous systems, will have to deal with real doctrinal, operational, morale and tactical problems, particularly when it tries to concentrate its forces. The movement of ground vehicles, for instance, will create noise, heat, and other observable phenomena that can be picked up by tiny but very discriminating sensors in airborne vehicles loitering over the battlefield and over other areas of high interest such as airfields and logistics areas. The enemy ground force command will face a number of bad choices. One choice would be to destroy the vast majority of these autonomous vehicles before he begins to move his forces in order to avoid suffering massive losses in the first few hours of major ground force movements. Destroying these systems will be difficult because they should be very small, very stealthy and very agile. In addition, those that will be destroyed could be easily and rather cheaply replaced by others.

Another choice for the ground force commander would be to deceive these systems — that is, to spoof them in some way. This could have some very positive results but it could also be very expensive. For instance, to produce the exact sound, heat and shape of a Soviet truck may be almost as expensive as creating the truck itself and bringing it to the battlefield. In short, decoys only make sense when they are considerably cheaper than the real thing.

A third choice for the ground force commander would be to concentrate his ground forces in such a way as to overwhelm these autonomous systems with too much data. This approach could fail, and fail massively, if the commander underestimates the capability and the numbers of these autonomous vehicles.

A fourth choice for the ground commander is to accept the losses that these systems will cause and hope that the opponent will run out of them. This can work against an adversary that has not procured large numbers of these systems or has not developed the logistical, transportation, and deployment systems to ensure that enough of these vehicles are available to launch and re-launch into the battlefield area where the enemy is contemplating an attack.

Enemy airfields will also face the devastation that these autonomous systems can cause. Turning on external power units, towing airplanes and taxiing aircraft may all become very risky operations if autonomous airborne systems are loitering over key enemy airfields. In the past, an airfield has been vulnerable to attack but launching of aircraft could still take place at night, in marginal weather and in between enemy air or missile attacks. In the future, a commander of an air base will have to deal with air attack by aircraft, glide bombs, missiles and autonomous systems. In the past, attacks on air bases were of short duration and after each attack, airfield repair and the recommencement of launch and recovery of aircraft could take place. By the year 2000, even the rapid runway repair vehicles may be programmed as targets in these overhead autonomous systems, and the repair of runways and taxiways may become much more hazardous than it has been in the past.

The 21st Century Air Base in Europe

Autonomous systems will not require air bases of the traditional size and scope, but planners must be creative in the deployment, launching and recovery of autonomous systems in order to take full advantage of their size and stealthy characteristics. There will remain, of course, many aircraft which must operate off hard surfaces. Dispersal will become increasingly important and technology, if properly exploited, can help a great deal in this area. Expert systems which provide help to maintenance technicians have excellent potential here. If each aircraft mechanic and each avionics technician had a small computer which contained the knowledge of some of the very best and most experienced supervisors, the overall manpower needs could be reduced and the ability to disperse aircraft in small numbers to diverse locations would be enhanced.

The great emphasis on very high reliability of aircraft systems will begin to pay off by the early part of the next century and the need for spare parts and supply personnel to provide and manage the spare parts will also decrease modestly. These factors will help to enhance the ability of an aircraft squadron to disperse quickly and operate out of austere locations. Tactical deception must become a high priority for commanders of fixed air bases. There are many things that an air base commander will be able to do to make his air base very difficult to find, and once found, to make it difficult to identify the 'real' targets.

Exploiting NATO's Technological Advantages

Over the course of the next few decades, there will be a technological race of extraordinary proportions. The United States and its NATO partners should be able to win it. The Soviet Union and Eastern European nations have deep abiding problems with the relationship between widespread public access to high technology and the need to maintain control over their populations. These problems will inhibit exploitation of high technology sufficiently to give the West an advantage that prudent public policy can exploit. Microcomputers, software engineering (the 'hacker' role here can be most important if the defence communities of the West can attract some of the best of the hackers), miniaturisation, expert systems, and intelligent computer-aided design can all make important contributions to air warfare. In short, the societies that have the most computer-literate populations and the populations with the most highly developed innovative and entrepreneurial skills should be the winners of this important technological race.

The real challenge for the Alliance, however, is not the development of these new systems. The challenge is how to share this technology between and among NATO nations and how to develop the doctrine and tactics for the optimal use of these systems.

This co-ordination of technology, doctrine and tactics should be accomplished prior to the operational deployment of these new systems.

Since changes in doctrine and tactics come quite slowly in the NATO environment, it is incumbent upon the leaders in the United States, Great Britain, Germany, and other nations who are developing exotic new systems, to share the basic technology and the operational capability with the leaders of the NATO operational commands. This sharing of information should take place at least a year before each new black programme becomes operational. Individual nations must take the initiative in disclosing this sensitive information since the NATO operational commanders will, in many cases, have insufficient background or insight to ask for it. It is clearly not enough that the Research and Development chiefs of each service and each nation share this information: the NATO operational commanders must be briefed in some detail so that they are aware not only of its existence but also of its importance.

The Changing Operational Environment

The battlefield of the 21st century will be dramatically changed by the ground and air systems that are being developed now and should be deployed over the course of the next 10 years. A period of budgetary austerity may even accelerate this trend towards exotic new systems since many of them are considerably less expensive than traditional ones such as manned aircraft, helicopters, tanks and artillery pieces. As service programmes in each of the nations of the Alliance are developed during upcoming austere budgetary years, decision analysis, mission area analysis and systems analysis should highlight the value of these new developments. In addition, these analytical techniques, which have matured materially in recent years, should help in the difficult, but important, divestiture process. For instance, it is likely that both the A-10 aircraft (the primary American close air support aircraft) and the RF-4 (the primary tactical reconnaissance aircraft of a number of NATO nations) will not be replaced by manned systems when they become obsolete in the early part of the next century. These aircraft will probably be replaced, in large part, by autonomous systems of low unit cost as well as very considerable mission capability. A great advantage of these autonomous systems, which was not discussed earlier in this paper, is that they should have the potential to accomplish a multiplicity of missions with only modest changes to the sensor software. In other words, a lethal autonomous system could be designed to do all of the following missions: close air support, battlefield air interdiction, interdiction, counter-SAM attack and airfield attack. A single weapons

PLATE 4.1. Tackling airfield vulnerability: A Tornado GR1 of 617 Squadron RAF in a hardened aircraft shelter at RAF Marham. *(Crown copyright: by courtesy of Air Clues Magazine.)*

system should be capable of being changed from mission to mission by changing a small software package in the vehicle itself.

The close air support mission in Europe will remain an important one but neither aircraft nor armed helicopters will play an important role in this mission area in the 21st century because of the vulnerability of manned systems to the air defence systems of the Soviets. Manned aircraft will still play a predominant role in interdiction, offensive counter-air, and defensive counter-air but they will be assisted by autonomous systems to a considerable extent. For instance, an airman who is planning an attack on a heavily defended airfield will be able to call upon autonomous systems to spoof the air defences in the area. Other autonomous systems will be able to attack key targets on the airfield so the manned aircraft can focus its full attention on those targets that will be particularly vulnerable to attack by a manned aircraft. In baseball terms, manned aircraft will become the 'clean up' hitters — that is the powerful force that comes in behind the autonomous systems with the knockout punch. The real challenge for airmen of the Alliance is not to consider autonomous systems as a threat to manned systems but as a very useful adjunct to them. Ground force commanders at all levels will welcome the addition of close air support systems that they can control and it will be the wise air leaders who are magnanimous about this.

A significant impediment to rapid development in the whole area of high technology is a residual 'Luddite' mentality that exists within the defence community of all the NATO nations. In fairness to those who are sceptical about the magic of exotic technology, there have been many unfulfilled promises in the last few decades. In addition, the Clausewitzian concepts of the 'fog of war' and 'friction' must be kept in mind when planning for the use of military forces in the demanding and confusing battlefield environment. Hence, thoughtful scepticism must be the order of the day when contemplating the long-range future. The long-range planner must, however, try to avoid putting on blinkers on and losing the opportunity to grasp the technological, doctrinal and tactical importance of the recent dramatic improvements in reliability and capability of miniaturized systems.

The 'technological slingshot' is a reality in the civilian world; it could become a reality in the military world, particularly if the advantages of development in the 'black' world can be fully exploited. Whereas it took decades to take the concept of a telephone, a radio and a television and turn them into fully operational and reliable systems, it has taken a much shorter time to do the same thing for the transistor, the semi-conductor and laser compact disk. Although the military has generally not taken full advantage of this 'technological slingshot', recent initiatives such as the United States Air Force Project Forecast II was designed to do just that; that is, to accelerate the exploitation of particularly promising technology. All the nations of the Alliance should consider emulating the Project Forecast II effort, since only by determined, sustained and innovative methods will the right technologies be given the proper emphasis and sustained support.

If I were to give advice to the RAF in this regard, I would suggest the initiation of a series of highly compartmentalised programmes which would be largely devoid of bureaucratic barriers. Britain, which for many years has been in the forefront of technological innovation in the field of aviation, needs to examine the possibility of restructuring its decision-making system in the research and development area and pushing hard to develop truly radical new systems. However, there are a number of areas of technological opportunity that have much less promise than autonomous airborne systems. For instance, the robotic soldier will not be a factor on the battlefield in the next 25 years. The technological and cost problems are just too large to put a thinking mobile robot with a lethal capability into the field. Hence, airmen will not have to figure out how to defeat robotic infantry troops. Happily, the ground forces of the Warsaw Pact in the early part of the 21st century will look much like the forces in the field today, with the exception of the air defence systems, which will be more sophisticated and will be able to identify and kill some of the early stealth systems.

Technological choices are twofold: what to develop and what not to develop. We Americans have developed lots of things that have been disappointing. Sorting out the wheat from the chaff requires enlightened leadership with a solid operational background, a healthy scepticism about technological schemes, and a willingness to spend some money and take some technological and bureaucratic risks.

Another major aspect of high technology which will have important military applications and which should be exploited over the course of the next decade will be in mission planning and training. Mission simulation has finally become both reasonably realistic and a lot of fun and the tank crews, the fighter pilots and lots of others can now learn a great deal by driving, or flying in, simulators. Leaders must understand that simulators will not be useful until the crews actually want to use them and learn from them. As new modifications are made to individual weapons systems, the simulator should get the modification first. In that way the crews can learn how to use the new capability of the weapons system before that capability is placed in the actual aircraft, tank or helicopter. This procedure will also ensure an interest by the crews in climbing into the simulator on a regular basis. By the early part of the 21st century, considerable training costs will be saved through realistic simulation. Hopefully, these cost savings can be translated into more and better systems.

Mission planning using small personal computers will also be much improved. Already the 'hackers' are showing us how much can be done on a small computer (a recent example is the very realistic and sophisticated computer game, licensed by the National Football League, called NFL Challenge, which uses over 120 thousand lines of code but can be played on a personal computer). Just before a pilot walks out to his aircraft to fly on a combat mission he will be able to glance at his portable personal computer, update it with the very latest intelligence data and re-plan his route to and from his target in an instant. By the year 2000, he will be able to do this again when he is en route to his target as he receives updated intelligence information. As long as the Alliance has to face a medium technology enemy, its ability to offset quantity with quality will remain strong, especially if strong R and D programmes exist in each of the major NATO nations' defence budgets. Compressed R and D cycles, institutionalised innovation and long range planning in each nation and in the Alliance as a whole, as well as close co-ordination among nations, should be the guidelines for the Alliance over the next 15 years.

In the years ahead the Alliance should focus more attention on concepts and doctrine and develop institutional arrangements whereby new conceptual ideas can be shared, debated and, in some cases, incorporated into NATO doctrine and procedures. Let me cite an example. In 1986, Colonel John Warden of the United States Air Force wrote a seminal paper at the National War College in Washington. It won a major research award, and yet there was no easy way to ensure that strategists and planners in the Alliance were exposed to his ideas. A clearing house for new conceptual ideas should be established in every major NATO headquarters and in every Ministry of Defence. If each major national and international headquarters had a small long-range planning division (five or six people should be adequate) with direct access to the top commander or leader, the Alliance in time could develop a better strategic vision. In addition, these long-range planning divisions could be the place where bright young people (from throughout each of the commands) with fresh ideas could interject them at a high level.

The military chain of command, for all of its strengths, is an impediment to innovation. It is time that leaders of the Alliance recognised this fact and took action to solve this problem. Conceptual thinking, based on a solid understanding of operational factors, has been largely lacking in recent years. Our concepts must keep up with our technology. Better still, our concepts should stay ahead of our technology if the advantages of our technology are to be fully exploited.

Radical Conceptual Approaches

Let me close this short paper with a discussion of the need for long-range planners to go beyond conventional wisdom and to think radical and heretical thoughts. So much planning done in the Alliance is not much more than the extrapolation of current policy and programmes into the distant future. Long-range planning must avoid fiscal, conceptual, organisational, technological, political, psychological and economic barriers to clear thinking.

As far as military planning is concerned, radically new concepts are worth examining even if the only purpose they serve is to stretch the minds of planners and decision makers. John Warden may be correct when he looks into the future and sees air superiority as the primary mission in the air-land battle; others with equally innovative concepts should be encouraged to come forward and advance their ideas with little or no risk to their military careers.

If the Alliance that wins the air superiority battle is the ultimate winner of the war of the 21st century, then, between now and then, major reconsideration of Army and Air Force (as well as Navy and Marine) doctrine needs to be undertaken. The further the nations of the Alliance are removed from the last war the harder they must work to ensure that their military forces and doctrine are relevant to the next war. The fact that most innovators are uncomfortable in large bureaucratic organisations means that there will always be a shortage of ideas and innovators within the military services. If the civilian and military leaders of the Alliance recognise this very natural tendency, they can compensate for it in a number of ways. A senior and very experienced analyst, who is presently a trusted member of Mr Weinberger's staff, points out that some of the very best intelligence work is being done by individuals and organisations outside government and one of the great advantages of contracting out more work is that this means fewer people remain inside government to provide bureaucratic barriers to the implementation of new ideas.

In addition, very influential individuals, like Senator Sam Nunn, are not only asking the tough questions but also are showing a greater discomfiture with the answers they are getting to questions relating to strategic planning and institutional innovation. The military must reach out for help in order to be able to overcome the personal and institutional impediments to innovation. Another serious problem the Alliance will face in the years leading up to the 21st century will be the widening differential in military capability between the high tech nations of the Alliance and those nations which for economic or other reasons do not move forward rapidly as far as military technology is concerned. Military leaders in an alliance must be able to discuss issues together. If the leader from a 'high tech' nation is constantly 'dazzling' his counterpart with the esoteric terminology of high technology, the communication barriers will only become more troublesome. It will be the task of all leaders to nourish the Alliance by understanding the barriers to good communication and co-ordination and breaking down these barriers on a regular basis.

The air battle in the early part of the 21st century may well be the decisive battle. As a result it demands our attention, our time and our best intellectual efforts. Too much time is being spent by leaders on current problems and too little time is being reserved for long-range thinking and planning. If this paper can, in a small way, be a catalyst for better planning and better thinking, it will have served its purpose.

TECHNOLOGICAL TRENDS, CAPABILITIES AND AIR POWER
Professor Sir Ronald Mason, KCB, FRS

The Conventional and Strategic Defence 'Initiatives' within the Western Alliance have certain objectives in common: to identify technologies and systems which could contribute, in a cost-effective way, to defence against a changing spectrum of the 'through-air (space)' threat. There is a sense in which there is little novelty of approach: the Alliance has looked to the rapidly changing technological scene as a force multiplier since the original Lisbon force goals discussion. But the management of technology, today and into the future, including issues of technology transfer and resources, is demanding more and more skill at all planning stages — from the laboratory to government.

Technology is the deliberate and systematic exploitation of scientific knowledge. In both the defence (and civil) sectors of the advanced industrial countries, the opportunities flowing from new technologies are enmeshed in a complex matrix made up of the threat (competition; industrial structures) and military requirements (market perceptions and forces). The threat is seen to drive the requirements; interactive integration of requirements with advanced technologies and subsystems provides for feasibility studies and project definition phases for the development of a weapon system; weapon systems and men make up defence capabilities which, in turn, should coherently provide a defence programme which is demonstrably in line with national and Alliance policies. The phases and time-scale of typical weapon system procurement, are, of course, well known, but I want to emphasise that the customer-contractor 'principle' is, at best, a management technique, and much deeper strategic skills need to be deployed to harmonise broadly stated requirements with state of the art technologies. At present, it is debatable whether we are succeeding; (consider, for example, the typical procurement time-scales and procedures for military communications and control equipment which serve, often, to exclude up-to-date computer hardware and software).

I take it, as a final point in these introductory remarks, that what is called air power is the sum of capabilities such as surveillance and reconnaissance, interdiction, close air support, counter-air and air defence. In spite of some semantic or definitional problems, air power must increasingly have a significant equation with capabilities in space. I argue that the space dimension, coupled with a broad range of enabling developments in information technology and materials and propulsion technologies, make it certain that the means of implementing these capabilities will change. The changes will not occur in a way which is simply related to technological opportunities.

Space Policies and Technologies

The evolution of the United States military space programme has been based on the six functions of reconnaissance, surveillance, communication, navigation, metereology and geodesy (comparable Soviet capabilities can be noted). It is difficult to overstate the value to the Alliance of the space-derived information base, and one can clearly anticipate the availability of real-time (measured in minutes) tactical information as well as strategic data. The way ahead in space will, *inter alia,* be determined by and will require:

Reliable launch vehicle(s) with increased lift capabilities.

Continuing development of multi-function satellites.

Optimal signal and data processing and communications.

An expansion of satellite survivability measures (including the improvement of robustness and redundancy of satellite networks, communications and control facilities).

A reduction of reliance on those capabilities which present problems of survivability; here, redundancy may imply that cost-effective alternatives to satellites — dedicated airborne and ground-based facilities — are essential complements for theatre surveillance and targeting requirements. The emphasis will lie on passive multi-sensor platforms such as that which may be defined by the Optical Adjunct Programme.

An enhancement of satellites' surveillance of other spacecraft activities; the development of long wave infra-red sensors for high orbit space tracking is deserving of priority.

These requirements are not intended to be comprehensive. Others are obvious and will enjoy a priority determined by the emergence, or otherwise, of arms control agreements. Anti-satellite weapons, and weapons postulated to be of value for ballistic missile defence, have much in common. The deployment of weapons in space, however, may have a certain inevitability — kinetic energy weapon systems in space may be seen to have great value in force projection and/or in constituting deterrence within a wide spectrum of scenarios. I make no judgement here on the strategic imperatives and liabilities of such a policy. The need for collaboration on investment in space, within Western Europe and within the Alliance, is starkly obvious. In the United Kingdom, the challenge to traditional resource allocation priorities is as sharp as exists in any section of high technology management.

Information technology

Information technologies and their connections with communications, command, control and battle management have some commonalities in the context of land, maritime and air power. But the demands of air power, including air defence, are quantitatively different from those which obtain in the land and maritime scenes. The airman will be cast increasingly in the role of a tactical manager of information, rather than being a primary part of a complex servo-mechanism!

I say that in no sense of being pejorative. Rather, the judgement refers to the pervasiveness of information technology (the integration of computing machines with telecommunications) and electronics, a pervasiveness that is already reflected in changing resource allocations within an airborne weapon system (avionics *vis-à-vis* airframe *vis-à-vis* propulsion plant).

Information and increasingly comprehensive data bases are derived from or may contribute to:

Sensors (infra-red, millimetric, optical, acoustic etc) coupled to advanced software for signal and image processing and fast transfer and integration into a data base and/or advanced displays. Sensors will cover larger moieties of the electromagnetic spectrum and seekers (sensors plus advanced algorithms for image processing) will advance capabilities ranging from night flying aids, aim point refinement, 'artificial agility' of weapon systems coming from quite simple 'add on' equipment such as helmet mounted sights and, in the limit, to autonomous guidance and control which we associate with advanced missile systems.

High resolution geographic information with respect to terrain reference mission systems and related requirements. The most demanding element of a digital base is that which will describe obstacles, and there can be little doubt that, combined with other sensors, the base will have great value as an aid, for example, to low level interdiction and to mission survivability. But it will remain of critical import — in the context of resource allocation — whether cost-effective applications of information technology will not, in the medium term, favour a shift towards unmanned rather than manned missions (*vide infra*).

Requirements related to the above remarks regarding the impact on the man-machine interface. Apart from 'conventional' improvements (for example in display technology and embedded microprocessors) expert systems will affect tasks ranging from fuel control to the fusion of tactical information. Again it is difficult to assess objectively whether these technologies will be driven, in cost-effective terms, by the manned platform or autonomous missile — to some extent that dilemma is advantageous, since it allows a recognition of the generic quality of these technologies.

Artificial intelligence. There is now adequate evidence that artificial intelligence — the embedding of information and logic in such a way as to allow some measure of inference, if not inductive reasoning — is realisable. While there are enormous potential applications across the board of defence capabilities (command and control, guidance, mission planning, simulation etc.) it is not obvious that the defence sector will drive the dynamic of research and development — the pace of the application of future generation languages may well be set by the civil programmes of Japan and the United States, with Western European industry and government or quasi-governmental research institutes in a less convincing position.

Electronic warfare. Over the past half-century, the development of air power has gone hand in hand with the evolution of electronic warfare: electronic support measures and electronic counter-measures reached a quite sophisticated level in World War Two and counter-counter-measures represent one of the most advanced areas for contemporary research and development. There is no doubt that the West enjoys an increasing advantage in deception and discrimination technologies, a situation which allows a control of the counter-measure — counter-counter-measure balance and the consequent ability to determine the 'cost-effectiveness at the margin' of deployed systems. Electronic warfare capabilities often take the form of 'information denial' and here passive and active stealth technologies are important. The science and technology and, even more importantly, the systems engineering of signatures are developing rapidly and it seems inconceivable that any weapon system in development will not have 'stealth' as a major design driver. There are views which assume that stealth — a shorthand for signature reduction, enhanced penetration and survivability and effective suppression of defences — will determine the defence-offence balance over the next 25 years or more. The implications for resource allocations — for ourselves and potential aggressors — would then be fundamental, particularly in any proposals for viable strategic (and theatre) 'through-air' defences.

There are two capabilities making up air power which, it seems to me, are particularly affected by technological changes in defensive and offensive measures: interdiction and air defence. I want to discuss these and also make a few remarks on close air support but before doing so would close this discussion of technological opportunities and their implications with some remarks on weapon systems looked at as a whole, and on materials technology.

Air Vice-Marshal John Walker, in his address to the RUSI in 1986, drew our attention to the Lenin dictum: 'quantity has a quality of its own', a sentiment echoed, albeit from a different standpoint, in Lanchester's equation. We are all familiar with 'structural disarmament', with 'the road to absurdity' and so on. Most nations have reduced the size of their aircraft fleets and the number of types of aircraft they employ. The viability of an air force comes into question when the maintenance of a force even at historically low levels has required a transfer of funds from other areas.

A 'systems look' at the situation would suggest that when a radically new system is introduced, improvements come rapidly and cheaply. But after several successive generations, progress is both slow and expensive and it becomes increasingly difficult to achieve the force multiplication from technology which we seek. If old technologies are *replaced* by the new technologies into new sub-systems and systems, then one can again move forward on a course which imposes greater costs on an opponent than *we* need experience. The Royal Air Force's initiative, more than three decades ago, of introducing high-speed, low-level aircraft attack techniques has required enormous investment in low-level air defence by our potential opponents, culminating only recently in effective airborne early warning and look-down intercept systems. But it is arguable whether we should now press this line when, at one extreme, we have within reach low-signature stand-off missiles which will require a totally different air defence regime.

There is, of course, no risk free path in security policies. What is clear, however, is that new or emergent technologies can only produce real advantages when they are allowed to replace what, in the past, I have called the baroque technologies. It is an unpalatable fact that the West is more effective at implementing new technologies in the laboratory than in front-line equipment. The development and production cycle of around 15 years for defence equipment is not consistent with the integration of today's technologies into equipment developed and in life for periods of up to 35 years. The current pressures on Western defence budgets and the likely cut back on research and development call for tackling production cycles and strategies for product improvement in an evolutionary way, rather than seeking quantum changes of capabilities. Such a procurement strategy does require greater collaboration amongst the Allies — to achieve real economies of scale — but it is a lower risk strategy for the management of technology in the defence sector than that which has characterised our equipment procurement in the last four decades or so of peace.

Manufacturing technology must emerge as the necessary systems approach to reversing structural disarmament. Design to production and design to cost are held by many to have no value beyond that of a slogan — yet we are beginning to see the value of such planning in advanced industries of the civil sector, and we shall see related benefits in certain defence programmes of the United States, particularly in the context of developments in materials technology and engineering being closely linked to cost and value production engineering, rather than simply to perceived performance characteristics under extreme environmental conditions.

Trends in Theatre and Tactical Air Power Capabilities

Close air support, the use of fixed wing aircraft in the anti-armour battle around the forward edge of the battle area, attracts varying priorities amongst the national capabilities of the Alliance. In analytical terms, discussion often centres around exchange ratios (dominated often by order of magnitude cost differences between land and air weapon systems) and perceptions of survivability; a 'defensive' response rehearses the traditional arguments of flexibility and rapidity of reaction.

There appear to be at least two developments in anti-armour capabilities which may call for some re-allocation of fixed wing aircraft to roles other than close air support. One is the development of land-based systems (such as MLRS) with a 'reach' of 30 kilometres or more, a large 'footprint' in the target area and rapid delivery of munitions coupled to real-time target acquisition through cost-effective low-signature remotely controlled vehicles. The other is the enhanced survivability and mission effectiveness of the anti-armour helicopter, given stand-off missiles whose characteristics can be less sophisticated than those launched from high-speed low flying aircraft and also given relatively simple 'no show' target acquisition. Stand-off capabilities are, of course, the response to issues of mission survivability, particularly when missions require extended penetration against comprehensive air defences. The technologies underlying defence suppression and penetration aids have been touched upon earlier and it is only the interdiction role of stand-off systems that will be further commented upon.

First, it is important to define interdiction requirements — how far?; against what targets?; with what 'multiplicative effects'? Having specified targets, one can then determine mission effectiveness in terms of such parameters as payload, penetrability and so on. Stand-off missiles with high survivability characteristics but relatively small conventional payloads can be assured of a significant role against static high value targets such as airfields, C^3 centres and certain choke points. Our understanding of their value against deep lying mobile targets is less complete, since mobility raises substantive issues of target acquisition and tracking and trades-off between, for example, flight time and required footprint in a target area. The claim is readily made that interdiction against mobile targets is optimally invested in manned aircraft supplemented by extensive defence suppression (and there is little doubt that third generation anti-sensor RPVs, coupled to other electronic counter-measures are contributing in a major way to perceptions not only of mission survivability but to more general deterrent and defence postures); but consistency of argument would then require that the traditional view of what is necessary to sustain aircraft survivability (increasing sophistication of single platforms) must be broadened.

That leads one on naturally to the subject that is at the centre of Alliance discussions at present: extended air defence. By extended air defence, at least for the purposes of the present discussion, one is concerned with the developing through-air threat in Western Europe which would include 'traditional' air breathing threats and cruise missiles, and the so-called aerodynamic or high performance threats made up from the short and intermediate range ballistic missiles (SS20, 21, 22, 23; the latter with conventional and chemical warheads). It is the case that little certainty can be attached to some critical qualitative and quantitative aspects of the threat as it may stand in 10–15 years time:

delivery accuracy, types of payload, re-entry vehicle signatures, total missile inventories, targeting strategies, and so on. Those parameters will determine the balance of (any) investment in passive, active and counterforce defences. Only three technical comments need be made here. First, aircraft dispersal must reinforce the already substantial arguments for STOVL capabilities. Second, counterforce (without major Alliance doctrinal changes equivalent to 'counter-reload') capabilities can be invested in highly accurate cruise or ballistic missiles coupled to real time surveillance and acquisition — the Alliance could deploy such capabilities in the very near future and such intentions may be necessary if the threat is to be removed by further arms control processes. Finally, the architecture(s) for active theatre air defences are under intensive study — one can already discern that the defence-offence balance, the measure-counter-measure balance, the resource determination of the balance between air platforms and ground-based missile systems will all pose major problems, largely of a political kind, within the Alliance over the next three years.

The technical limitations to developments in 'through-air' or 'from space' capabilities are not significant. The most fundamental challenge to the management of technology comes in the evolution of control. There is an understandable preoccupation with control in the context of nuclear operations and deterrence but the interaction of political, strategic and control processes is not something which is well understood. Conventional and, *a fortiori,* chemical munitions on advanced delivery systems can be deemed to be approaching strategic value when they are directed, with great specificity, against targets of the highest political and military value. Control in crisis stability, in arms race stability, in escalation *and* de-escalation must be demonstrated by those advocates of the primacy of air power who rely, *inter alia,* on the qualities of flexibility and responsiveness.

The Economic Dimension

THE AFFORDABILITY OF AIR SYSTEMS
Professor Keith Hartley

Air systems are costly. Over 30 per cent of the defence budget is spent on the Royal Air Force. This expenditure buys equipment, manpower, bases and the supporting infrastructure required for the provision of air systems and their contribution to United Kingdom defence. We need to know whether this expenditure provides good value for money and whether there are opportunities for savings. Questions have to be asked about the efficiency of current arrangements for *procuring and using* equipment and manpower. What are the costs of buying British air systems compared with collaboration or importing? Are there opportunities for using more reserves in the Royal Air Force and for making a more intensive use of existing equipment and personnel? These are questions to which economists can contribute by providing evidence on the costs and benefits of alternative policies. Any consideration of affordability has to start from an assessment of likely future trends in United Kingdom defence budgets: how much will be available for the Armed Forces? Stress will be placed on the need for the Royal Air Force to bear its share of difficult decisions. Economic principles will be used to outline a range of possible choices. It will be shown that there is considerable scope for improving efficiency but such opportunities will be opposed by established interest groups likely to lose from change.[1]

Choices and the Defence Budget:
Is There a Budgetary Crisis?

Defence budgets reflect a complex set of choices. Judgements have to be made about the current and future threat, the best ways of responding to the threat (the United Kingdom's commitments) and the willingness of society to spend on defence rather than social welfare programmes and private consumption. A limited defence budget then has to be allocated between manpower and equipment, between nuclear and conventional forces, between air, land and sea forces, and between the United Kingdom, NATO and the rest of the world. These choices have to be made in a world of uncertainty about the future (e.g. potential allies and enemies, ruling political parties, economic growth, technical change and arms control). Since these choices have to be made *continuously*, questions arise as to whether current claims of a crisis in defence funding are unique. The actual and forecast trends in defence spending in the 1980s are central to the debate.

Between 1979 and 1986, the United Kingdom accepted a NATO commitment to raise real defence spending by three per cent per annum. By 1985–86, the defence budget was some 20 per cent higher in real terms than in 1978–79, excluding Falklands expenditure. As a result of the three per cent commitment, not only were more real resources devoted to defence, but the proportion allocated to equipment increased from almost 40 per cent in 1978–79 to some 46 per cent in 1985–86 (Table 5.1). Within this growing equipment budget, the Royal Air Force approximately maintained its share, whilst the Army and Navy increased their shares, with implications for United Kingdom defence industries supplying air, land and sea equipment.

The ending of the three per cent commitment in 1986 signalled a major budget squeeze during the rest of the decade. A number of factors cannot be ignored in any debate about a crisis in defence funding:

i   The 1981 defence review was required because the Government believed that even with three per cent growth it would not be possible to fund adequately all the existing force structures and the plans for their further improvement (Cmnd 8288, 1981). The Falklands campaign led to a reappraisal of the 1981 defence review. However, with the ending of the three per cent commitment, the underlying budgetary pressures which led to the 1981 review are likely to re-emerge.

ii   Total real defence spending is planned to fall from an estimated £18075m in 1986–87 to £17120m in 1989–90 (1985 prices: Cmnd 56-II, 1987). Compared with 1986–87, this gives a *cumulative* reduction of £2.3 billion (1985–86 prices) over the three years 1987–90, of which at least one billion pounds will be in conventional equipment, with implications for both the Forces and United Kingdom defence industries. In 1985, Ministry of Defence officials believed that, following the end of three per cent, there would be broadly level funding in real terms (HCP 399, 1986,

TABLE 5.1
United Kingdom Expenditure on Manpower and Equipment

	1975–76	1979–80	1985–86	1986–87
1. *Expenditure*				
Total defence expenditure				
current price, £m	5419	9316	17959	18588
constant 1984–85 prices, £m	15024	14753	17197	16962
Manpower expenditure –				
as per cent defence budget	47.3	42.6	34.7	36.4
Equipment expenditure – as per				
cent defence budget	33.5	39.7	46.3	44.6
Equipment expenditure by				
Service –				
as per cent of total equipment:				
RAF	38	37	36	34
Army	24	20	22	21
Navy	29	34	36	38
Other	9	9	6	7
2. *Size of Armed Forces*				
Numbers of United Kingdom				
Service personnel (000s):				
RAF	95.0	86.3	93.4	93.1
Army	167.1	156.2	162.4	162.1
Navy	76.3	72.5	70.4	68.2
Total	338.3	315.0	326.2	323.5
Numbers of RAF squadrons:				
Strike/attack/ground support	19	19	16	16
Air defence	9	9	9	9
Maritime patrol	5	4	4	4
Reconnaissance	5	5	3	3
Transport	18	10	11	12
Tankers	3	2	3	4

Source: Cmnd 9763-II, 1986

pxvii).

iii The buying power of future real defence spending will be affected by variations in the exchange rate and in the relative price effect for equipment and pay. For example, between 1979 and 1986, the relative price effect for the total defence budget averaged about plus one per cent per annum (HCP 399, 1986, p134). As a further example, an allowance of 4.5 per cent was made for the Armed Forces pay award for 1986–87. Each additional one per cent awarded above the assumed level cost the defence budget some £33m per annum (HCP 399, 1986, p135).

iv With a limited budget, the Armed Forces have substantial demands for new equipment which is not only expensive but is becoming costlier with each new generation. The Royal Air Force wants new Harriers, AWACS and a new European fighter aircraft; the Army wants a new main battle tank and, in addition to Trident, the Navy wants three new frigates per year, a new helicopter, more submarines, torpedoes, missiles and a new amphibious force. Table 5.2 shows examples of the levels and trends in costs for new equipment. Inevitably, the result of rising costs is declining numbers of each new type of equipment, reflected in the strength of front-line units and in orders for new equipment.

v   Against this background, the Parliamentary Defence Committee has expressed serious doubts about whether future budgets would be sufficient to provide the capability needed to meet the United Kingdom's defence commitments. The Committee mentioned the need for some hard decisions and the possibility of a defence review by stealth (HCP 37–I, 1985, p. xli; HCP 399, 1986).

vi   The problems could be accentuated in the late 1980s and 1990s with the reductions in the numbers of 16–19-year-olds in the population, so increasing the difficulties and costs of maintaining the current size of all-volunteer forces.

A combination of a budget squeeze and substantial demands for costly new equipment suggests that it will be increasingly difficult for Britain to continue meeting all her defence commitments at the current levels of effectiveness. Logically, there are four broad policy solutions, although in practice it is likely that any government will adopt a mix of policies:

i   Increase real defence spending. This option is unlikely since all political parties have expressed support for the Conservative Government's defence spending plans to 1990. Also, a successful arms control agreement might contribute to reduced international tension and a reduced threat.

ii   Accept a gradual reduction in the combat effectiveness of United Kingdom Forces and in their ability to continue meeting all their current commitments. This is likely to mean delays in ordering new equipment and in reaching required stocks of ammunition, together with a squeeze on the training programme. This is a politically attractive option since a vote-conscious government can continue to claim that it is meeting all its commitments and so avoid a major defence review. For a time, it might also be a sensible option, involving only a marginal reduction in defence output or protection, which society might willingly accept.

iii Reduce or eliminate a major commitment. The obvious options

TABLE 5.2
United Kingdom Equipment Costs

Equipment	Programme costs: development & production £m, 1985–86 prices
Tornado GR1, F2 (385 units)	9200
Harrier GR5 (60 units)	1200
European fighter aircraft (estimated United Kingdom costs: 250 units)	6600
Nimrod AEW (11 units at cancellation)	1257
AWACS (6 units)	860
EH101 helicopter (50 units for Navy)	1450
Skyflash	800
Alarm	300
JP 233	700
Trident	9265
Type 23 frigate – per ship	110 +
Challenger tank – per copy	1.5 +
Average annual running costs of forces (1986 prices)	
Tornado GR1 squadron	19
Polaris submarine	55
Challenger regiment	12
Type 23 frigate	7
Life-cycle cost of Type 23 frigate (procurement and running costs over 20 years)	270

Cost trends in real terms – relative production costs of successive generations of equipment:

Harrier GR1	=	3.75 × Hunter
Tornado F2	=	2.75 × Lightning
Sea King helicopter	=	1.75 × Wessex
Sea Wolf missile	=	3.25 × Sea Cat

Ratios of development to unit production costs

Combat aircraft (based on average production costs of first 100 units)	100 +
Missiles (based on average production costs of first 1000 units)	1000

Life-cycle costs of a combat aircraft (15 year life)
Acquisition costs

Research and development	12 per cent
Production	33 per cent
In service costs	
Repair and maintenance (including initial support and spares)	35 per cent
Operations and training	15 per cent
Post-design modifications	5 per cent
	100

Sources: HCP 399, 1986; HCP 37, 1985; Kirkpatrick, 1983; Pugh, 1986.

TABLE 5.3

Cost of Major United Kingdom Commitments 1986–87

Commitments	£m 1986–87 prices
1. Strategic nuclear deterrent – Polaris	283
– Trident	375
Total	658
2. United Kingdom home base	2045
3. Central Europe – BAOR and Berlin	2602
– RAF Germany	897
Total	3499
4. Maritime operations – Eastern Atlantic	2618
– Channel	552
– Amphibious capability	115
Total	3285
5. Out of area – Falklands	251
Total	554
6. Others – ACE Mobile Force and United Kingdom Mobile Force	305
7. Defence research and development	
– military aircraft	648
– guided weapons	311
Total	2327
Total (1–7)	12673

Note: Items 1–7 relate to expenditures shown by the first seven sections of Table 2.5 of Cmnd 9763-II, 1986.
Source: HCP 399, 1986, pL36.

include abandoning the independent deterrent (Polaris and Trident), reducing the size of land and air forces in Central Europe and of naval forces in the Eastern Atlantic, withdrawing from out-of-area roles or reducing the commitment to support a domestic defence industrial base. Table 5.3 shows the costs of the United Kingdom's major commitments.

iv   Improve efficiency within the military-industrial complex (better value for money). This is the Government's preferred solution to enable the Country to continue to meet all its commitments after the end of three per cent growth. It embraces more competition, fixed price contracts, contracting-out, privatisation, collaboration, MINIS, Responsibility Budgets, rationalisation and transferring Service personnel from support areas to front-line units.

Choices for the Royal Air Force

Everyone accepts that over the next 10 years, the Ministry of Defence will have to make some 'difficult decisions' (Cmnd 9763, 1986, vol. I, p.

40). Here we have to focus on *the need for the Royal Air Force to make some difficult choices*. With only limited resources, the Royal Air Force cannot have everything it ideally needs. Something will have to be sacrificed. Questions arise about the range of available options and the criteria to be used in choosing.

Choices and efficiency are central to economics. Four basic economic principles can be used in considering choices for the Royal Air Force:

First: *The principle of outputs*. Admittedly, the output of the Royal Air Force, and of defence in general, is difficult to measure. Reference can be made to peace, protection, security and the valuation of human lives. Nevertheless, the emphasis on the output of the Royal Air Force requires all air systems activities to be related to this objective and shows the limitations of focusing on inputs such as a 50 squadron air force or a 50 ship navy or a commitment to maintaining 55,000 troops in Germany. The crucial question is what contribution do these air, sea and land forces make to the protection and security of the United Kingdom; and what would be the implications for protection and security if the Royal Air Force were, to be reduced in size by, say, 10 per cent?

Second: *The principle of substitution*. There are alternative methods of achieving protection and security. In principle, the Royal Air Force is faced with a range of possible substitutes:

Air systems can replace, or be replaced by, land and/or sea systems. Manned aircraft and cruise missiles could replace Trident submarines; Tornado aircraft in Germany could replace soldiers in BAOR; RAF maritime patrol aircraft can replace Navy frigates and aircraft carriers.

Equipment can replace manpower.

Within equipment, there is a range of alternatives:

- Quality versus quantity
- Manned aircraft versus missiles
- New equipment versus the continued use of existing equipment through longer in-service lifetimes and mid-life up-dating
- Platforms versus weapons and multi-role versus single role
- Equipment versus stocks
- Expensive purpose-built equipment versus existing civilian equipment
- British versus foreign equipment.

Within manpower, there is a further range of alternatives:

- Regulars versus reserves. For example, the average annual cost of a Regular Army soldier is £12,800 compared with £2,800 for a TA soldier and £770 for a member of the Home Service Force (HCP 399, 1986, p. 147). Although the Royal Air Force already uses some auxiliary forces, and is experimenting further, there remain opportunities for expanding their role. After all, nations such as the United States, Israel and Sweden make more extensive use of reserve formations, including using reserves to fly modern combat aircraft.
- Younger versus older personnel. With a declining population of 16–19 year olds, it might be increasingly worthwhile to focus on retaining existing trained but older personnel rather than seeking to recruit new untrained manpower (e.g. run-on existing labour force just as you run-on existing equipment).
- Skilled versus unskilled labour, with implications for training budgets. This also raises the wider issue of whether the Royal Air Force is obtaining a worthwhile return on its substantial investments in training.
- Men versus women.
- Military versus civilian personnel (e.g. contracting-out).

Economists would expect the Ministry of Defence and the Royal Air Force to substitute relatively cheaper for more expensive forms of protection, regardless of the traditional property rights of each of the Services. This is what happens in the private sector of the economy where there is a continuous search for cheaper production techniques, new products and new markets, a search which leads to continuous change in the profitability and size of firms and industries. But in the private sector, the incentive to substitute cheaper production methods is provided by competition and the profit motive.

Third: *The principle of contestability and rivalry.* Actual and potential rivalry promotes efficiency. Defence offers massive opportunities for introducing and extending rivalry and for creating contestable markets. Here are such possibilities for more competition:

i   Rivalry between the Armed Forces. The aim would be to allocate defence budgets on the basis of each Service's comparative advantage (i.e. specialising in what it is good at). Why not allow the Army with land-based guided missiles to compete with the Royal Air Force and manned fighter aircraft for the air defence of the United Kingdom? Similarly, Royal

.   Air Force Germany could compete with BAOR for the defence of Central Europe. For example, the expenditure on a Harrier with six BL 755s could be used to purchase twenty Multiple Launch Rocket System (MLRS) launchers each with a supply vehicle and 36 rockets (Davies, 1985). In other words, there are opportunities for reducing the entry barriers associated with the traditional monopoly property rights for each of the Services, thereby creating contestable markets. The recent reorganisation of the Ministry of Defence and the creation of a unified Defence Staff might lead to an improvement, although there must be doubts as to whether genuine competition will be offered. There is a danger that the three Services will engage in collusion and a continuation of the principle of 'Buggins's Turn.'

ii   Rivalry between the Armed Forces and private contractors. Firms could be allowed more opportunities to bid for a whole range of activities traditionally undertaken 'in-house' by the Royal Air Force. Examples include catering, cleaning, the repair and maintenance of equipment, the management of stores, air transport, air traffic control, search and rescue and the whole range of training activities (e.g. pilot training). Whilst it is recognised that recently there have been some moves towards contracting-out, these have been relatively limited and there remain considerable opportunities for further experimentation with the policy (c.f. NHS and local government: Hartley, 1987).

iii   Rivalry between firms seeking defence business, ranging from standard items and services to the supply of high technology equipment. For example, in buying defence equipment nearly 95 per cent of Ministry of Defence orders go to British companies. This 'buy British' policy excludes foreign competition and forms a barrier to achieving substantial cost savings in weapons procurement. For Royal Air Force equipment, the Ministry of Defence is a dominant customer for the aerospace industry, accounting for 50 per cent of its output. The industry is characterised by domestic monopolies in aircraft, helicopters, missiles and aero-engines (British Aerospace, Rolls-Royce, Westland). Large producers with domestic monopolies form a major pressure group with an obvious interest in seeking to persuade governments to 'buy British' (cf. GEC and Boeing on AWACS).

Fourth: *The principle of individual self-interest.* The search for cheaper substitutes and better value for money depends upon the motivation and behaviour of individuals who have to implement policies. Individuals have no incentive to co-operate in policies aimed at improving efficiency if they bear all the costs and receive none of the benefits (i.e. are made worse-off). Currently, individuals and groups in the Forces and Ministry of Defence have every incentive to spend since there are no inducements and rewards for economising and not spending. The Royal Air Force is unlikely to economise if all the savings are used to buy more tanks for the Army or more frigates for the Navy, or if the savings accrue to the Treasury. This suggests that devices such as MINIS and Responsibility Budgets are unlikely to be successful unless they are associated with employment contracts for military personnel which reward efficient behaviour and penalise inefficiency. In this context, it is interesting to note that whilst the Ministry of Defence has reported substantial progress in introducing MINIS and military and civilian Responsibility Budgets, it has never provided any evidence on the magnitude of the cost savings resulting from these measures. Not only is there scope for experimenting with efficiency-promoting employment contracts for military staff (e.g. bonuses, sharing in cost-savings, promotion, firing and so forth), but similar principles can be applied to defence contractors. Here, there are opportunities for experimenting with fixed price and incentive contracts which provide defence firms with inducements to reduce the *life cycle* and not only the acquisition costs of Royal Air Force equipment (Table 5.2).

Both military and civilian personnel and defence contractors are also central to the broader problem of 'gold plating' as the over-elaboration and technical sophistication in equipment requirements is known. One official study reported cost escalation in real terms of 91 per cent on a sample of 12 British development projects, at a cost equivalent to £938m which could have been spent on other defence equipment (HCP 104, 1987). Solutions to 'gold plating' require an understanding of its causes, especially the role of military and civil staffs, scientists and technologists as well as defence contractors, each pursuing their own self-interest. Some recent policy changes are to be welcomed (and long overdue), particularly the Ministry's use of fixed price and incentive contracts for development projects and its acceptance of the need to assess the extra costs of meeting a full Staff Requirement compared with something less ambitious (HCP 104 1987, p. xiii). Nevertheless, at least three doubts remain about the real effectiveness of these policy changes. First, fixed price contracts need to be determined on the basis of competition and, so long as the market is restricted to the United Kingdom, there will remain single sources of supply where prices have to be negotiated (aircraft, missiles, helicopters, aero-engines). Second, the Ministry of Defence has publicly stated that if contractors encounter problems on fixed price development contracts, 'the Ministry is not in the business of putting the companies out of existence' (HCP 104 1987, p. vii). Third, decisions about Staff Requirements are made by amorphous committees where no individual is at risk and where there are no financial incentives and penalties for good or poor performance. Mistakes can always be blamed on the committee which will defend itself by showing that it followed 'proper procedures' and the taxpayer and the rest of the defence budget will bear the consequences. If the Ministry is serious about seeking information on the costs of meeting Staff Requirements and alternative specifications, it needs a system which generates cost information on alternative proposals under genuinely competitive conditions. To safeguard the public interest, its procedures for allocating contracts following a genuine competition could be monitored through investigations by the Office of Fair Trading which is the Government's competition regulatory agency.

The Limitations on Royal Air Force Choices

The Ministry of Defence's current efficiency programme has produced some useful savings which will ease the budgetary problems for the Services. However, it has been suggested that the efficiency savings will not be sufficient to avoid cuts or delays, particularly in new equipment (HCP 399, 1986, p. xvii). For example, a 25 per cent saving from contracting-out an annual expenditure of £5m is useful but no more than marginal in terms of the costs of air equipment and the cost escalation on high technology projects (e.g. Nimrod AEW). Indeed, critics have suggested that any gains from the efficiency programme will simply be used by the Forces to fund their preferences for technically-sophisticated (gold plated) and costly new equipment.

Consideration needs to be given to the results of the efficiency programme. It will be argued that further savings are available but are unlikely to be achieved so long as there is a reluctance to tackle some of the major barriers to extending competition in the military-industrial sector. There is opposition to contracting-out, to creating contestable markets between the Armed Forces and to allowing foreign firms to bid for British defence contracts. All of this means that, in making difficult decisions, the Royal Air Force will encounter a number of restrictions on its range of choices. Economic principles cannot be applied independently of the existing organisations, institutions and the defence industrial base.

The efficiency programme: claims and results. When the competitive procurement policy was launched in 1984, significant cost savings were expected and an average saving of over 30 per cent was quoted (Cmnd 9227-I, 1984, p17). In fact, only a small number of examples of cost savings from competition have been reported, such as a saving of £60m or 35 per cent on the RAF's new trainer aircraft. From the small number of reported examples, the median saving is 20 per cent, substantially less than the original claim of savings exceeding 30 per cent (HCP 399, 1986, p. xii). Overall, the Ministry of Defence plans to save 10 per cent on the procurement budget over the period 1985–90, although the Chief of Defence Procurement has stressed that it will be impossible to demonstrate whether such savings have been achieved (HCP 399, 1986, p, xiv). To this end, the proportion of Ministry of Defence equipment contracts by value let by competitive forces increased from 38 per cent in 1983–84 to 64 per cent in 1985–86, whilst the share of cost-plus contracts fell from 15 per cent to nine per cent. Nevertheless, these trends conceal a variety of experience. For example, for GEC and Plessey, the share of non-competitive military equipment contracts by value was above average, although it had declined from some 75 per cent in 1983–84 to about 50 per cent in 1985–86 (Cmnd 9867, 1986, p. 45).

Contracting-out has also led to total savings estimated at £30m per annum in 1986–87, with examples of a 25 per cent cost saving from using contract staff at flying training stations (Cmnd 56–II, 1987, p. 45; HCP 37–II, 1985, p. 251). There are opportunities for a major extension of the policy. For example, in 1984 the maintenance and repair of Royal Air Force aircraft and equipment cost the Ministry £1.5 billion per annum, of which only 10 per cent was spent in private industry. An internal Ministry of Defence report estimated that closing three Royal Air Force repair units and transferring their work to industry would save 5000 staff and £16m per annum. Such a transfer would also benefit the United Kingdom defence industrial base.

Interestingly, a 1984 Public Accounts Committee Report on Royal Air Force maintenance concluded that civilians are undoubtedly cheaper to employ on maintenance than servicemen and have a higher productivity, and yet the Royal Air Force used 38,000 servicemen and only 3,000 civilians on maintenance work! The usual justification is that servicemen are essential for 'operational reasons', especially for servicing at front-line units. Apparently, there are 'operational difficulties' in employing a combination of servicemen and civilians and possible security problems if contractors' staff had access to secret equipment. This is rather a strange argument in view of the extensive use of civilians in the development and production of air systems by private industry. Also, it has to be recognised that operational considerations are not costless. The Royal Air Force has to choose between the operational advantages of using a high proportion of servicemen for maintenance work and other things, such as less flying training or buying less equipment. Similar choices have to be made when considering the purchase of British equipment.

Procurement options and the defence industrial base. The defence industrial base and the efficiency with which it provides equipment is a major 'input' into the protection of the United Kingdom. If buying British means paying more for some defence equipment (e.g. an extra 20 – 50 per cent on some aerospace equipment) and waiting longer for delivery (e.g. Nimrod AEW), the result is smaller defence forces and less protection for our citizens (Hartley 1985, p. 180; RAS, 1987). Choices are required between a smaller and more efficient defence industrial base or a defence review, either by stealth or by official policy.

Sensible debates about the national defence industrial base need to start from a clear definition of the concept of the defence industrial base, why it is needed and how much the country and the Forces are willing to pay for domestic defence industries. References are sometimes made to the experience during the Falklands crisis and to the need to maintain 'those industrial assets which provide key elements of military power and national security' (HCP 518, 1986, p. xxxvii). However, these 'essential, key national assets' have never been clearly defined by governments and political parties. In 1986, on the single issue of Westland, differences of view emerged between members of the same Government! The Royal Air Force needs to ask whether it is necessary to maintain a United Kingdom aerospace industry of the current size with major development and production capabilities in aircraft, helicopters, missiles, engines and avionics. The answer will depend upon assessments of the costs and benefits of the current national aerospace industry, compared with one which is, say, 10, 20 or even 50 per cent smaller.

As part of the defence industrial base, the national aerospace industry provides military, strategic and economic benefits. These include independence, security of supply, the ability to be an informed buyer, lower support costs, a responsiveness in emergencies and war, as well as equipment tailor-made to national requirements. There are also claimed to be wider economic benefits, with the United Kingdom aerospace and electronics industries presenting themselves as thriving dynamic sectors, working at the frontiers of technology, providing jobs, contributing to exports, saving on imports and generally contributing to the maintenance of the national manufacturing base. An opposing view asserts that defence, and especially aerospace, claims 'too high' a proportion of society's scarce R&D resources, which could make a greater contribution to improving the economy's competitiveness and growth rate if they were used in the civil sector. Much of the debate is dominated by myths, special pleading and nationalism. Procurement policy is formulated and implemented in the political market place where it will be influenced by vote-conscious political parties, governments seeking re-election, bureaucracies aiming to protect and raise their budgets and defence producers lobbying for new contracts.

Economists can contribute to sensible procurement choices by critically evaluating the arguments used by the different groups in the political market, by exposing myths, by seeking evidence on the various arguments and by pointing to the costs and benefits of alternative solutions. For example, there are alternative and often better ways of achieving national economic benefits in the form of jobs, exports and high technology. More jobs might be created if defence spending were re-allocated to education, health, housing and roads (Hartley, Hussain and Smith, 1987). This also raises the question of whether these wider economic benefits should properly be the concern of the Ministry of Defence or the responsibility of other Departments (e.g. DTI, MSC, HM Treasury). Such a re-allocation of responsibilities would leave the Ministry of Defence and the Royal Air Force to concentrate on identifying the military benefits of a national aerospace industry and their willingness to pay for these benefits.

The traditional Ministry of Defence commitment to buy British has been a major barrier to achieving substantial cost savings in the procurement of air systems. Government-created barriers to entry and exit means that existing firms are protected from rivalry, especially from foreign rivals. The scope for inefficiency is increased where there are domestic monopolies, as in aerospace, and where government regulation of defence profits provides firms with incentives to pursue non-profit objectives (e.g. a quiet life; luxury offices). There are various indicators of the extent of inefficiency in United Kingdom defence equipment industries:

i   Ministry of Defence studies show an average saving of over 30 per cent following the introduction of competition (Cmnd 9227–I, 1984, p. 17). However, in the long-run, the pursuit of a competition policy might lead to the creation of domestic monopolies at which point further rivalry might require the opening of the United Kingdom market to foreign firms.

ii   Supporting a national aerospace industry can be costly. For example, the United Kingdom's work-sharing arrangements on its purchase of American Phantom aircraft raised unit costs by an extra 23 – 43 per cent compared with buying directly from the United States (Hartley, 1983, p128). On the F16, the European co-production deal is estimated to have involved the Europeans in a 34 per cent cost penalty compared with buying directly from the United States (Rich et al., 1981). Both the United Kingdom and European examples also show that there are alternative methods of maintaining a domestic capability which also provides jobs, balance of payments and some technology benefits (i.e. work-sharing, co-production, licensed production).

iii During the debate on the Westland helicopter company, it was stated that 'the European helicopter industry is characterised by over-production, over-manning and lack of profitability' (HCP 169, 1986, p62).

iv   United States aerospace firms enjoy advantages of scale, with output being a major determinant of unit costs via economies of scale and learning. Typically, learning results in a 10 per cent reduction in aircraft unit production costs as output is doubled (Kirkpatrick, 1983). In the United States, domestic orders for combat aircraft are often in the range 1500–2800 units (F15, F16, F18) compared with British orders of 200–400 units for their Armed Forces. As a result of its greater scale of activity, the American aerospace industry benefits from more new projects, longer production runs at higher production rates, a number of competing large airframe firms and greater competition amongst its suppliers (Hartley, 1983). Table 4 shows the differences in size and productivity between the American and European firms.[2] In this context, however, care is needed to ensure that comparisons

TABLE 5.4
Airframe and Engine Companies 1985

	Sales (ECU millions)	Employment	Labour Productivity (ECUs)
Airframes – Europe:			
British Aereospace (UK)	4534	75823	59797
Aerospatiale (F)	3595	34889	103041
MBB (WG)	2693	36915	72951
Dassault (F)	2412	16123	149600
Aeritalia (It)	1430	12321(1)	116062
Dornier (WG)	605	6904	87630
Fokker (NL)	532	11613	45811
Westland (UK)	528	12195	43296
Agusta (It)	523	3585	145886
Saab (Sweden)	505	6443	78380
Casa (Spain)	352	10238	34382
Fiat (Italy)	308	3604	85460
Shorts (UK)	276	6265(1)	44054
Sabca (B)	57	1458	39095
Engines – Europe:			
Rolls Royce (UK)	2742	41700	65755
SNECMA (F)	1380	13862	99553
Matra (F)	838	4846	172926
MTU (WG)	536	6613	81052
SEP (F)	333	4000	83250
Turbomeca (F)	299	4291	69681
Volvo Flygmotor (SW)	248	3463	71614
FN Division Moteurs (B)	215	2308	93154
Airframes – USA:			
Boeing	18237	98700	184772
McDonnell Douglas	13916	83310	167039
Lockheed	12752	70200(1)	181652
General Dynamics	10919	85100(1)	128308
Rockwell	7100	45700	155361
Northrop	6763	46900	144200
Martin Marietta	5092	27962(1)	182104
Grumman	4145	32000	129531
Cessna	3826	8269	462692
Vought	2479	10000(1)	247900
Engines – USA:			
General Electric	7811	37818	206542
Pratt & Whitney	7019	47842	146712

Note (1) Data for 1982 or 1984
Source: EEC 1984, 1986

are based on *actual* British and American aerospace industries and not on actual United Kingdom experience in relation to some 'ideal' United States model.

Against this background, there is considerable pressure for the Europeans to collaborate to reduce excessive and wasteful duplication of costly R&D, to achieve longer production runs and to create a more competitive aerospace industry capable of competing with the United States. From a NATO perspective, the preferred solution emphasises the military and economic benefits of standardisation along the lines of the Warsaw Pact solution where there are long production runs of a few basic types of equipment. But international collaboration creates a new set of problems and costs. The time-scales involved also mean that collaboration is unlikely to make a major impact on the United Kingdom defence budget in the short to medium term.

The benefits and costs of international collaboration. International collaboration involving the sharing of design, development and manufacture is presented as the solution to American competition. However, any evaluation of European collaboration encounters major difficulties. There is a limited and heterogeneous population of joint projects (such as combat aircraft, trainers, helicopters, missiles and space systems) involving different partner nations and different organisational arrangements. As a result, collaboration is only one element in a complex model in which it is necessary to hold constant all other relevant influences (e.g. complexity of project, type of contract). Problems also arise with the counter-factual: what would have happened without the joint venture? Further difficulties arise in any evaluation since different partner governments use collaboration to achieve a variety of policy objectives, not all of which will be clearly specified at the start of a joint project. Nonetheless, supporters of European collaboration stress three major benefits:

i   Cost savings for both R&D and production (including the production of spares). Partners can share R&D outlays and, by pooling their national orders to achieve a longer production run, they can obtain economies of scale and learning. For instance, on the Tornado project, three nations shared the R&D costs and combined their national requirements to give a combined *initial* order of some 800 units (385 for the United Kingdom, 324 for West Germany and 100 for Italy): this was substantially greater than the requirements of any one nation and was much closer to American scales of output. Similarly, on the United Kingdom- Italy EH101 helicopter, initial requirements are 50 for Britain and 38 for Italy, giving a total order of about twice that of each partner nation's requirements.

ii   Collaboration enables the creation of a European aerospace industry able to compete with the Americans in military and civil aircraft, helicopters, missiles and space systems. This has been reflected in the creation of a number of European aerospace companies, namely, Airbus Industrie (airliners), Panavia (three-nation Tornado), Eurofighter (four-nation European Fighter Aircraft), Euromissile Dynamics and the European Space Agency. For helicopters, there are bilateral agreements resulting in EH Industries (Agusta-Westland) and Eurocopter (Aerospatiale-MBB). International collaboration enables Europe to undertake aerospace projects which would be too costly to undertake on a national basis. In this way, Europe can continue to compete in high technology aerospace products, whilst retaining its own defence industrial base and preventing an American monopoly. Without collaboration, each European nation has too small a home market to compete with the United States. For example, United Kingdom national orders for military helicopters are in the region of 40–200 units of each type. Estimates show that the European military market probably represents 100 helicopters per year of all types. In contrast United States military orders for the Sikorsky Blackhawk are expected to exceed 1750 units and might well exceed 2500 units, produced at a rate of 150 helicopters per year (HCP 169, 1986, p273, p394).

iii There are military and political advantages from collaboration associated with a greater standardisation of equipment among NATO forces and a practical demonstration of the cohesion and credibility of the Alliance (HCP 626, 1984; Hartley, 1983).

In view of the frequent official references to the benefits of collaboration, especially its cost savings, there is a surprising absence of publicly-available information on the magnitude of the benefits and savings. An official British report concluded that 'In reviewing the outcome of projects, it proved extremely difficult to establish the extent to which the potential benefits of collaboration — which in principle are very significant — were fully secured in practice' (HCP 626, 1984, p1; Vredeling, 1986, vol.2 p. 109).

Various pieces of evidence provide some limited information (e.g. on acquisition rather than life-cycle costs) which would need to be incorporated into a proper study of the benefits and costs of European collaboration. For example, it has been suggested that British involvement in a joint European battlefield helicopter project might lead to savings in development costs equivalent to six Sea King helicopters or some £60m (HCP 169, 1986, Q230). On the United Kingdom-Italian EH101 helicopter, savings to the United Kingdom from collaboration have been estimated at £100m when compared with a national venture: such savings seem surprisingly small on a project likely to cost the United Kingdom £1.5 billion of which £650m will be spent on R&D (1985 prices: HCP 169, 1986, p297). Finally, the savings to the United Kingdom from its involvement in the four-nation European Fighter Aircraft have been estimated at some £1,000m, or some 20 per cent when compared with a national project (HCP 169, 1986, Q1541).

Collaboration should also lead to longer production runs approaching American scales of output and greater export sales. The Anglo-French helicopter package (Gazelle, Lynx, Puma) has been successful in terms of sales. Initial forecasts for Anglo-French needs were 835 helicopters; at the end of 1985, total production was 2582 (HCP 169, 1986, p395). For the proposed five-nation NH90 helicopter, total production is estimated to be about 700 units which considerably exceeds the home market of any one of the European partners (HCP 160, 1986, p384). Finally, sales of the Tornado aircraft exceed 900 units, which moves the project closer to American scales of output.

Collaboration rarely resembles the ideal model. It has some major disadvantages and costs. Bargaining between partner governments, their bureaucracies and armed forces, together with lobbying from interest groups of scientists, engineers and contractors, can lead to inefficiencies. Critics claim that there are three sources of inefficiency in collaboration:

i   Work can be allocated on political, equity and bargaining criteria and not on the basis of efficiency and comparative advantage. During the 1985–86 debate on the future of the United Kingdom Westland helicopter company, it was suggested that the European helicopter industry was characterised by over-production, over-manning and a lack of profitability. It was never made clear precisely how European collaboration would rationalise the helicopter industry and make it more competitive. Critics of the proposals for European collaboration in helicopters feared the creation of an inefficient cartel supplying a protected European market, with all the costly features of the Common Agricultural Policy! Some critics have claimed that industry welcomes joint projects since they are much more difficult to cancel!

ii   Collaboration is believed to involve substantial administrative costs with claims of excessive government bureaucracy, duplicate organisations, frequent committee meetings, paper-work and delays in decision making.

iii   There are likely to be compromises in operational requirements as the armed forces, scientists and industries of different nations try to reach an acceptable agreement. Problems arise in harmonising requirements and schedules for deliveries. It is not unknown for each partner to insist upon modifications for its own national order, so raising R&D costs and reducing the economies from a long production run of one type.

As a result of these various pressures, joint ventures might take longer to develop and involve higher costs than a national programme. Evidence that European joint ventures take more time to develop than national European programmes is mixed and not yet conclusive (Hartley, 1986; Rich et al., 1981, p32). On costs, estimates show a collaboration premium on aircraft R&D of an extra 20–35 per cent, depending on the complexity of the project, the number of partners and the previous collaborative experience of the partners (e.g. problems of doing business with strangers). On production work, the inefficiency premium ranges from an extra one or two per cent to an extra 10 per cent for a given output. Some analysts have suggested that unit production costs are unchanged and that the real savings from collaboration are in development (Kirkpatrick, 1983; Pugh, 1986, p357). Even with such inefficiencies, collaboration results in cost savings for each partner compared with an identical national project. Of course, further cost savings, possibly up to 25 per cent, might be available if a nation were willing to purchase its defence equipment from the cheapest supplier in the world market (Hartley, 1985, p. 180).

Conclusion

Air systems are extremely expensive and increasing cost pressures on limited defence budgets will require the Royal Air Force to make some difficult choices. Decisions are required in situations where no one can predict the future accurately. Today's high technology air systems might be tomorrow's dreadnoughts and castles. Increasingly, economic pressures will require the Royal Air Force to think more radically about the current constraints on its range of choices.

The search for lower cost solutions to obtaining air systems will require the Royal Air Force and Ministry of Defence to think again about the procurement of new personnel and equipment and the use of existing stocks. The recruitment, training and retention of manpower is costly and there are possibilities of replacing Service personnel with civilians and with reserves (even if operational standards have to be reduced). Similarly, in procuring new equipment, it will be increasingly necessary to think again about such issues as:

i   The United Kingdom aerospace industry as part of the defence industrial base and the costs of buying British. This raises basic questions about the aims of defence policy and what is being bought by the defence budget. Is it buying protection and security for our citizens, or support for the aerospace industry which probably weakens our defences through buying fewer, costlier pieces of equipment with delays in delivery (structural disarmament)?

ii   A willingness to allow foreign firms to bid for United Kingdom defence contracts, where foreign includes both European and American manufacturers (e.g. Dassault, McAir). To maintain some British defence capability, offsets could be required as part of any policy of buying from abroad. It has been suggested that, as a result of competition policy, the United Kingdom's defence industry is now more efficient, so that buying from abroad is unlikely to be substantially cheaper. But, of course, a number of domestic monopolies remain and collaborative projects are far from efficient. Moreover, if this view is correct and the British defence industry is now competitive, there should be no objections to opening the domestic defence market to foreign firms!

iii Improving the efficiency of collaborative projects. Where nations find independence too costly but are unwilling to import defence equipment, they are likely to prefer international collaboration. There are massive opportunities for allocating work on joint projects more efficiently, for example through introducing more competition between firms in the partner nations, allowing outsiders to bid and applying the principles of specialisation and comparative advantage. Collaboration with the United States as well as with Europe should not be ruled out in the search for worthwhile and mutually advantageous transactions.

The vigorous pursuit of a genuinely competitive procurement policy will encounter massive opposition from established interest groups likely to lose from such a policy. But a failure to achieve substantial savings from increased efficiency means that other difficult defence choices cannot be avoided during the 1990s (e.g. a review of commitments). There are no free lunches and no costless options.

NOTES

1. The Author is grateful for assistance from Dr F. Welter of NATO, for a NATO Research Fellowship 1986–87 and for comments from Nick Hooper. The usual disclaimers apply.
2. The productivity figures are based upon turnover rather than on value-added and can be regarded as no more than suggestive indicators.

References

Cmnd 8288, 1981, *The UK Defence Programme: The Way Forward*, HMSO, London.
Cmnd 9227, 1984, *Statement on the Defence Estimates 1984*, vols. 1 and 2, HMSO, London.
Cmnd 9763, 1986, *Statement on the Defence Estimates 1986*, vols. 1 and 2, HMSO, London.
Cmnd 9867, 1986, Monopolies and Mergers Commission, *The General Electric Company PLC and the Plessey Company PLC*, HMSO, London, August.
Cmnd 56-II, 1987, *The Government's Expenditure Plans 1987-88 to 1989-90*, HMSO, London.
Davies, J., 1985, 'The guided missile and its role in the air-land battle', *Air Clues*, MOD, London, November.
EEC 1984, 1986, *The European Aerospace Industry: Trading Position and Figures*, Commission of the European Communities, Brussels.
HCP 626, 1984, National Audit Office, *Ministry of Defence: International Collaborative Projects for Defence Equipment*, HMSO, London.
HCP 37, 1985, House of Commons Defence Committee, *Defence Commitments and Resources and the Defence Estimates 1985-86*, HMSO, London.
HCP 169; HCP 518, 1986, House of Commons Defence Committee, *The Defence Implications of the Future of Westland*, HMSO, London.
HCP 399, 1986, House of Commons Defence Committee, *Statement on the Defence Estimates 1986*, HMSO, London.
HCP 104, 1987, Committee of Public Accounts, *Control and Management of the Development of Major Equipment*, HMSO, London, February.
Hartley, K., 1983, *NATO Arms Co-operation*, Allen & Unwin, London.
Hartley, K., 1985, 'Defence procurement and industrial policy', in Roper, J. (ed.), *The Future of British Defence Policy*, Gower, London.
Hartley, 1986, 'Defence, industry and technology: problems and possibilities for European collaboration', in Hall, G. (ed), *European Industrial Policy*, Croom Helm, London.
Hartley, K., 1987, 'Competitive Tendering', in Jackson, P. and Terry, F. (eds.), *Public Domain*, 1987, Public Finance Foundation, London.
Hartley, K., Hussain, F. and Smith, R., 1987, 'The UK defence industrial base', *Political Quarterly*, vol. 58, no.1, January–March, pp 62–72.
Kirkpatrick, D., 1983, 'Costing aircraft projects', *Air Clues*, MoD, London, January.
Pugh, P., 1986, *The Cost of Seapower*, Conway, London.
RAS 1987, Royal Aeronautical Society, *Development Time Scales: Their Estimation and Control*, Symposium, February, London.
Rich, M., *et al*, 1981, *Multi-national Co-production of Military Aerospace Systems*, Rand, Santa Monica, California.
Vredeling, H., 1986, *Towards a Stronger Europe*, Independent European Programme Group, Brussels.

OBTAINING VALUE FOR MONEY
Peter Levene

I normally describe my primary objective as Chief of Defence Procurement as 'to acquire for the Armed Forces the equipment they need to maintain their effectiveness and credibility against the developing threat; to acquire that equipment *when* it is needed and at a price that can be afforded within the resources available'.

But if I had to find one word to describe our main preoccupation in the Procurement Executive, 'affordability' might well be it. Of course, it is fairly easy to coin a simple phrase like that but not quite so easy to define what it means. But I think that, from the procurement point of view, affordability must mean, first and foremost, value for money. Again, this is not as simple as it sounds. As a concept, getting value for money is something which anyone who has been shopping instinctively understands, but there is no easy formula for measuring it. Moreover, the problem is compounded in defence procurement because the range of equipment we buy is enormous — from the obvious large items such as warships, submarines, tanks and aircraft to, quite literally, the nuts and bolts. It does not always make sense to buy the cheapest product, nor does it make sense always to buy the most complex. According to the particular needs, circumstances and timing, different choices have to be made. However, before describing the policies and procedures we have adopted in the Ministry of Defence to meet our objective, I would like to set the scene by saying a few words on the economic background against which we are now working.

Over the last seven years there has been a large increase in the defence budget — an increase, overall, of 20 per cent in real terms. Within this budget, the proportion spent on equipment procurement increased from about 40 per cent to about 45 per cent. Thus, procurement expenditure by 1985–86 was over 40 per cent higher in real terms than in 1978–79. We have now reached the end of the commitment within NATO to the three per cent per annum real growth target. Nevertheless, the fact that the defence budget is now on a plateau, albeit a high one, makes it all the more important that we, in the Procurement Executive, achieve our objectives.

To do this we must concentrate hard on getting the best possible value for our money. This is the overriding theme in all our procurement procedures and leads, in turn, to two keynote objectives:

—Putting greater emphasis on more, and sharper, competition;

—Making the PE more commercially minded.

I would be the first to admit that these aims are neither new, nor original. They are exactly the aims that any large private company would have in dealing with its own purchasing. For the Ministry of Defence, with more than £8bn to spend in any one year, and — it must be emphasised — the necessity to demonstrate publicly that we have spent the taxpayers' money wisely, it is even more important to ensure that we get a good deal from our suppliers.

However, although our objectives are hardly revolutionary, the climate within which the Procurement Executive is operating has changed dramatically in the last two or three years. The competition policy with which we began has now accelerated into a much more broadly based strategy for improving the effectiveness of our procurement. And I think we have now created within the Procurement Executive, and also within the Ministry as a whole, a climate which allows us to operate with the freedom and flexibility necessary to achieve our aims.

As I indicated, the central element in our strategy is the competition policy. I hardly need to explain the benefits which can be derived from competitive tendering, rather than reliance on a sole supplier. In addition to the cost benefits, competition also promotes the most efficient use of industrial resources, greater export success for British industry and, perhaps most importantly, the stimulation of new ideas. These benefits are also obtained by seeking a closer alignment with industry and by changing the means by which we define our requirements for industry.

In earlier days it was customary for the Ministry of Defence to define equipment down to a very detailed level, almost to the last nut and bolt. Industry would then be requested to produce the requisite kit. We have now largely moved away from this scheme to ensure the maximum contribution from industry in determining the way in which the Services' requirements can be met. Through the medium of regular presentations to industry, Systems Controllers give information on the Ministry's perception of the threat and the direction in which we see equipment development in the coming years.

Draft Staff Targets are circulated widely within industry so that their comments and ideas can be taken into account before any feasibility studies are undertaken. I might add here that we specifically ask for details of any relaxation of the requirement which might lead to significant cost savings, earlier completion or enhanced export potential. But the most important change has been the move towards the use of Cardinal Points Specifications (CPS). Whenever possible, rather than rigidly defining the exact specification, we express the requirement in terms of performance criteria and leave it to the contractor to determine the best way to meet those criteria and to produce the detailed specification. This may be — at one extreme — the design of an entirely new piece of kit; or — at the other extreme — an off-the-shelf purchase. Or, of course, it could be some mixture of the two. We then make our decision by assessing the degree to which the proposed solution meets the specification and provides value for money.

I should like to emphasise that the Ministry of Defence adopts an intelligent approach to competition. As I said earlier, getting good value for money is not judged solely by the price at the end of the tender documents. We recognise that a short-sighted competition policy which merely resulted in driving prices so low in the short term that it became no longer worthwhile for companies to bid for our contracts, or which drove all suppliers except one out of business, would hardly be beneficial in the long term. No — getting good value for money means taking account of *all* aspects of a proposal and judging whether the package *as a whole* makes sense. There would be no sense, for example, in taking the lowest bid if we had no confidence in the record and reliability of the supplier. We would also have to be convinced that he fully understood and could achieve our requirements within the required time-scale. We would need to take account of the arrangements under which payments would be made, the associated and running costs of the equipment in the longer term, export prospects, and so on — and only if we have a good measure of trust and understanding with our suppliers can we ever hope to consider proposals in an informed fashion.

Judging how successful we are in the making of savings through competition is not easy; we only know the bargain actually struck on the day and not what might have been achieved under other circumstances. A saving against our original estimates of what we might have to pay may, in part, reflect inaccurate estimating as well as good bargaining. However, using that yardstick, one gratifying example was a large project where the final price in the contract was £60m less than our original estimate. Now, I know I cannot be completely certain that this price was, in fact, the best which could have been achieved but I am quite convinced, in my own mind, that, without competition, the price quoted by whoever had been the chosen supplier would have turned out to be very close to our estimate.

A much better measure of the success of competition is provided in circumstances where we can make a direct comparison between the cost of the same item or service when procured competitively and non-competitively. This can work in two ways. First, by throwing open our tender to competition, it is always possible for companies who have not been in the business before to tender for Defence work; if they produce a better proposal all round than the incumbent supplier, then competition will have achieved its object. One example in this category was a 30 per cent saving on procuring certain items from a different source. Secondly, there are also circumstances whereby the introduction of competition does not result in a change of supplier, but can produce a sufficient incentive to the existing supplier to produce better prices.

To ensure that competition is spread as widely as possible, we are encouraging the greatest possible competition at sub-contract level. In the interests of good project management, it is now our policy to appoint a prime contractor wherever possible to take overall responsibility and control of the project. However, for all contracts over £1m in value we shall be reviewing the contractor's plans for manufacturing in-house and for sub-contracting. In the case of the large industrial groups, this requirement will hold true even in the case of sub-contracts being awarded to subsidiaries of the main company. We do not in any way object to this, but the subsidiary must win the business competitively. In addition, we have agreed with the CBI and trade associations a code of practice on competition at sub-contract level. This code advises contractors of our requirements for maximum effective competition to be obtained at all levels and provides guidance on the conduct of such competition.

Moreover, competition is now run at almost all stages of a project. The days when the contractor who carried out the development phase was assured of obtaining all the production work are gone. Competitiveness must be proved at all stages — although, of course, we appreciate that, normally, a first tranche of production should go to the design and development contractor, in part to ensure that all development and production problems have been ironed out. But we keep this first order to a minimum in order to maximise the scope for competitive future orders.

Another measure which is intended to increase the number of potential suppliers at both prime and sub-contract levels is a new procedure to ensure the open announcement of tender and contract opportunities for suppliers. We are now making announcements of these opportunities by way of a fortnightly bulletin which is disseminated through a commercial publisher who distributes it to industrial subscribers. Each tender or contract announced in this fashion is broken down into sufficient detail for potential sub-contractors to identify opportunities for themselves within the overall package and approach those competing for the prime contract. Building on the success of the booklet *Selling to the MOD* — recently re-published — we have also established a small firms advice division to help newcomers to the defence market.

Before I leave the subject of competition, I must make clear that genuine competition means that we will not buy British regardless. We do, of course, recognise the strategic importance of a strong indigenous industrial base, but industry must prove that it can provide value for money in order to sustain this. We will not neglect to look at the foreign competition where appropriate. We buy British whenever it is sensible, economic and consistent with our international obligations to do so; but we acquire from overseas when the advantages of performance, cost or timescale offered by the overseas option outweigh the longer term benefits of procuring the British alternative. However, foreign firms — or British firms for that matter — will not be invited to tender merely to sharpen up competition.

By the same token, and particularly in the context of a static defence budget, we take very positive steps to help defence industry's exports. The Defence Export Services Organisation is set up specifically for this purpose within the Ministry of Defence — headed by a businessman on secondment. And, as I intimated earlier, our procedures stipulate that every Staff Requirement or other equipment proposal must contain an assessment of its export potential. We have made a number of procedural changes within the Ministry which are designed to monitor sales activity, to identify sales potential at an early stage and to take a long term view of key concepts with sales implications. We look to contractors to tell us how changes to the stated requirements would help export prospects.

Offsets, reciprocal deals or licence manufacture are essential components of defence sales in some markets. We ourselves may benefit from a flexible approach. Reciprocal purchases for example can be an effective way of avoiding unneccessary duplication of development.

Some firms may be disappointed as a result while others benefit, but if the outcome is a more efficient and competitive industry such arrangements will be worth pursuing.

The overall effect of our policy now is to ensure that very substantial savings are being made as a result of our increasing the proportion of contracts let by competition from some 38 per cent four years ago to some 60 per cent today.

However, competition is of little value if it does not lead to a taut contract which provides the maximum incentive for the contractor to live up to his promises. It is just as important to get a good contract when, for one reason or another, competition is impracticable. This is one of the things implicit in a commercial approach. Our preference is for a firm price — what we say is what we pay — or fixed price, which makes allowance for inflation according to agreed indices, nowadays running only to scheduled rather than achieved dates if there is slippage. Under such contracts an efficient contractor may do well — and good luck to him.

There will continue to be some cases, particularly in the early stages of a project, where the uncertainties are such that a price cannot sensibly be fixed. We look then for a target price with the Ministry of Defence and the contractor sharing the benefits if the work costs less than anticipated and similarly sharing the cost of any overrun, up to a maximum beyond which the contractor must assume full responsibility.

I spoke earlier about the creation of a more flexible environment within which we could behave more commercially. One key element in this is the fact that, as far as spending on equipment is concerned, we are now able, to a certain extent, to move away from the strict year-on-year annuality approach to a more sensible and responsive system of carry-over. In the past, money not spent in any one financial year was lost to the Defence Budget — it was not possible to carry it over into the next year. As you might imagine, this greatly constrained the way in which Project Managers did their business. Success was measured by whether a programme was able to live within its cash limit, rather than by whether the equipment was being delivered to the customer in the most cost-effective way. Far too much time was being spent on managing the cash and not enough on managing the programme. It is quite understandable that Parliament, which votes expenditure annually, expects our spending to accord reasonably closely with that provision. But efficient procurement requires some measure of flexibility and that we have now been able to agree.

Under the new procedures, the Procurement Executive has been authorised to carry forward about 10 per cent of its budget if it remains unspent on 31 March. The money can now be devoted to the programme for which it was originally voted and authorised, instead of being lost to the Defence Budget. However, I do not think it will matter if, in the end, we do not use this facility but instead end up spending very close to our cash limit. The important thing is that project managers will be able to take sensible decisions against the background of a flexible budget, knowing that hitting the cash limit exactly on one arbitrary date in the year is no longer to be regarded as the main measure of success. Coupled with this, the end-of-year control measures which are operated within industry ensure that we can avoid overspend problems, and so can adopt the flexible approach we shall need.

The Procurement Executive has also revised its approach to making interim payments to contractors during the course of a contract, intended to ensure that throughout the life of that contract the supplier is also investing in the development, thereby providing him with a greater incentive to perform well. Over the past 10 or 15 years, a regime of interim payments, far more generous than is the case commercially, ensured that in many cases firms continued to receive cost *and* profit from the Ministry of Defence even when projects had fallen behind schedule and deliveries had been delayed. In the past, we have made payments of up to 100 per cent of the costs incurred by a contractor. We are now reducing these payments on major contracts and the interim payment of profit will discontinue, in order to supply an additional incentive to our contractors to supply goods on time. A significant part of payment will not be made until such time as the goods are produced, proved to meet our requirements and are suitable for the use of the Armed Forces.

Another area in which a fresh commercial look should pay dividends is spares purchasing. We have recently completed some very extensive studies into the prices we pay and the value they represent. This work has shown that, in many cases, we do indeed appear to be paying rather more than we need. There are, no doubt, instances of over-pricing, but sometimes the problem is of our own making, through buying in uneconomic quantities. The efficient management of numerous, individually small purchases represents a different form of challenge from a single major project, but it is a very important challenge. We are pursuing a number of ideas for improvement with those responsible for provisioning and stockholding as well as with industry. One very important, and very simple action we are taking is to arrange for the packaging of spares to be clearly marked with the price. I want those who hold or use spares to know what the cost is — and to tell us if this seems excessive. By this and other means, I am looking for an overall saving on our spares bill of perhaps 10 per cent over the next two to three years.

I should like now to touch on international collaboration, and especially collaboration within Europe. This is not just because of the need for equipment which is interoperable and standardised. The fact is that technology and market structures are changing at a very rapid pace and there is no doubt that we can no longer afford to sustain expensive national programmes to produce relatively small numbers of equipments. We must try to share development costs and achieve more economic production runs. Britain and Europe possess the scientific and engineering skills to match this challenge but we cannot succeed while these skills are dissipated in national projects which duplicate each other, which have inadequate home markets for economic viability and which compete with each other, as well as with American equipment, in export markets. Collaboration can cut out this wasteful duplication of effort, both at the governmental and at the industrial level. If we do not collaborate, in Europe and elsewhere, we will be left behind in the technology race and we will be unable to compete in the world market place which is bad for NATO, bad for Europe and bad for business.

I must make clear that I stress collaboration in Europe not through any anti-Americanism. There is nothing anti-American in wanting a strong European base. Indeed, pressure to maintain this comes as much from America itself as from within Europe. And the reason is to ensure that Europe pulls its weight within the Alliance to the maximum possible extent, which is good for us and for the Americans. However, collaboration will not succeed if it leads to inefficient procurement. We must recognise that our partners, from either side of the Atlantic, have their own policies and their own methods of working. Account may have to be taken of differing legislative backgrounds and methods of Parliamentary control of budgets and programmes. Industrial strategies are important to every Government.

Inevitably, then, we must be prepared to compromise in return for the benefits of collaboration. But the compromise we settle for must be one which gives confidence that the project will be well run. This calls first of all for sound management on the part of both Government and industry, and we cannot commit a lot of money until we are satisfied with these arrangements. Collaborative projects may require set shares of the work to go to each nation but this need not rule out competition. International consortia may be formed to compete for the prime contract. Work packages may be opened to international competition, leading to selection of the most cost-effective combination of winners consistent with national shares. Arrangements for payment and other contract terms require close attention. The solutions adopted may not be quite the same as those we would obtain in national procurement, but the underlying principles of clear definition of what is to be done, and terms which provide an incentive to achieve it, hold good.

I would like to turn now to the people in the Procurement Executive. After all, if we are pressing our contractors to become more efficient in our drive to obtain the best value for our money then we must ensure that our own house is in order. We must do what we can to widen the experience of our staff and to give people the opportunity to acquire the skills which are relevant to procurement in a competitive environment. For example, we need greater interchange of staffs between the Ministry and industry in order to ensure that each side is exposed to the environment in which their counterparts work. We have made good headway on this recently — in 1985 just over 100 Ministry of Defence staff were seconded to industry and commerce. This was twice the level of 1984 and last year the figure exceeded 200. We are working to encourage this even further and to increase the number of staff from industry who come to us on secondment. We are also placing greater emphasis on training now, including the provisions of courses leading to relevant professional qualifications.

I should like to conclude by looking to the future. A lot may change over the rest of this decade and the next, but the problem of equipping the Armed Forces as technology advances and with limited resources is unlikely to go away. Value for money will continue to be vital, and I do not foresee a time when the Chief of Defence Procurement will be able to sit back and relax.

Much recent public debate has concerned the running of major projects. Within the Procurement Executive we have pressed very hard to ensure that we now have prime contractors with full responsibility under a taut contract. I am certainly not claiming that we now have it exactly right but I do believe that we have learned the main lessons. We need to concentrate on ensuring that in practice, and at each stage, every project is on a sound footing. We must continue to work on fine tuning our procurement strategies, in consultation with industry; even a very small percentage of £8.5 billion spent inefficiently is to be taken seriously.

One of the areas in which I hope to see considerable progress is in the use of life-cycle costing. Hitherto it has been difficult to make full use of life-cycle costs because of the difficulty of predicting them with sufficient confidence. As we become more proficient, competitions will increasingly be judged on through-life rather than initial acquisition costs.

I aim not just at predicting costs but at reducing them. If equipment is less reliable than it should be or is harder to maintain, then money and personnel are unnecessarily diverted from the teeth to the tail. Modern technology provides the opportunity to offer higher availability as well as higher performance, all the more important when equipment of a previous generation cannot always be replaced on a one for one basis. But I am not convinced that we always obtain, in practice, the full benefit available in theory, and we are considering where there is scope for improvement.

A MILITARY PERSPECTIVE
Air Vice Marshal Roger Palin, RAF

The papers by Dr Hartley and Mr Levene throw up a veritable pot pourri of issues. There is not enough space available to enable me to tackle them all, so I shall concentrate on the major points of principle, bearing in mind that Mr Levene has already responded to some of the points made by Dr Hartley on the procurement side.

An important point that I would like to make about the new procurement practices, from a military point of view, relates to timeliness. Nobody disputes the eminent good sense of seeking maximum value for money and the part that competition can play in this: examples now abound. But the process of competition can slow down the actual acquisition of the new equipment we need. Our requirement for new equipment stems for the most part from an assessment of the threat, and I have to remark how little reference was made to this fundamental factor by Dr Hartley or Mr Levene.

Now one can accept that threat assessments are highly judgemental; one can also accept that we cannot be precise about the exact date at which changes in a potential enemy's capability will occur and therefore precisely when new equipment would be needed in service. Nonetheless, the threat remains the prime determinant of the way we, the military, go about our business and must therefore be a prime consideration in the procurement process.

This problem is exacerbated as our emphasis on seeking collaborative partners gathers pace. Not only is there the need to harmonise the operational requirement — itself a particularly difficult task (witness the EFA programme) — but the acquisition/procurement process is further delayed by the need to bring into line different national procurement practices, not to mention overcoming differences in industrial objectives, which are themselves often driven by different national objectives. Delay normally means more expense, not only in higher procurement costs but in the need to run-on obsolescent equipment. The danger from our perspective is that we could get the worst of both worlds: price advantage due to competition eroded by extended overheads (which will appear elsewhere in the programme if not in that specific project) and increased maintenance costs in the interim. It also means lost capability. And of course developments in the threat do not await the outcome of our national procurement process.

Turning specifically to the issues raised by Dr Hartley, it is difficult to know where to begin. He has used a sort of shotgun approach, and, as with any shotgun, some of the pellets will be near enough to hit the mark, while almost inevitably many will fall by the wayside. Certainly, where he talks of the need to emphasise output, to examine trade-offs between platforms and weapons, manpower and equipment, investment in new equipment versus running-on old, greater use of reserves and civilian resources of all kinds, including contractorisation, and the need to look at our requirements across traditional Service boundaries, the principle that lies behind his remarks is very much to the point.

However, we should not underestimate what is already happening in these areas. Much water has flowed under the bridge since he started publishing articles along these same lines in the early 80s. The range of functions either already contractorised or planned to be so in the future, is very wide — and one only has to consider (although this is not a Royal Air Force example) commercialisation of the Royal Dockyards to see how fundamental some of these are. The Royal Air Force is expanding its use of reserves, including in the flying role, although in this respect it must be said that initial experience is somewhat disappointing. A great deal of repair is carried out in industry, but let us not forget that the many thousands of servicemen involved are all required to support the front line in war. New equipment, and indeed new concepts, are now examined across Service and systems boundaries, the entry barriers no longer exist and trade-offs are the very stuff of the Ministry of Defence's long-term planning.

No doubt we have not yet gone far enough in some of these areas, but as we search for the right balance to strike I would stress two points which tend to be uppermost in our minds. First, economic principles and commercial practices are not sufficient in themselves to determine what we should buy or how we should carry out a particular function. Cheaper substitutes do not necessarily give better value for money. There is, for example, no point in employing reserve forces, even if they are cheaper, if they cannot carry out the job; nor for contractorising support functions to the point where you have insufficient people to fill the war establishments. Secondly, it behoves us, the military, to use some circumspection when considering radical changes. We are not necessarily against change (although there is an in-built tendency to feel more comfortable with traditional practice, as in any large organisation of long standing). Rather, we are dealing with the military security of the nation and it would be a dereliction of our military responsibility if we were to implement radical changes which, in the event, diminished our security rather than improved it. And, of course, during the process of change itself, we have to maintain the efficient working of our current structures.

Turning now to some of the other more radical ideas Dr Hartley has put forward, I have to say that some of these give me particular difficulty. Leaving aside his implied suggestion that we lower the skill levels of our personnel and that we should reduce our operational standards, the idea of relying for the air defence of the United Kingdom on land-based missiles manned by Army personnel fills me with horror, not because of the colour of their uniform, nor because it would do me out of my current job, but because the idea is patently deficient from an operational point of view; I would have thought there were enough examples in recent history to show why. Tornados for RAF Germany in place of BAOR manpower is a plain case of apples and oranges; MLRS Phase III against Harriers with BL755 would be a better case study, because of the obvious overlap in some roles, but this is a notoriously difficult equation, since it ignores the tasks that the Harriers can perform and which the MLRS cannot. As for RAF Germany competing with BAOR for the defence of the central region — this seems to me to be an idea born not of imagination but of fantasy and is best, I think, left still-born.

One perspective of the problem of affordability for the Royal Air Force which deserves much more attention is the inherently high costs the Service faces. We require highly skilled manpower, which is expensive. We incur high initial training costs; continuation training costs are also heavy, particularly when oil prices are high. We incur high capital costs, for both platforms and weapons (there is some evidence in recent years that air systems have suffered a higher pay and price increase than land and sea systems). We also incur high infrastructure costs because, unlike the other two Services, we would fight largely from our peacetime estate, which must therefore be prepared in peace as in war. Faced with these almost inexorably high costs, the message I personally draw is the imperative need to focus on output/capability; hence the drive to reduce the support infrastructure to the bone, the search for significant advances in capability from both platforms and weapons, and the realisation of the need for a holistic approach to further increase overall capability.

The Tornado F3 may well cost 2.75 times as much as a Lightning, but its capability is immeasurably greater than that of the Lightning today and will be yet further improved as the weapons planned for the future come into service. The same is true for the Tornado GR1 armed with JP233 when compared with its predecessors, and for the Harrier GR5 if armed with the weapon postulated to AST 1238. There are plenty of other examples. With such quantum leaps in capability, some trade-off in numbers is at least contemplatable. If it is then a question of a fixed budget, the extent of any such trade-off between quality and quantity will be determined very much by the success of our efforts to reduce support costs. And here the next great leap forward we look for should come in reliability. There is no doubt that reducing repair and maintenance costs could bring enormous spin-offs throughout the whole Royal Air Force infrastructure. That to me is among the most important challenges for the aerospace industry today.

PART TWO

Roles and Missions

CHAPTER 6

Air-to-Ground Operations

BATTLEFIELD OFFENSIVE AIR SUPPORT AFTER THE YEAR 2000
Lieutenant General Sir Jeremy Reilly, KCB, DSO

It is evident that both NATO and the Warsaw Pact, like any group of forces throughout history, will seek to retain mobility: strategic, operational and tactical. Conversely, they will seek to reduce the equivalent mobility of their opponents. Without mobility it is obvious that an attacker cannot attack, nor would he if he thought that he might lack it! Equally, no defender can be strong everywhere — nor should be: 'If there is no place he does not make preparation, there is no place he is not vulnerable' wrote Sun Tzu — and the defender therefore requires mobility to reinforce against the attacker's success and to restore the situation with counter-offensive operations. Without this capability, the defender would not have the ability to respond, the attacker would know that the option to achieve tactical decision rested in his hands alone, and deterrence would be degraded.

But this mobility cannot just be plucked from a tree. The fastest car is impotent in a traffic jam, the swiftest airliner of no purpose when stacked above an airport: under these conditions mobility is lost and investment in the means of mobility, at least temporarily, negated. And so the question is, how much mobility can be achieved, or denied, by forces under the conditions of actual battle when factors such as the enemy, the weather and the availability of suitable munitions would determine the attainment or restriction of potential mobility?

This takes us straight into the historic relationship between mobility and firepower and the undulating balance derived from it between advantage to the defender on the one hand and to the attacker on the other, from which we can, I suggest, draw several general deductions. First, the basic element is firepower; mobility is subordinate. Second, although effective firepower can prevent movement, it has been rare for mobility to be eliminated, common for it to be, for a time, degraded, and usual for it to be restored by counter-measures: a process, I suggest, which is likely to occur, at least in degree, during the service life of most major weapon systems. Third, mobility will remain a feature of warfare which all forces will make substantial investment to retain and deny.

The key thing is that the ability to move — and I mean on or above the combat zone — will be relative to the effect of enemy fire, and this implies two underlying priorities:

— to suppress the fire of the enemy whilst movement takes place and, because this could never be perfect;

— to provide the moving elements either with protection or with the ability to move fast and with agility, preferably both.

These practices represent nothing new in the history of warfare: Zulu domination of Southern Africa was ended when the dismounted spear gave way before the Maxim Gun and horsed mobility. The British Army of 1914 had developed an admirable concept for mobile operations but it lacked the firepower and battlefield mobility necessary to execute it when the freedom of Salisbury Plain was displaced by the reality of war. For similar reasons, heavy pre-war investment in the daylight bombing capability of a certain distinguished service, despite much gallantry, was brought to naught in 1940.

Of course today, when we use the term 'firepower', we are not only imagining the delivery of lead and explosives — by whatever means — but also a wide spectrum of destructive and suppressive capabilities such as electronic radiation, lasers and other novel developments, and chemicals. But it is convenient to group all these capabilities under the general heading of 'firepower'.

Let me now focus a bit more specifically on the area of ground operations, even if these can never be separated from those in the air (and not only in the air immediately above them). Just as there is a need to generate enough firepower to cover our own movement there is, on the coin's reverse, a need to deal with the volume and energy of the enemy's attack. For checked he must be, and unbalanced too, at least in places, before we ourselves can attack.

In the first instance, the deployment of Soviet Operational Manoeuvre Groups would probably merely reinforce the scale of the Warsaw Pact First Echelon attack and, by mathematical process, reduce the priority attaching initially to follow-on forces. After all, if the First Echelon is not defeated, then the existence of further echelons of forces is to a large degree academic. Nevertheless, these further forces must be delayed to provide the time necessary for the leading echelons to be destroyed.

But leaving this aside, and to add some perspective, let us dwell for a moment on a Warsaw Pact tank division in the attack mode with two regiments — 200 tanks — in its leading echelon. Forget for the moment their heavy back-up support in the form of ground attack aircraft, armed helicopters, conventional and chemical artillery and immediately following and flanking forces.

Let us suppose that these 200 tanks advance in a box six kilometres across and three in depth, covered by modern smokes, across reasonable terrain which has not been fully prepared for defence, and that they have a mobility performance comparable with the United States Army M1A1 tank. Not an unreasonable supposition I suggest. In purely illustrative terms, the effect of this would be that all these tanks, on a frontage appropriate for the defensive deployment of no more than one NATO battle group, might pass through the direct fire engagement zone of that battle group in a mere five minutes, i.e. at a mean rate of 40 tanks per minute, or one every 1.5 seconds. And we are only considering the first echelon of a single division!

What emerges from any examination of such factors is that it would be quite impossible and hopelessly unaffordable for NATO to have everywhere sufficient in-place firepower and prepared defences to halt the enemy wherever he might choose to concentrate on this sort of scale. Realistically, this deficiency can only be offset cost-effectively by the use of mobile army reserves — at all levels but particularly by the committal of reserve armoured divisions and airmobile forces on army group direction — and by the co-ordination of flexible and non-local (if individually more expensive) methods of applying fire, such as air power and rocket artillery.

There are, of course, other considerations. For example, the problem for the defender can be redressed to some extent by reducing the momentum of the attacker, his energy being a product of his density, volume, speed and general tempo:

His density can be reduced by forcing him to disperse.

His volume can be lessened by causing him casualties during the overture to battle.

His speed can be slowed by mines and obstacles, natural and artificial.

And his tempo can be lowered by the actual and psychological effects of attacking his headquarters, communications and ammunition arteries.

Then there is the heavy weight of fire with which his attacks would be supported. If nothing was done about this, NATO anti-armour units,

PLATE 6.1. A Harrier GR5: the latest addition to the battlefield air support arsenal. *(Photo: Peter Shephard of Air Clues Magazine.)*

including armoured reserves, would be neutralised and their concept of operations would fail. Consequently, the ability to locate and engage his artillery units quickly and to provide an effective defence against aircraft and helicopters, must, for this reason, remain of very high priority. And this takes us full circle to the same capabilities which we need to support our own offensive intentions.

Well what can be drawn from this? Primarily, I suggest, three essential tasks which Northern Army Group needs the 2nd Allied Tactical Air Force to undertake, namely:

To keep the enemy air 'off the Army Group's back';
To create a vacuum between the Warsaw Pact leading and follow-up echelons, and
To attack enemy armour which has been canalised and concentrated as a result of our own ground action.

I will touch on each of these in turn, starting with 'keeping the enemy air off the Army Group's back'.

Fortunately, this army requirement fits very nicely into what the airmen would see as the very *raison d'être* of a tactical air force — that is the need to engage enemy aircraft in the air and destroy their airfields on the ground. But, of course, the airmen would see the air force's role as being larger than simply one of supporting the Army Group — crucial as that would be. As we will never have all the assets we think we would need on the day, air priorities would have to be set — and those might not always be set to the Army Group's satisfaction.

There could, of course, be other concerns from an Army view point, and understandably so. The first of these would be the placing of an excessive priority on offensive counter-air at the expense of defensive capability and tasking. Whilst I applaud the concept of offensive counter-air operations, and have no doubt that, individually, they would be successful, taken as a whole and without effective longstop provision, they involve an unavoidable risk of not achieving adequately the Army Group's — and indeed 2 ATAF's — requirement to suppress the enemy offensive air potential.

This risk is inherent in some question marks applicable to such air operations, for instance:

> Is the number and hardness of airfields to be attacked and subsequently neutralised within the scope of the number of aircraft and munitions available?
>
> What would be the battle effectiveness of operationally unproven munitions?
>
> What would be the actuality of the long but inconclusive debate about attrition rates, and the likely percentage reduction in operability of fixed runway airbases when subject to attack, even allowing for dispersal techniques and the provision of companion support?

Seen through khaki eyes, such questions add point to the importance of our defensive counter-air capability. Yet here too there may be latent concern, and on two counts:

> First, that although much reliance in forward air defence has been placed upon the SAM belt concept, SAM systems are likely to remain vulnerable to enemy counter-measures and ground penetration, and to provide only degraded effectiveness against low-level targets in the forward combat area.
>
> Secondly, that air interceptor operations, for sound enough reasons, may provide little direct defence of forward Army corps; a situation exacerbated by continuing difficulty in resolving the problem of air space control in the area of the contact battle.

Next let me turn to the second Army Group requirement I mentioned, namely 'to create a vacuum between the Warsaw Pact leading and follow-up echelons' — in other words, 'interdiction'. Interdiction means isolating the battlefield, essentially by destroying —

and keeping closed — choke-points that the enemy follow-on forces would have to pass through. But past experience has shown how difficult this task can be, however desirable the aim. It is also one that does, in many cases, require weapons tailored to the target type. There are therefore many question-marks over the role.

The main problems associated with interdiction in a NATO context are that the number of targets would be large, that many repeat attacks might be required to ensure that the battlefield remained isolated, and that the aircraft used would also be needed for other tasks. Nevertheless, there is an apparent symmetry between the capabilities required for the attack of enemy airfields and those needed for interdictory operations which suggests that, warhead design apart perhaps, harmonisation of systems with resultant economy might be possible.

There are those, of course, who believe that missiles might be rather better for the attack of targets in depth than aircraft flying from bases which might be disrupted by enemy attack. Proponents of this idea envisage variously either ground-launched missiles or those carried in quantity in large stand-off aircraft operating from relatively secure bases outside the area of tactical operations. However, and not unnaturally, each concept has a wide range of pros and cons.

The third important task which I suggested the Army Group needs the Royal Air Force to undertake is the attack of enemy armour which has been canalised and concentrated as a result of our own ground action. By definition this task is unlikely to arise so early in war as the other two, and by the time it did, as a result of the manoeuvring and intensity of fighting which would have ocurred, the enemy air defence envelope in the ground battle area might be expected to have been downgraded to an extent which would provide 2 ATAF with an acceptable air environment for ground attack operations.

I do not envisage this task as being continuous in nature or requiring dedicated aircraft, acting almost as a branch of army artillery, as was practised in World War Two by the German Stukas and, later on, by the Soviet Sturmovik fighter-bombers. I see it rather as a response to the periodical requirement to mass firepower from all sources, with that delivered from the air being an essential component, to take quick advantage of the opportunities of war — such as the Falaise pocket in France — at critical points in both time and place. Clearly, given what I said earlier, the flexibility, speed of response and firepower of aircraft provide great potential in meeting this task, although the need to mass a suitably heavy weight of attack would require priorities to be agreed quickly and harmoniously at Army Group/ATAF level.

Some people, of course, continue to press for their own preferred solution to the problem of getting the right firepower to the right place at the right time — be it by aircraft, by attack helicopters, or by rocket artillery. My own view is that such a partisan approach is wrong. There are pros and cons to each solution, and no solution is cheap. I am convinced that we have to look at the various elements as complementary weapon systems — each of which has a synergistic effect on the other, and all of which are dependent on the progress of the counter-air campaign — both offensive and defensive.

Let me conclude with a few observations.

First, all the tasks which I have touched on, and notably the correct committal of Army reserves and allocation of air priorities, depend on timely and well informed command decisions. These require, as an absolute essential, provision of a surveillance and target acquisition capability which is responsive, reliable and robust against the inevitable counter measures. Furthermore, this capability must be effectively integrated with the command and control system at all appropriate levels and with the vital process of fusing and distributing intelligence. This is an area which seems, unfortunately, to have been more notable for argument than for progress in recent years.

Secondly, I must emphasise how crucial are the command links between the Army and the Royal Air Force at the NATO Headquarters level. There will obviously be more tasks to carry out than those for which we will have resources. And I have to say that I am not yet happy in my own mind that the links we have put in place so far are really good enough to ensure that the right decision could be made in the hurly-burly of war without lengthy discussion on priorities — just when time was at a premium. We have suffered the operational consequences of this occurring in the past, and today the Russian system has, of course, been designed to overcome this risk.

Thirdly, I do sometimes wonder at the implications of multi-role aircraft. On the face of it, it seems a great idea and I am a firm believer in the flexibility endowed by everything having an alternative capability. But how much does this cost to achieve? And how much can actually be achieved? I don't know, but it must surely be that, unless flown by a multi-role man, who has been multi-role trained in multi-role tactics, and unless it has readily available multi-role weapon and sensor fits, that a multi-role aircraft may be little more than an optimistic presentational statistic.

If this heretical thought were to have some grain of truth in it then I suppose it could be argued that the cost of buying an airframe which matched both interceptor and ground attack roles might be unnecessary, and that buying something less compromising and cheaper — but in greater numbers — could be better. Because, at the end of the day, at least as seen from the ground, numbers do still count and the Warsaw Pact has them. However, as I say, I realise that this is heresy!

Overall, I hope that there is today a healthy understanding that operations on the ground and operations in the air are both part of the same battle, and that if the Army is to fight and win, the *sine qua non* is that the Royal Air Force has to succeed in its tasks. The motto of RAF Odiham is emblazoned on a plaque on my office wall: 'Promise and Fulfil'. Much hangs on that last word!

*Editor's footnote:
Because of the change of date of the Conference, General Reilly did not attend. We have included his prepared text as it complements so well General Guthrie's presentation.

THE FUTURE OF BATTLEFIELD AIR SUPPORT
Major General Charles Guthrie, LVO, OBE

After the year 2000, much on the Central Front will be similar to today. The conventional threat facing the Allied ground forces will be from mass: superior numbers of tanks and helicopters, supported by guns, rockets and aircraft, whose aim would be to roll over NATO forces and their reserves as quickly as they could. The increasing numerical imbalance in army equipments could well continue until 2000 and beyond. The enemy's mass will enjoy a mobility which does not exist today.

The Allies will continue with the concept of forward defence but also recognise the folly of an over-literal interpretation of this term and the awful dangers in trying to defend everything or to be strong everywhere. The thin red line may have worked against the Russians at Inkerman but it would not work now. With the number of Allied soldiers that could at best be made available and the frontages to be covered, it is mathematically impossible to cover everywhere, much as Western European politicians would like us to. Demographic studies already tell us that our predicament over numbers will become worse. We will have to plan on holding what really matters and having reserves ready and waiting to react to the battle, to destroy enemy forces.

Just as it is today, important terrain will be selected and held. Some of these positions will be in depth. They will all be held strongly and have a degree of mutual support. They will contain and canalise the enemy's mass and, having depth, give time and space for effective Allied reserves to react and seize the initiative. The forces on the important terrain can reduce the momentum of the attacker, making his very mass militate against his momentum.

NATO commanders will continue to be faced with the dilemma of getting the balance right between their terrain-holding troops, which could be said to shape the battlefield, and their mobile reserves, consisting of tanks and helicopters and armoured infantry supported by guns, rockets and aircraft. The former, the ground holding element, can be likened to a shield, the latter, the mobile reserves to a sword. These reserves will have to be in sufficient strength really to damage the enemy's mass and to seize the initiative. Inadequate numbers of reserves, which can only achieve a flea bite on the enemy's mass, will only lead to having our soldiers killed for no good purpose.

After the year 2000, movement is likely to become even more difficult than it is today. Top attack weapons, scatterable mines, improved surveillance and target acquisition, more and more urbanisation of Western Europe will, I suspect tend to favour the defender. But even so, God will still incline to be on the side of the big battalions, at least to start with. The importance of the attack helicopter and air assault/mobility will increase after 2000 for both NATO and the Warsaw Pact. We in the Army will require post-2000, indeed we require today, attack helicopters, in airmobile formations, which can wait in the rear area in comparative safety and when the need arises destroy enemy armour through shock action. The speed with which they can react, their ability to fly over the most difficult terrain (which may be impassable to ground forces) and their hitting power will be priceless assets. As a commander I would view them in many ways as similar to a tank.

Until a few years ago, the corps of the Northern Army Group fought what could be said to be independent Corps battles with little regard to what was happening to the other National Corps in the Army Group. Today, that is different and further advances will have been made by the year 2000. Large Army Group reserves will be in existence and practised, for use throughout the Army Group area. Inter-operability and training will be advanced. It should be much harder for an enemy to pick off Allied formations piecemeal.

A new factor is emerging which will I think be even more important after 2000: FOFA. It has always played a part in war but without much effect; in the year 2000 and beyond it could have a dramatic effect on the Army Group's battle. FOFA will remain a joint Army/Royal Air Force operation, but the Army will have to remember that their priority task is still to win the FEBA battle and the necessary resources for this must not be jeopardised.

What can be drawn from all this? As General Reilly has already said, the three essential tasks which the Army will need the Royal Air Force to undertake post-2000 are:

First: To keep the enemy air, including enemy helicopters off the Army Group's back. (Enemy helicopter sites will become an even more important target post-2000.)

Second: To create a vacuum between the Warsaw Pact's leading and follow-up echelons by attacking vulnerable choke-points and major command and control facilities, in depth, at critical stages in the battle in order to prevent the enemy's follow-on forces joining the battle while our own forces engage and defeat the leading formations: in other words, Interdiction.

Third: To provide concentrated air support when it is required in support of essential ground operations. Examples include attacking enemy armour which our ground forces have canalised and concentrated, attacking an enemy formation which could interfere with the movement of our own reserves and regrouping, or the destruction of a sudden armoured breakthrough or an air assault. The Royal Air Force may have to plug the gap whilst ground forces manoeuvre.

Two comments apply to all these three tasks. First, the order of air priorities cannot be predetermined and the actual priority will be decided according to the operational circumstances. Secondly, air forces must be prepared to extend air action throughout the 24 hour period.

In touching on the three principal needs the ground forces have from the air, I will attempt to highlight the main concerns I have as an Army officer. First, keeping the air off the Army Group's back. This coincides with the first mission of the Tactical Air Force which is to conduct defensive and offensive air operations against targets vital to the enemy air force and nuclear capability. But the coincidence is not precise because the Air Force mission is wider in scope than the Army Group's direct needs and, in the absence of adequate resources to meet all the tasks of the day and the night, a conflict of priorities might be inescapable, with detrimental effect on the Army Group's requirement.

Next let me turn to the second Army Group requirement I mentioned, namely to create a vacuum between enemy leading and follow-up echelons. The mission arising would primarily involve the destruction of points at which follow-on forces would cross significant obstacles, and thereafter keeping those crossings closed. Historically this has proved to be a mission more easily identified than achieved and one for which munitions with appropriate warheads and guidance capabilities are essential. This leaves a number of 'ifs' but the big if stems from the facts that the number of targets would be considerable, that the mission would need to be sustained, and that many of the aircraft involved — if manned aircraft are to be used — would be in demand for other tasking.

There is, of course, the proposition that the interdictory role, the attack of ground targets in depth, might be more cost-effectively undertaken by missiles than by very expensive manned aircraft operating from airfields which would themselves be subject to attack. Through my khaki eyes I would certainly like to see the Army Group having a rapidly responsive surface-to-surface conventional missile system of their own that was effective against mobile formations and would give the ground forces the ability to attack the enemy in depth. It should have a high degree of survivability and a delivery capability throughout the Army Group's area of responsibility. It should be very accurate and capable of inflicting heavy casualties. The surface-to-surface missile would certainly not replace the aircraft, but complement it. Aircraft-delivered weapon systems will generally require time for preparation before being brought to bear on the target. Surface-to-surface missiles could react more quickly.

The third need was for concentrated air support of essential ground operations. Inherently, this could be the most lucrative area for fixed-wing aircraft and helicopter alike, but both must be properly orchestrated into the all arms battle — which implies effective and robust C^3, including ground and helicopter based LTM for use with smart weapons and on-board weapon-aiming systems. By the year 2000, much progress needs to be made in the field of IFF, as the proper co-ordination of air forces and army plans, and the mutual support this affords, is crucial. Present systems are inadequate.

All the tasks which I have touched on, and notably the correct committal of army reserves and allocation of air priorities, depend on timely and well informed command decisions. These require, as an absolute essential, provision of a surveillance and target acquisition capability which is responsive, reliable and robust against the inevitable countermeasures. We need ground and air based systems to locate targets for attack by air, artillery and missile. This capability must be effectively integrated at all appropriate levels with the command and control system and the vital process of fusing and distributing intelligence.

I would highlight the need for war-worthy command relationships between the Army and the Royal Air Force at NATO command levels. I have already alluded to a disparity between identifiable tasks on the one hand and force numbers on the other, and I am not personally convinced that development so far avoids a risk that, under the strain of war, the timing of a command decision might be placed in jeopardy by debate over a conflict of priority at that very moment when there was no time for debate.

One does hear from time to time that after 2000 Command and

Control will be easier. Surveillance equipment and techniques will be more advanced, it should be much easier to acquire targets, and, theoretically, it should be easier to hit what you see. But I think this is a dangerous delusion. Certainly after 2000 it will be possible to transmit and process information faster than ever before but *more and more* information will become available and there will be a great danger of commanders losing the gold amongst the trivia. What is relevant and crucial will be lost amongst the irrelevant. Opportunities may be missed and we should beware of having too many people being involved in the decision-making process. Technology will not invalidate Clausewitz who said that a great part of the information obtained in war is contradictory, a still greater part is false, and by far the greatest part is uncertain.

In conclusion, there will be nothing very clever about the Army's concept from the year 2000 and beyond. It will obey the principles of war. It will demand a degree of mutual support for containment, depth to give time and space to react, and effective reserves (not necessarily transported along the ground) with which to react and seize the initiative. FOFA could well have a dramatic effect. It will still be dangerous to have tailor-made plans, too finely tuned for a few scenarios. We could still be attacked before we are ready, with NATO ground forces being unbalanced and requiring a heavy pre-planned initial air response of close air support and battlefield air interdiction to support the forces covering the Army Group's deployment.

I suggest we must resist those who will advocate either aircraft, attack helicopters or rocket artillery as their preferred method of delivering firepower in the Central Region. There are dangers in a selective approach. Each system — admittedly all are very expensive — has its own characteristics, advantages, disadvantages and alternative roles.

I suggest that they should be seen, together with all other elements involved, as mutually complementing instruments in the orchestra of war, acting in concert, with their effect in union being greater than the sum of their individual contributions.

We do need to develop armed helicopters and fixed-wing aircraft in tandem. Joint planning and funding must be essential to get the right mix, and we have a long way to go in learning to conduct and co-ordinate the orchestra properly before the turn of the century. We have to have the ability to concentrate weapon systems and the right mix of weapon systems very quickly in order to destroy an enemy breakthrough. The interdependence of air and land operations will be as important as ever, even increasingly important, and it will be crucial for the Royal Air Force to achieve its missions if the Army, for its part, is to fulfil its war role successfully.

DEEP INTERDICTION AND OFFENSIVE
COUNTER-AIR AFTER THE YEAR 2000
Air Vice Marshal John Walker, CBE, AFC, RAF

The Need for Interdiction

What is the need for interdiction? Will not the battle be decided in the front line and should not our concentration, mental and material, acknowledge this? That could prove a plausible but shortsighted policy. The Soviet doctrine is based on *mass* and *momentum*, for the mathematicians, MV^2. Soviet divisions are long on firepower but short on sustainability. Unlike NATO, they will fight them to exhaustion, then reinforce through them with fresh divisions. For that they need the freedom of communication and the protection from the delay and disruption, or what Slessor called it, 'aggravated muddle,' which an interdiction campaign imposes. The very mass they possess gives them almost an embarrassment of riches, for it is difficult for them to get all their tanks on a sensible frontage, and they need ground, shallow and deep, for assembly and preparation. Given adequate surveillance, there should be rich pickings for air forces with the right weapons.

Mass and momentum also add up to high consumption of stores, ammunition and fuel. The Warsaw Pact has increased its forward holdings considerably in recent years to lessen reliance on lines of communication, but even then, in the forward area, those materials have to be moved. Further, if too much is dumped forward, it can become a target in its own right.

One of the most convincing arguments for interdiction is one that is too rarely rehearsed. Increasingly, night, the soldier's friend, which allows him to sleep and recuperate, is being removed from the battlefield by technology. Without respite, troops will very quickly become exhausted, even more so if forced to wear NBC equipment. If the enemy can be made to engage with his own exhausted troops, at least a balance of disadvantage is obtained. However, if he is left with the freedom to bring fresh troops to the fray, the battle will be soon decided — for NATO is critically short of reserves.

Few, if any, British commanders have up-to-date experience of interdicted lines of communication and it is very difficult to play interdiction realistically in exercises. Consequently, the grossly debilitating effect of air attack can go unrecognised. In such circumstances, reference to those commanders who have experienced interdiction is profitable, and the works of Guderian and Rommel, to mention only two, leave no doubt about their profound respect for it and the disruptive effect it can have upon the conduct of operations.

There is a need to ensure that the enemy has no 'safe ground'. There must be no *sanctuary* and the knowledge of this is an essential part of the deterrent posture upon which we rely to prevent conflict in the first instance. How deep the interdiction should be will always be a difficult question to answer. Soviet concern for the sacred homeland is well known, but can it be assumed that the Soviet leadership will have any great concern about war fought on the territory of the vassal states? Probably not, so it is the homeland itself that must be threatened if Soviet minds are to be concentrated. With the buffer states to the fore, the homeland is very deep from the tactical point of view but at least those Soviet formations and facilities within reach of NATO must be given no quarter. To accomplish that, NATO air forces need *range*, more range than is common at present.

In the past, some interdiction campaigns have not proved to be successful. When they have not, they have lacked the essential land/air character. Enemy forces which are not being forced to manoeuvre or to expend their materiel will be less vulnerable to interdiction and it is the land forces' task to ensure this essential input into the scenario; thereafter the air forces must get amongst the targets thus offered.

Modern weaponry is opening up more target systems to effective interdiction, targets which, until now, have been deemed suitable only for nuclear attack. Conventional warheads are increasing in effectiveness and some fuel-air effects are said to be equivalent to localised nuclear bursts. The dominant improvement by far is that in accuracy. Modern aircraft attack systems are producing very impressive results and the possibilities for the terminal homing of missiles, through the whole range from the ballistic, through cruise, to the MLRS, is equally encouraging.

Parallel with this, and helping to increase greatly the overall effect, is the trend towards increasingly sophisticated, and thereby militarily more vulnerable, target systems. A steam railway with manual signalling presented a multitude of small targets but a modern electrified system, with computerised signalling, presents only a handful of targets. Once attacked the system is not merely damaged — it is stopped, and very nearly completely. Modern power stations work at much higher pressures than those of yesteryear and have within them the seeds of their own destruction. Chernobyl has already demonstrated that you do not need to take the 'bang' — it is already there — you only need to take the initiator. Power transmission at very high voltages, using large and scarce transformers, is now proliferating and if 25,000 volts cannot be stepped-down it is useless to most subscribers. It is time for the military to pay more attention to this approach to targeting in the light of the emerging weapons capabilities.

Offensive Counter-Air

Let us now turn to offensive counter-air. We should not think that the Israeli attack on the Egyptian Air Force in 1967 was unique — remember what the Luftwaffe did to the Second Tactical Air Force on New Year's Day 1945 — but it did start the modern drift towards airbase defence. Hardened aircraft shelters appeared in the Warsaw Pact within 18 months of the Israeli initiative and followed in NATO later. They left the offensive forces with no weapon-to-target match short of nuclear attack. Even now the new generation weapons — JP233, MW-1 and Durandel — are optimised against the operating surfaces rather than the primary target, which remains the aircraft. There are answers to these weapons; dispersal is the obvious one, helped in part by the trend towards high-agility aircraft and power-to-weight ratios which give STOL almost as a natural fallout. The intelligent use of tankers takes away some of the urgency for recovery into damaged bases and can be used to give a measure of airborne dispersal as well. Perhaps the best defence is concrete. This is not a popular solution — the R&D is a bit thin — but a look at some of the old Luftwaffe bases will show just how quickly over-target requirements can be made ridiculous for a quite modest investment in concrete mixers.

In the future, weaponry must catch up with the target system and be able to take on the primary target. For this both aircraft in the open and those in HAS must be attacked, and a HAS-buster is required. The advantage here is that the HAS is in a fixed and known position. Given good surveillance, putting a weapon system over it is not going to present a major problem. The hardness is becoming less of a protection as weapons technology improves and the cratering sub-munition of the JP233 is the sort of warhead which could be used profitably against a HAS. The recent demonstration of a Tomahawk exploding over an aircraft in a revetment gives an insight into what may soon be possible. The disadvantage of the HAS attack is that it is something of a shell game, and an empty structure may be the one selected. In this respect a lot of small HAS are perhaps a better defence than a few large ones.

Whether the manned aircraft will be found in the future OCA package depends a lot on the developments in accuracy. High accuracy can equate to small warhead requirements which can be satisfied by missiles of one sort or the other. Until those accuracies materialise, large warloads are best carried by aircraft. The overall balance in the argument will probably swing with cost-effectiveness and that, in turn, depends on two things: the relative cost per damage function at the target, and the probability of arrival, or, put another way, attrition.

Cost-Effectiveness

On probability of arrival the ballistic missile scores heavily and the United States Counter-Air 90 proposals showed what may be possible. Some of those proposals involved very high throw-weights and impressive amounts of terminal ordnance. Cruise missiles, on the other hand, are more vulnerable — but that should not automatically rule them out. Even the present generation are formidably difficult to intercept and they lend themselves to stealth technology in the future. Their relatively slow speed makes them vulnerable to terminal defences — but that, again, is dependent on the sub-munition design and *modus operandi*. Cost is widely held against the missile solution but care needs to be taken. Most current missile costs relate to weapons built for a nuclear role and the engineering and redundancy requirements for nuclear systems are far greater than those needed for a conventional application. Further, a conventional missile approach pre-supposes quantity. Few missile projects so far, ballistic or cruise, have been favoured by long production runs.

The great advantage held by the aircraft is its flexibility. Although most weapon systems have some element of multi-target application — JP233 against choke-points and bridges for example — the warheads of missiles may need to be more specialist in nature. Cruise missiles, to take an actual example, may not lend themselves to large area targets. Airmen must guard jealously this precious flexibility of the manned aircraft. In air power terms that largely means range, or more descriptively, 'reach'. It cannot be stressed too strongly that 'reach' is the absolutely vital function in the flexibility, and thereby the effectiveness, of air power.

The greatest argument against the aircraft compared with the crated missile is *life-cycle costs*. Here the trend is not in the aircraft's favour, although there are things which can be done about it. Of the two major items in the budgeting, both can be expected to become progressively more expensive; fuel, for example, can scarcely be expected to get any cheaper in the next century, and even its availability may one day become a problem. Personnel costs are unlikely to drop, particularly if we stay with the all-volunteer force and system complexity continues to increase. There is at least a partial answer to the problem but one which is difficult for the financial planner to accept, and that is to *spend-to-save* and invest heavily at the front-end of programmes on reliability and maintainability. In this way, spares and manpower demands can be held in check, to the benefit of life-cycle-costs.

A lot of nonsense is talked about attrition — both by those who would have it that we shall emerge from the Third World War with the historical campaign norm of one to two per cent, and the others who forecast that little will be left after the first day. The truth, as always, probably lies between the two extremes. Unfortunately, there is no widespread recognition of attrition mathematics and when we cannot rely on massive reinforcement of aircraft and crews, even quite modest loss rates debilitate the force well within the limits of the 30-day war. Remember that in World War Two a single month's aircraft production in the Third Reich exceeded the total in-place aircraft in NATO's Central Region today.

A couple of examples may not go amiss. At typical sortie rates an attrition rate of five per cent leaves less than a quarter of the aircraft available after 10 days; a 10 per cent attrition rate leaves only five per cent. Perhaps of greater importance is that over a 10-day period the higher attrition rate results in only 60 per cent of the sorties generated at the lower attrition level. Particularly in the face of numerical superiority, *it is the generation of sorties which counts most.*

Can attrition be kept in check? Certainly not without a good deal of effort but, given this, it is more than possible. The Soviet AWACS and the look-down, shoot-down fighter between them have removed the previous low-level gap, and ground-based defences do not suffer the weight, or size, or power, or crew, restrictions of the aircraft. Thus far it is a one-sided affair, more so when the profusion of Soviet systems is considered. Some say *stealth* combined with other equipment and tactics, will overcome the defences — and perhaps, in certain specialist applications, it may (the SR-71 operation springs to mind) — but radar is no longer the only surveillance means. IR detection, even acoustics, could be brought into play and, again, we must not forget the basics; the Mark-1-Eyeball and the small arms barrage will be as effective in the next war as they have been in the last half dozen.

It is unlikely that the aircraft alone will be able to protect itself for some time to come and an integrated campaign utilising a number of different approaches will be needed. HARM and ALARM are examples of specialist defence suppression missiles and there are specifications issued for self-protection missiles. Clearly, drones have an important part to play, particularly in the forward area, where the air defences are likely to be so dense. I have always found it strange that they have not proved to be more popular since they offer one of the few areas in which NATO can operate on the right side of the cost-effectiveness curve — surely an SA-6 or an SA-10 engaging a drone must be attractive to the side with the drones? Electronic warfare equipment together with chaff, (still as effective as ever, when used intelligently), will also remain an important, if expensive, part of the complete suite.

OCA/DCA Balance

There is always enthusiastic discussion about the OCA/DCA balance. Whilst there is no choice but to penetrate to accomplish interdiction, some would have it that there is an option with the counter-air battle. Rather than penetrate, the argument goes, wait for them to come to you. It is superficially attractive because, in so doing, only offensive aircraft are engaged. What is the point of risking losses and expending effort to engage aircraft which are defensive in nature, *for they do not win wars*. Further, offensive aircraft are usually heavily laden with fuel and ordnance, and defensive fighters, operating close to their own bases, and in the air defence fit, will have a useful performance advantage. They may not even need that, because as soon as offensive aircraft jettison their loads to defend themselves so is the target perfectly defended and the fighters can disengage.

So goes the theory, but the practice could be different. Trenchard warned that the aircraft was an excellent weapon of offence — but was shockingly bad at defence. Did he have in mind, I wonder, the fact that the flexibility of aircraft can be used in the offensive to *concentrate* and thereby to saturate the defences? This would certainly be the offensive plan and could be successful unless there was very good surveillance and warning. Without that, the defences have to be eternally vigilant and that means, in practice, holding combat air patrols. CAP is very expensive in just about everything, but primarily can cause the butter to

PLATE 6.2. The counter air punch: a Tornado GR1 releasing JP-233 runway cratering sub-munitions. *(Photo: by courtesy of British Aerospace.)*

be spread too thinly which, full circle, better enables the offensive concentration and saturation to work.

Again, the answer is not to be found in the blacks and the whites. There will be circumstances where sensible use of capabilities can enhance overall effectiveness. For example, NATO is a defensive alliance of 16 sovereign nations and that means, almost by definition, that the other side will be able to exploit the inestimable advantage of tactical surprise. NATO may well have to take the first blow on the nose. In addition, it may take time to get the political clearance to begin offensive operations and, during this time, it would be wasteful to keep offensive aircraft on their bases, to be mere targets, when many of them have a tidy, if secondary, air defence capability with their missile armament. In effect, this would be using the force in defensive counter air, and most sensibly so, but it does not make a strong case for doing it for the complete campaign.

Why not? Four main reasons. First, that it would enable the enemy to operate his bases undisturbed and that would allow him to optimise his sortie rate. Second, it could result in fewer total offensive sorties penetrating, and so allow the enemy to concentrate his fighters better on those aircraft which do penetrate. Third, a lower offensive threat may allow the enemy to re-role defensive aircraft into offensive roles, and last, but by far the primary reason, is that defending against an air threat is a resource-hungry business and it is much better for us if the opponent is spending his war-like rouble on defensive rather than offensive systems.

Multi-Roling, Dual-Capability and Flexibility

We touch now on the thorny subject of multi-roling. There are as many opinions on the merits of multi-roling and dual-capability as there are airmen. In the past, Spitfires and the like doubled very adequately as multi-role aircraft. The same guns which fought Messerschmitts did a passably good job against trucks. The performance figures and aerodynamics of the day were tolerant of amazing liberties taken to hang some unglamorous armament aboard. At that time the 'system' as a whole was only two-part, the air-frame and the engine. It was with the advent of devices like air intercept radar and H2S bombing systems that the balance started to change in cost and complexity to a three-part balance: airframe, engine and avionics. As time went on, the cost of the avionics increased and in aircraft like the EF-111 and the AWACS it probably costs a good deal more than the airframe and engines combined. Recently, the fourth element entered the balance: the new expensive and complex weapon systems themselves which enable the pilot to spend impressive amounts of money by a single pressure on his weapon release button. In such a situation, is it possible to build, equip, train for, or utilise a multi-role aircraft?

Consider the past. The might of the United States and the European aircraft industries have engaged in two attempts to produce the Multi-Role Aircraft. In the States, Mr McNamara's dream of the single type ended up as the F-111, perhaps the best offensive aircraft in NATO, but even its ardent supporters would not claim it was an air superiority fighter. In Europe, what is now the Tornado started life as the Multi-Role Combat Aircraft and, indeed, it is to be found in a number of roles, but the air defence version has a different fuselage, cockpit and radar and modified wings and engines. Its admirers, and they are many, would probably concede that the necessary compromises in the design resulted in a good, rather than a great, aircraft. In other words, in that time-scale anyway, technology did not seem to be able to produce the multi-role dream on either side of the Atlantic.

Conversely, there have been a series of aircraft which have made a very acceptable job of the multi-role function. In all cases, they started life as specialist single-role aircraft. The Canberra, as a high-altitude bomber, ended up in the B(I)8 form as a good, sound, low-level interdictor. The Hunter, as a high-altitude fighter, made a splendid ground attack aircraft in the FGA-9 and an excellent fighter reconnaissance aircraft in the FR-10. Pride of place must be conceded to the McDonnell-Douglas F-4 Phantom. Conceived as a high-altitude fleet defence fighter it has since performed, seemingly in more roles than not, with great distinction. Is it possible that the same firm is to repeat the experience and make the impressive F-15, born under the slogan 'not-a-pound-for-air-to-ground', into an interdictor *par excellence* with the F-15E version?

It is not only the problem of building the multi-role aircraft but also of operating it. The training difficulties are often ignored, partly on the false argument that modern systems take the load off the crew and thereby allow more roles to be undertaken. This ignores the fact that flying the aircraft is only one part of the total tactical package; the other is the knowledge and exploitation of the tactical situation or, as operators prefer to call it, *tactical and situational awareness*. The differences in this essential quality between the BVR missile attack against a swarm of high-altitude bombers and the synchronised mass attack against a highly defended target at low level are as chalk is to cheese. It is not an area in which to make economies, because modern combat, (in whatever role), is becoming more lethal. If the other fellow, the single-role specialist, is better than you are, it is not a matter of coming second, it becomes a matter of not coming anywhere at all.

That point may be dismissed as emotionalism by those who prefer figures, but they too have their reasons for questioning multi-roling. Long gone are the days when weapons were cheap, and multi-roling means the provision of large inventories of weapons. A salvo of JP233 costs a seven-figure sum; a full load of Mavericks just as much; initial estimates for the AMRAAM indicate a price closer to half a million dollars than to the cost of previous generation weapons.

Yet for the 30 or so sorties which can be expected from an aircraft in war is the multi-role aircraft provisioned with 30 loads of Maverick and 30 loads of AMRAAM? Very extravagant if so, because half of this very expensive inventory will go unused. Yet without it, is the aircraft multi-role? After all, no matter how well the aircraft flies, it is the *weapon* which ultimately does the deed. *No weapon — no role!* Or is an apportionment made — perhaps, say, 30 per cent air defence and 70 per cent ground attack? If the initial demand, as it might be, is for air defence, then what multi-role capability is possessed on sortie 10? The Maverick is a magnificent weapon but it has its limitations in a dog-fight!

If nations are going to get caught in the costs of training and in provisioning and are not therefore going to be able to exploit to the full their multi-role capability, and if the cost of having it in the first instance is compromised performance, for a higher initial purchase cost, then should they not ask themselves whether it is really worth the candle?

When a fighter has you in his gunsight, it does not matter whether or not you are a multi-role aircraft, because whatever you are, you are just about to be a dead one. Nor does it matter that your designers have been so clever in producing a multi-role aircraft, for the operator's definition of technological superiority is fairly simple. If the enemy is in your gunsight, you are technically superior; if he is in your rear-view mirror, you are technically inferior. To paraphrase von Richtofen, 'Anything else is Rubbish!'

CHAPTER 7

Air Defence and the Theatre Nuclear Role

AIR DEFENCE AFTER THE YEAR 2000
Lieutenant General Thomas McInerney, USAF

The challenges which face future offensive air operations have been described in detail in other chapters. However, all military operations will be much more difficult, if not impossible, if NATO cannot attain and maintain a favourable air situation. I will focus here on the mission area most responsible for providing this favourable air situation: air defence operations. I will concentrate on Allied Command Europe's Central Region, since the high density of deployed weapons there provides possibly the greatest challenge for air defence systems. Most aspects of the threat to the Central Region and the concept of future air defence operations there apply directly also to the defence of the United Kingdom and the United Kingdom Air Defence Region.

Any discussion of military operations must begin with a consideration of the Threat, since it drives all military requirements. Hence, I would like to begin by portraying the Threat, as I see it, which NATO air defences will face in the year 2000 and beyond. The air threat posed by the Soviet Union and the Warsaw Pact will be diverse, technically advanced and numerically superior. Tactical and strategic aircraft will combine the latest technologies with greater lethality. Highly manoeuvrable fighters, such as the Flanker and Fulcrum, will likely be complemented by an even newer generation fighter with longer range and more potent air-to-air weapons to challenge our air superiority fighters. The Backfire bomber will be joined by the Blackjack to provide long-range attack capability. The presence of longer range, sea-based attack aircraft on the new Soviet aircraft carriers will give the Warsaw Pact the capability to project power in locations that are difficult for them to reach today. Aircraft will be armed with precision-guided munitions, as well as long-range air-to-air

169

and air-to-surface missiles to give Warsaw Pact forces greater ability to stand off from NATO defences.

Soviet cruise missiles, unmanned air vehicles, anti-radiation missiles, and ballistic missiles will be capable of carrying conventional as well as chemical and nuclear warheads. These weapons may be launched from air, ground, sea or sub-surface platforms. TBMs are likely to become an integrated part of, and a precursor to, Warsaw Pact offensive air operations. Advanced attack helicopters, capable of air-to-air combat, such as the Havoc and Hokum, will also be present in large numbers along the forward edge of the battle area, and ample numbers of radio-electronic combat (or REC) platforms, in concert with attack aircraft, will attempt to degrade or destroy NATO air defence weapons and command and control systems. Soviet and Warsaw Pact air forces are likely to combine large numbers of escort fighters, attack fighters, bombers and REC assets into large, mass raids that will severely tax NATO's air defences.

As I mentioned earlier, a favourable air situation is of paramount importance for *all* NATO military operations — air, land or sea, offensive or defensive. While it may not be necessary, or even possible, to achieve complete air supremacy, the most salient contribution of air power in any conflict is to provide a favourable air situation — and this axiom will remain valid in the year 2000 and beyond. Such a situation may involve localised air superiority only, limited in space and time, but a favourable air situation will, nevertheless, still be necessary to permit successful friendly air, land, and sea operations. In order to attain and maintain this condition during the early stages of conflict, Allied Command Europe will respond with a heavy emphasis on defensive counter-air operations. Initially, this will require the maximum use of multi-role fighters in an air defence capacity. To counter the Warsaw Pact's large mass raids, we must co-ordinate and integrate the employment of all air defence assets, including maritime anti-air warfare systems. A properly co-ordinated and integrated air defence will reduce mutual interference and fratricide, and avoid redundant targeting of hostile aircraft and missiles.

The Warsaw Pact's development of longer-range weapons will dictate that the NATO air defence umbrella be moved farther forward, even over hostile territory if necessary, to permit unhampered friendly air and ground operations. Likewise, increased use of fighter escort and fighter sweep missions will be necessary to support deep interdiction and offensive counter-air operations. This concept of fighter employment will hinge on the development of an aircraft with revolutionary capabilities: it should be highly manoeuvrable through the use of vectored thrust and fly-by-wire flight controls; it must be capable of short take-off and landing, so that it can continue to operate out of airfields with damaged runways; it needs to be able to cruise at supersonic speeds without requiring afterburner or re-heat, to give it a greater combat radius; it must be armed with long-range fire-and-forget missiles to provide the capability to engage multiple targets simultaneously; and finally, it must incorporate low radar, optical, and infrared signatures to enhance survivability.

A key element of the air defence system is the Recognised Air Picture, or RAP. In the year 2000, it will be obtained by integrating inputs from ground-, air- and space-based sensors, and will be disseminated to all air defence components using secure digital data links. The RAP will incorporate positive aircraft indentification, using a combination of direct, indirect and procedural methods to minimise fratricide. The RAP, which will be more complete and accurate than the equipment we have now, will permit new tactics to make more effective use of our scarce air defence assets — tactics such as detached mutual support for fighters and the employment of SAMs and fighters together in the same air defence zone.

The TBM defensive challenge is such that *it* may become the long pole in the air defence battle management system: it will drive the tempo of operations, which will force us to automate and streamline our defensive reactions — with most human decision-making accomplished prior to the launch of the missiles. The threat posed by conventional TBMs will also force NATO to step out sharply and develop direct defence options, in lieu of a retaliatory response. The air defence system will use a variety of air-, land- and space-based sensors and weapons to provide protection from these tactical missiles, as well as unmanned air vehicles. Finally, defence against Warsaw Pact attack helicopters will be accomplished through the co-ordinated use of fixed-wing aircraft, air-defence-capable helicopters, and both line-of-sight and non-line-of-sight ground-based weapons.

In order for this futuristic concept of air defence operations to become a reality, NATO nations will need to take a logical and coherent approach to the development of future weapon systems and future national defence budgets. Investment in air defences should provide a balance between active and passive measures. Passive measures, such as the hardening of facilities, dispersal of assets, concealment, and tactical deception, provide a significant contribution to a credible air defence, and much remains to be accomplished in these areas.

Active defence measures include the development of air defence fighters, SAMs and AAA. In this area, the United States development of the Advanced Tactical Fighter will help provide NATO with the capability to extend the air defence umbrella farther forward and to ensure qualitative superiority over the new generation of Warsaw Pact fighters. However, additional numbers of air defence aircraft will be required to respond to large air attacks. Therefore, multi-role fighters will be necessary to give air commanders flexibility in tasking appropriate numbers of air-to-air and air-to-ground missions. Long-range, area defence SAMs, such as the Patriot system, will be necessary to provide defence against both aircraft and tactical missiles. However, the Patriot must be complemented by shorter range systems such as the Hawk, Rapier, Roland, and a follow-on system — the M-SAM. Point air defence missile systems with a non-line-of-sight capability will be required to complement the normal line-of-sight missiles and AAA to defend against helicopter attacks.

Effective battle management requires improved command, control and communications systems. Of course, surveillance systems form a key portion of the air defence C^3 network, since they provide tactical warning and assist in the employment of air defence weapons. The use of mobile, ground-based early warning and ground control intercept radars must be supplemented with manned and unmanned airborne sensors and space-based systems to ensure adequate surveillance and control capability. To keep pace with the threat, improvements will be required for our airborne early warning force, including possibly the development of a follow-on aircraft. The NATO Air Command and Control System should provide a long-range blueprint for the acquisition of secure and ECM-resistant systems and facilities that will furnish the connectivity and interoperability required between all air defence elements. The development of the multi-functional information distribution system, called MIDS, will be required to enable us to disseminate the Recognised Air Picture to all air defence elements, including airborne fighters. Of course, we still need to pursue development and acquisition of the NATO Identification System, or NIS, so that the possibility of fratricide can be minimised. Effective battle management will also require more real-time intelligence information, which must be fused automatically with other command and control information to assist the air commander in making wise combat decisions.

As I discuss NATO's future needs for air defence, I would be remiss if I did not mention a critical issue — the affordability of weapon systems

PLATE 7.1. A MiG-29 at an air-show in Finland in July 1986: evidence of the increasing sophistication of the Soviet air threat. *(Courtesy of Air Clues Magazine.)*

and defence programmes. This issue has several important and relevant aspects, the first being the co-operative development of weapon systems. Although, in the past, the strong economies of many western nations have permitted them to develop similar weapon systems simultaneously, the cost of today's high-tech weapons and the current austere fiscal climate provide strong arguments for greater co-operation in the development of NATO armaments. The duplication of effort and inefficient use of funds for research and development are evidenced today by the simultaneous development of two aircraft designed to occupy the same niche in NATO's family of defensive systems: the Advanced Tactical Fighter and the European Fighter Aircraft. Fortunately, we can point to positive recent examples of co-operative armaments ventures, such as the NAEW and F-16 aircraft, and the AMRAAM and ASRAAM weapons. However, more needs to be done in this area in the future.

The issue of affordability also places greater emphasis on reducing life-cycle costs for weapon systems. By improving the reliability and maintainability of weapon systems, we will be able to support higher combat sortie rates, which, in turn, may help to offset NATO's numerical disadvantage.

Future armament developments must also exploit promising new technologies, such as the use of composite materials in airframes and advanced microprocessors in avionics. Electronic systems represent, perhaps, the West's last major area of qualitative superiority over the

Soviets, but the margin is decreasing. In order to retain our lead, we must aggressively exploit advances in computer hardware and software to produce, for example, integrated counter-measure systems that enhance the survivability of our aircraft. Future weapons must use technological advances to provide greater stand-off capability and improved lethality. Space systems must also be exploited to provide improved tactical warning, targeting, command and control and survivable communications.

A last area which needs to be explored is how to achieve more cost-effective training by using innovative methods and advanced technology systems. One example of such a future application is an advanced flight simulator for air-to-air combat training, such as those currently under development by British Aerospace and McDonnell-Douglas. These advanced technologies offer us the opportunity to improve our combat capabilities at decreased operating costs.

In conclusion, I hope that I have not just presented a 'wish list' of what *might* be, but that I have been able to provide a realistic picture of air defence operations in the year 2000 and beyond. I would like to emphasise again that air power's most important contribution in any conflict is to provide a favourable air situation, which, in turn, permits all other military operations to proceed as planned. Therefore, NATO's air forces must give very high priority to improving our air defences, so that we will be prepared to respond to the Warsaw Pact threat in the decade ahead and even into the 21st century.

THE ROYAL AIR FORCE AND AIR DEFENCE
Group Captain Marten Van Der Veen, RAF

Few would disagree with the view that the prime concern of any government must be to provide for the security of its citizens. In the same way, the prime function of an air force must be to protect the nation's air space. Thus, in a wider context, the NATO air forces must jointly protect Alliance air space. It is, of course, a truism to say that defence posture is driven by the threat — but in air defence this fact is perhaps even more self-evident than in other fields. Recent Statements on the Defence Estimates make it clear that the British Government continues to see the Soviet Union as the prime threat to our security. It is therefore worth looking briefly at Soviet air doctrine before examining NATO's air defences and the contribution made to them by the Royal Air Force.

The Soviets well understand that Western views on deterrence hinge on an assured retaliatory capability. In war they would almost certainly aim to destroy as much as possible of NATO's European-based theatre nuclear stockpile, using conventional weapons alone. To put such a strategy into effect, the Soviet Union would make enormous use of its air power. Both now and over the next decade and more, they would use manned bombers to target that nuclear arsenal, employing such aircraft as Badger, Blinder and Backfire, Fencer, Flogger and Fitter. To secure a high rate of advance for their ground forces, they would also use much of their air power for direct army support. The Royal Air Force, together with the other NATO air forces, seeks to deter, and if necessary to counter, such a Soviet offensive.

Air Defence in the Central Region

Deterrence by no means depends solely on having a retaliatory capability, important as that may be — in the conventional as much as the nuclear arena. The possession of defences likely to deny success to a potential aggressor is clearly also a key factor. In the Central Region, NATO therefore needs robust defences against the Soviet air threat.

But in Germany we cannot opt for an outer air defence screen hundreds of miles beyond West German borders, in the same way that we can (as we shall see later) in the defence of the United Kingdom. In the Federal Republic of Germany, NATO's air defences can start no further forward than the Inner German border. Warning time would therefore be short, and the air battle would be fought within a relatively small geographical area. Both these factors have an enormous impact on the structure of NATO's air defence system.

In the Central Region, it is the surface-to-air missiles (SAMs) that provide the first line of defence. The belt of Hawk SAMs runs not far from the Iron Curtain borders, from the south of the Federal Republic of Germany right up into Denmark. Further back, from Bavaria to Schleswig-Holstein, is the Nike belt. Nike missiles are now being replaced by Patriot — a transportable SAM system with a much greater capability. But SAMs, useful as they are, are not enough. We will therefore continue to need fighter aircraft to plug the holes the Soviets might make in the missile belts, and to catch those Soviet aircraft that get through or around them.

Currently we base two squadrons of Phantoms in Germany for just this role. But by the mid-1990s these aircraft will be more than 25 years old, and we are therefore aiming to replace them with the new European Fighter Aircraft. However, it is not merely age that is forcing us to replace our Phantoms. As the Soviets bring into service ever more capable bombers, and fighter aircraft to escort them, so the Phantom's capability to take them on successfully is reduced. The new Soviet fighter aircraft Fulcrum and Flanker — both excellent aircraft today — will undoubtedly be modified and improved as the years go by; and we also anticipate some being deployed in an air-to-ground role over the next decade. In a Soviet air attack against the West, we would expect to see large numbers of these aircraft over the whole of North West Europe — either in the fighter escort role or in an offensive role.

Other offensive aircraft, like Fencer and Frogfoot, will remain in the Soviet inventory for the next few decades, and the Soviets continue to deploy ever more capable assault helicopters. If we wish to continue to be able to counter the Soviet threat, we must upgrade our air defences. The European Fighter Aircraft (EFA) will reverse the adverse trend, and restore our ability to fight and win. The Royal Air Force sees such a capability as essential for a nation obliged by treaty to defend West German air space, and for one that maintains sizeable ground and air forces in the Central Region — forces that are, of course, vulnerable to air attack.

The European Fighter Aircraft (EFA)

In the Fulcrum and Flanker, in particular, EFA will face two formidable opponents. Fulcrum has a similar layout to the American F-18, although it is a little heavier and has more powerful engines. Flanker is rather similar to the American F-15, but is again slightly heavier and a bit faster. Both, of course, have a look-down, shoot-down capability, and both will undoubtedly be improved over the years. Fulcrum would be the greater threat to EFA in close combat, whereas Flanker would be the greater threat in Beyond Visual Range (BVR) combat.

Given the relatively small amount of air space in the Central Region, EFA needs good acceleration to get to the right point for BVR missile release, before the enemy aircraft penetrate too far. Once those missiles have been fired, EFA needs the speed and agility to turn in behind the enemy for a second pass using heat-seeking missiles and its gun. And, of course, the likelihood of large and numerous enemy raids, together with the fog of war, makes some close combat inevitable. EFA therefore needs to excel in both BVR and close combat. This, in turn, demands both supersonic and subsonic agility, as well as a radar and weapons fit at least comparable in performance to those of the enemy. And if EFA's radar is to detect Flanker before Flanker detects EFA, EFA must have the lower radar cross-section. Stealth technology is therefore vital. EFA must also be able to operate from bomb-damaged runways, and therefore needs to have a short take-off and landing (STOL) capability.

The European Experimental Aircraft Project (EAP) demonstrator aircraft, which first flew in 1986, has proved many of the technologies required for high agility in the year 2000 and beyond — in particular, the aerodynamics and the fly-by-wire systems. Whilst the design of the radar remains to be decided, the weapon systems — the Advanced Medium Range Air to Air Missile (AMRAAM) and the Advanced Short Range Air to Air Missile (ASRAAM) — will be the very systems the Americans too will use in this time-scale. Both will be 'launch and leave' missiles with an off-bore-sight capability. AMRAAM will permit salvo launch against multiple targets — so providing a jump in effectiveness that will compensate for the Soviet advantage in aircraft numbers to a considerable degree. Furthermore, EFA's radar and weapons system will allow it not only to take on Soviet fixed-wing aircraft, but helicopters, cruise missiles and remotely piloted vehicles too. We are also confident that EFA's radar cross-section can be reduced to a battle-winning degree; radar absorbent materials were, after all, a British invention. As to STOL, we believe the projected power-to-weight ratio, combined with advanced aerodynamics, will give EFA a take-off distance little worse than a Harrier GR3 with an air defence warload, and a landing run of no more than 500 metres. Whilst the advantages of VSTOL cannot be denied, such performance will reduce those relative advantages considerably. Overall, we think EFA is the ideal air defence aircraft for Europe in the year 2000 and beyond, and current indications are that it will be affordable.

None of this is to suggest that a defensive counter-air capability in the Central Region is enough. Missile belts would undoubtedly be breached, and some hostile aircraft would get through to their targets. Near the very confused and fluid Forward Edge of the Battle Area, NATO's defence against offensive air support aircraft might consist of no more than army short-range SAM systems. Rather than try to tangle with enemy aircraft in such a situation, what the NATO air forces could do much more readily is reduce the number of hostile aircraft that could operate — by attacking their airfields. NATO's offensive counter-air capability is therefore a vital complement to its air defence posture. Both are required for successful defence, as Air Vice Marshal Walker's paper in this volume makes clear. Furthermore, in the year 2000, offensive missions by the NATO air forces are also likely to demand fighter escort, which EFA would be well able to provide.

Air Defence of the United Kingdom

But the Soviet air threat would not be directed solely at targets on the Continent of Europe. In war, the United Kingdom would be of crucial importance to the NATO Alliance. We serve as a major base for maritime forces operating in the Eastern Atlantic and the Channel areas, and we would be a vital reinforcement base for Northern and Central Europe. Any Warsaw Pact attack on Western Europe would therefore almost certainly include a substantial air offensive against targets in this country. To attack these targets, the Soviets would undoubtedly use their air forces. And to achieve an adequate weight of effort with the current conventional weapons, the Soviets will, for the foreseeable future, continue to depend on their medium bombers, using free-fall bombs and air-to-surface missiles. We therefore face a threat which is in many ways very similar to that of 1940 — and we are all aware of that extraordinary moment in our history when our very survival depended on the men and aircraft of Fighter Command. It is indeed this continuing threat from a large Soviet manned bomber force

PLATE 7.2. The RAF's newest interceptor: two Tornado F3s of 29 Squadron RAF. *(Photo: John Upsall. Courtesy of the RAF Public Relations Department. Crown copyright.)*

that has prompted us in the United Kingdom into the largest air defence re-equipment programme since the early 1950s.

The heart of our future air defence system is the air defence variant of the Tornado, which is now taking over the role from most of our Phantoms. In war, we would expect to have some of these fighters on combat air patrol — directed by airborne early warning aircraft, and refuelled by air-to-air refuelling tanker aircraft. They would be the first to engage the enemy. But the warning we would get from our airborne early warning aircraft would also enable us to judge when best to commit our fighters held at high readiness on the ground — which is, of course, a much more economical way of operating. These would then be our second line of defence, intercepting — as they would — those hostile aircraft that penetrated the outer screen.

For the second layer, we would again use our radar equipped fighters (Tornados and Phantoms) in conjunction with some of our Hawk training aircraft. The latter have no radar, but carry missiles and are highly agile. Our mixed fighter force tactics — that is using a Tornado or a Phantom to shepherd a Hawk — have proved themselves in exercise after exercise. We have, in this way, boosted our air defences considerably at very small cost. For our third line of defence, we would use yet more Hawks to defend key targets, and we also have a number of surface-to-air missiles. Our relatively old — but still very effective — Bloodhounds are deployed in Lincolnshire and East Anglia to protect the high concentration of key airfields there. And some of these airfields, as well as others further afield, are also protected by Rapier — used with success in the Falklands War.

Our concept for the air defence of the United Kingdom is therefore a layered one. Not only would this provide many more firing opportunities, and so a higher attrition of enemy aircraft, but it would also allow us to destroy many of those Soviet bombers carrying long-range air-to-surface missiles before they could release them. And thirdly, such a concept lets us provide a robust air defence for the Fleet throughout much of its European operating area.

Our investment in the air defence of the United Kingdom is large — approaching 10 per cent of the total British defence equipment budget. One hundred and sixty-two Tornado air defence variants have been ordered to replace our current United Kingdom interceptor force, bar two Phantom Squadrons which will be run on into the 1990s. The first two squadrons of Tornados are now operational. Seven Boeing E-3 early warning aircraft will be bought, and new transportable ground-based radars are entering service for use around our coasts. We are now halfway through a programme to procure new air-to-air refuelling tankers. A new secure, jam-resistant, high-capacity data link system (the Joint Tactical Information Distribution System) will connect all these elements together. And work is advancing well on the new air-to-air missiles mentioned earlier — AMRAAM and ASRAAM. Overall, we believe we have, and will continue to have, a realistic and an effective defence against a sizeable (but by no means invincible) Soviet threat.

But the threat against the United Kingdom is changing in some respects, just as it is in the Central Region. Long-range conventionally-armed cruise missiles are likely to pose a more significant challenge over the next few decades, and the greater their stealth, the greater the problem. But such advances, and their counter-measures and counter-counter-measures, are the inevitable result of the onward march of technology. We see no reason why we should not be able to meet such challenges. For the moment, aircraft remain the key component in countering cruise missiles. The introduction of more agile Soviet aircraft — both bombers and fighters — also requires an effective response, particularly in the eastern and southern approaches to the United Kingdom.

We believe that EFA can provide that response. On current plans, EFA will replace those United Kingdom-based Phantoms run-on into

PLATE 7.3. The Hawk T1A will provide useful support to the Tornado in the air defence of the United Kingdom. *(Photo: courtesy of British Aerospace and Air Clues Magazine.)*

the 1990s. We see EFA as complementing our air defence Tornados. Tornado would engage the bombers, whereas EFA would take on the fighter escorts — in very much the same way that the Luftwaffe used their Me110s and Me109s in World War Two. EFA's acceleration, agility, and stealth will make it a vital component of our United Kingdom air defences into the next century.

It is also worth noting that EFA will be designed with an excellent ground attack capability too; this will enable one aircraft type to take over the role, not merely of our air defence Phantoms, but also of our remaining Jaguars in their air-to-ground role. We believe that technology will permit such multi-role operation, with all its attendant cost-saving advantages; indeed, we watch with interest the very successful multi-role concept the Canadians have introduced with the F-18s in Europe today. Furthermore, thanks to EFA's combined air defence and air-to-ground capability, we will have much enhanced flexibility for projecting tactical air power out of area at the turn of the century.

But although the way ahead for air defence is very clear in most respects, one or two difficulties remain. The development by the Soviets of an improved tactical ballistic missile is one such difficulty. Until now their relative inaccuracy has restricted their role to nuclear warhead delivery, but technological advances have boosted accuracies to such a degree that use with conventional warheads would now be worthwhile against some types of target. Currently the United Kingdom faces a lower threat from conventionally armed tactical ballistic missiles than the Central Region, which is vulnerable to shorter range weapons that cannot reach us. The only effective counters today — as in 1944/45 against the V2s — are offensive action against their launch sites, or passive measures, such as redundancy and hardening, although that may possibly change if the American SDI programme proceeds successfully. In any event, it is, of course, possible that the longer-range tactical ballistic missile threat to Europe may soon be removed, if the Super Power proposals on INF go ahead.

One of the other major problems today is that of Identification Friend or Foe. Neither side has a foolproof system, and some fratricide is inevitable. However, the NATO Identification System project is now well established, and we can hope to see some practical results by the mid-1990s.

Summary

Overall, despite some obvious difficulties, we in the Royal Air Force believe our future plans for procurement and research are well structured to provide the air defence expected of us. EFA will provide exactly what NATO needs in the Central Region, and the combination of Tornado and EFA will provide a formidable barrier to any Soviet attempt to wage war against this country. By deploying such systems, we can but hope that they will never be tempted to try.

THE THEATRE NUCLEAR ROLE
Dr John Roper

If we are to examine what might be the future theatre nuclear role for the Royal Air Force, we need first to examine the strategic context in which such a role might be played. That will require a consideration of the case for and the role of theatre nuclear forces, the case for British theatre nuclear forces and finally the case for air-launched British theatre nuclear weapons.

Before doing this it is perhaps worth noting that in the public controversy over theatre nuclear weapons in the last decade, air-launched systems have been very largely ignored. The doubling of the number of American F-111 aircraft in the United Kingdom in the late 1970s, the replacement of Jaguars and Buccaneers by Tornados, and the introduction of F-16s by the United States and some NATO countries in the 1980s, certainly represented a more significant increase in the quantity of NATO's theatre nuclear forces than the widely publicised introduction of GLCMs and Pershing IIs.

It is difficult to get accurate figures for the numbers of warheads available for theatre nuclear operations but a recent authoritative American study has suggested that there were 1,740 American nuclear bombs available for NATO use in 1985, the bulk for use by the United States itself but over 300 held by them for use by Belgium, Greece, Italy, the Netherlands, Turkey and West Germany.[1] In addition there were some 600 bombs available in the United Kingdom for the American F-111 aircraft based here and 360 on aircraft carriers operating in European waters. These 2,700 bombs represented about a third of the 8,000 American nuclear weapons available for NATO use in 1985. The same study estimated that the modernisation programmes underway for American nuclear forces would lead to a reduction in the total number of United States weapons available to NATO by 1992 to 6,500 but that within that total the number of nuclear bombs for aircraft would have increased to 3,200, therefore representing almost half of the inventory and more than five times as many as the number of warheads on all the GLCMs and Pershing IIs. In terms of the total deliverable megatonnage, the preponderance of air-launched systems is even greater, although the greater accuracy of the land-based systems will offset this to some extent.

The size of the inventory of British and French nuclear bombs is not publicly known but some estimates have suggested about 300 for Britain and rather fewer for France. Together they may represent some 15–20 per cent of the total of United States weapons deployed to Europe but rather more than the total number of bombs held by the United States for the six European NATO countries who operate nuclear weapons on a 'dual-key' basis.

Air-launched systems are unlikely to maintain their anonymity in the future. If an agreement is reached to remove the LRINF and SRINF missiles from Europe, the importance of aircraft as the only remaining intermediate nuclear forces will become much greater. This is likely to lead to political debate with pressure on the one hand to increase their effectiveness to compensate for the removal of land based systems matched by pressures to secure their removal as part of the 'denuclearisation' of Europe.

As with nuclear weapons in general there have been varying rationales for theatre nuclear weapons. The 1957 Defence White Paper announced that 'the fact that some of the squadrons (of the Second Tactical Air Force) will be provided with atomic bombs' was an offset to the decision to halve our air force in Germany.[2] As with the equipping of our land forces with 'atomic rocket artillery' it was thought that theatre nuclear weapons were an economical way of balancing Soviet conventional strength. More generally, such weapons were seen as instruments for war-fighting. As Walter Slocombe has recently written, 'In the heady early days of tactical nuclear weapons, it was argued that their use would produce victory in the field by destroying the very armoured forces whose overwhelming power made the use of nuclear weapons necessary. For many years, however it has been generally accepted that NATO use of nuclear weapons is very unlikely to produce a militarily decisive advantage.'[3]

The next stage in the development of the rationale for theatre nuclear weapons was as a component of the deterrent doctrine of flexible response in the 1960s. With Soviet nuclear capabilities beginning to threaten the United States, it was felt that strategic nuclear forces only served to deter the other side's strategic nuclear forces. The use of such forces was no longer considered credible in the case of war in Europe and thus the deterrence of such a war required theatre nuclear weapons in order to be able 'to respond appropriately to any level of potential attack and . . . pose the risk of escalation to higher levels of conflict.'[4]

Flexible response does 'not rule out the use of nuclear weapons....if that should prove necessary to contain or repel a major conventional attack by the Warsaw Pact.'[5]

There is a continuing controversy about the operational effectiveness of the doctrine of flexible response in a situation where the Warsaw Pact has substantial nuclear forces and the possibility of NATO obtaining 'escalation dominance' is reduced. There are those who argue that this reduces the importance of nuclear weapons and that NATO should devote greater resources to raising the nuclear threshold by improving the effectiveness of conventional forces. While demographic trends and pressures on financial resources make such proposals to lower the emphasis on the nuclear component of theatre force planning extremely unlikely at an Alliance level, it remains to be seen how much weight should be given to it in British decisions on modernising our own air-launched systems.

In spite of Mr Gorbachev's repeated call for a 'nuclear-free' Europe, and the proposals from responsible figures in the United States for NATO to move to a 'no first-use' posture,[6] it seems fairly unlikely that NATO will wish to move away from a position in which there is a significant role for theatre nuclear weapons in deterrence.

In these circumstances one must consider the case for British theatre nuclear weapons, by which I mean nuclear weapons where the warhead has been designed and built in the United Kingdom — like the present 'free-fall' bombs — and therefore under the ultimate political control of the Prime Minister, rather than those like depth-bombs for Nimrods and the Lance missiles and artillery weapons in Germany which, while operated by the British forces, have American warheads and therefore ultimately come under the control of the President of the United States.

The fact that we now deploy British nuclear bombs with the Tornado squadrons is to some extent an accident of history. These weapons, reputed to be based on a 1966 design, were originally built for the V-bomber force which, although assigned to NATO, had been seen as a contribution to Britain's strategic deterrent rather than as a theatre nuclear force. The Tornado aircraft are descendants both of the Canberras which fulfilled the strike role in Germany in the 1960s and the V-bomber force, whose weapons they have inherited. Thus weapons which were strategic when they were carried in the V-bomber force become theatre when they are carried in a Tornado aircraft.

Ten years ago at a conference on the future of airpower held at the University of Southampton[7], David Greenwood argued against the continuation of the deep strike/interdiction role for the Royal Air Force into the next generation of aircraft.[8] His arguments included those of the dubious cost-effectiveness of interdiction in an increasingly hostile air defence environment, the reluctance of politicans to authorise deep attack at the critical early stage of a war, the relative ease of defensive counter-air when compared with offensive counter-air and the availability of alternative weapons delivery modes in cruise missiles, RPVs and more accurate surface-to-surface ballistic missiles. Some of these arguments look less impressive now than they did then but Air Vice Marshal (as he then was) J. A. Gilbert in questioning the Greenwood proposals argued that such a decision would mean that 'we would be seen, as a nation, leaving the most demanding role for air power to the United States Air Force. Could we really do this without attracting severe political disadvantages within the Alliance?'[9]

Later, in returning to the question of aircraft roles, he referred to 'British tactical nuclear weapons — a vital element in NATO's strategy of deterrence'. Speaking in his personal capacity he went on, 'we have no separate doctrine for the employment of these weapons, which are intended for use according to Alliance plans'.[10] If this is so and there is a distinction between these theatre weapons and the strategic nuclear weapons which Britain does reserve the right to use independently in situations where supreme national interest is at stake, then the case for developing our own warheads for theatre nuclear weapons is perhaps weakened and we could consider operating on the same basis as the six non-nuclear members of NATO by arming our aircraft with American nuclear weapons.

The argument against this is perhaps developed implicitly in the Open Government Document of 1980 which argues the case for the additional deterrence afforded to the Western Alliance as a result of 'second centres of decision' created by the existence of French, and particularly British, nuclear weapons.[11] What that document describes as the 'lower-level components' of our nuclear forces are seen as contributing to deterrence, but only because they are part of a set of forces including effective strategic forces which provide 'an independent capability fully under European control'.

It can be argued that British strategic nuclear forces if they existed in the absence of British controlled theatre nuclear forces could be seen as having a primary role of deterring nuclear attacks against the United Kingdom. The existence of British theatre nuclear weapons deployed into Germany and integrated in SACEUR's nuclear planning can be seen both by European allies and adversaries as a clear European contribution to NATO's deterrent posture. In some ways they increase the integration of British nuclear forces into Western European defence. This would not be the case if those theatre nuclear forces, while operated by the British, were under the ultimate control of the United States.

Following the Reykjavik summit there is considerable concern in some circles in Germany about the possible reduction in the United States nuclear commitment to Western Europe. So far, as Lawrence Freedman has shown, there has been much more interest in West Germany about a possible French nuclear guarantee than about the existing British commitment of its nuclear forces to NATO.[12] There is inevitable political diffidence in Britain about the discussion of such nuclear issues; 'out of sight, out of mind' seems very often to be the principal maxim in this area. Britain, however, through the provision of theatre nuclear weapons for NATO seems to be incurring both a major financial obligation and a major military risk. There is no doubt that, because of our inhibition about discussing it more explicitly, we are failing to get the political credit for it in wider European discussions. If we are now to contemplate significant further expenditure to modernise such forces, we need to consider whether we should continue to be so reticent.

The case for British theatre nuclear weapons in the form of free-fall bombs inherited from earlier strategic programmes has been easy to make, as they have been at relatively low cost. The problems now arise when twenty year-old bombs become technically unreliable and militarily obsolescent. While, at least in theory, nuclear weapons can be repeatedly reworked, and so their technical reliability maintained, it is still the case that these would be 'dumb weapons in smart aircraft' and that the case for a stand-off capability is substantial. We will thus need to face in the near future the difficult political and resource questions of how, if at all, Britain should maintain a theatre nuclear capability.

Before considering the various nuclear alternatives, it will be necessary to determine whether nuclear warheads are still required to undertake the military tasks which they have carried out until now. The improvement of non-nuclear warhead technology might enable many of the roles previously assigned to nuclear weapons to be undertaken by conventional warheads by the time any new system came into operation. However, the political importance of nuclear weapons for purposes of deterrence may necessitate a nuclear solution, even if the technical arguments become more evenly matched in the future.

Until the recent progress in the INF negotiations, the case would not necessarily have been overwhelming for a replacement of the free-fall bombs by another weapon to be launched from a manned aircraft.

Now, however, ground-based systems are likely to be restricted, if not prohibited, by an arms control agreement. There will no doubt be some discussion about submarine-launched cruise missiles as theatre systems. They will face the usual problems of command and control and either of conflicting roles if dual capability is suggested, or of platform cost if a dedicated system is desired. Either way, they do not seem likely to be cost-effective nor to provide militarily or politically desirable solutions.

It therefore seems probable that any future British theatre nuclear weapon will be airborne. Most commentators have suggested that any replacement should not be a free-fall bomb but should have a stand-off capability.[13] In the hostile air defence environment likely to be encountered, such a capability will be essential. What cannot be asserted by someone with access only to the open literature is the range that such a stand-off weapon should have. It has been suggested that the 100 kilometre range of the existing French ASMP weapon is too short and 300 kilometres is frequently cited as a desirable range. There would therefore be two procurement programmes, one to build the stand-off missile and one to build the nuclear warhead. The first could be either a British programme, a collaborative programme, or, following the precedent of Polaris and Trident, the purchase of an American (or French) missile. The second — the warhead programme — for the reasons we have seen earlier, would have to be a British programme.

Before examining the options for such programmes, there are certain wider implications of a decision to go ahead with such a development that must be considered. Nuclear weapons have become increasingly controversial in domestic politics in the past decade. While the present government's majority in Parliament is such that an early decision would present no problems there, its implementation would have barely started by the time of the next election and it might therefore be something of a hostage to subsequent political developments. This might be increasingly likely if the costs of such a programme were seen to have a further adverse effect on other items of the defence budget. There seems a general tendency for an adverse public reaction to any new nuclear weapons development. Public opinion is both anxious to maintain existing nuclear defence capability and reluctant to have it enhanced.

It seems unlikely at present that nuclear arms control in Europe would have reached a point that would restrict air-launched systems by the time these weapons would be developed and there is no evidence that any other nuclear weapons state is at present inhibited in its weapons development. There is, however, another aspect of arms control which could be relevant. Mr Gorbachev has talked about the need to consider reducing asymmetries in the force postures of NATO and the Warsaw Pact. While we complain incessantly about the Warsaw Pact's preponderance in tanks, they complain about our advantages in offensive air power. It seems difficult to see how one would work out a trade-off of tanks against offensive air, but if one were to be negotiated it could affect aircraft with nuclear strike and interdiction roles.

Depending on the pattern of collaboration decided upon for the development of the missile, such a programme might be able to be cited as a strengthening of the European pillar of the Alliance. The fact that we were modernising a section of our nuclear forces which contributes directly to European defence could also have political dividends in West European relations in some circumstances. If there is a continuing perception of diminished United States commitment to European defence, our decision could be seen as a way of sustaining European deterrence. On the other hand, some will argue that undue publicity could lead to negative reactions in West Germany, with the risk of demonstrations outside RAF bases.

It is very difficult, without knowing more about the costs of the various options, to give any assessment of the impact of such programmes on the rest of the defence budget. For reasons to do with physical constraints on the nuclear weapons establishments, examined in more detail below, it seems unlikely that the major spending on such a programme could occur until after the end of the major expenditure on Trident. It would, however, overlap with the EFA programme. Like all nuclear programmes there will be significant political as well as military arguments involved in the decision. It clearly has important intra-Alliance political implications. The analysis of these will be very difficult, as they cannot be quantified in the financial framework used elsewhere for determining priorities.

Turning to the various options for a stand-off missile, it seems unlikely that Britain would develop a new missile for this purpose on her own, but it has been suggested that the long-range British Aerospace sea-skimming anti-ship missile 'Sea Eagle' could be developed for this purpose. There is, of course, no reason why a stand-off missile should be developed to carry nuclear warheads exclusively; the German— United Kingdom—United States project to develop a Long-Range Stand-Off Missile (listed in the current Statement on the Defence Estimates) could presumably be developed for a nuclear role.[14]

Alternatively there is considerable evidence of French interest in joint

Anglo-French development of a successor to their ASMP missile. It seems that cooperation on such a project would be less likely to run up against American opposition as a potential infringement of the 1958 United States/United Kingdom Nuclear Co-operation Agreement than cooperation in some other areas. There are clear political advantages in strengthening cooperation between Western Europe's two nuclear powers and this would appear to be one of the few ways available to do this. Such Anglo-French cooperation might even be extended to include West Germany, which could then use such missiles either with conventional warheads or, possibly, with British or French nuclear warheads held in time of peace by British or French custodial units on a basis parallel to that operated by the United States. This latter option could be seen as a significant step forward in European nuclear co-operation.

The final option would be to purchase an American missile. There are a number under development which might be available. It is not clear whether these would include the next generation of cruise missile incorporating 'stealth' technology. This obviously has many military advantages but would not have the political advantages of European collaboration. It is, of course, not clear whether the American Government would permit the transfer of such technology.

Irrespective of the missile selected, the warheads would have to be developed independently at Aldermaston. The possibility of Franco-British cooperation on warhead development raises significant problems both in terms of the Non-Proliferation Treaty and the United States/United Kingdom agreements. There are reported to be delays in the Trident warhead development programme and this may prove the most serious constraint on any decision to develop a new air-launched weapon. *The Economist* claimed that the production of Trident warheads will not start until 1991 and that production will then take some four years.[15] This could imply that production of warheads for an air-launched system could not begin until the mid-nineties which would mean that such a system would not be in service until two or three years after that.

Decisions on nuclear weapons are inevitably among the most political of all defence decisions. This one will be no exception. Although theatre nuclear weapons do not have all the political symbolism of strategic systems, in a period during which there may be significant changes in West-West as well as East-West relations as well as growing competition for resources from an inadequate defence budget, the decision will be difficult to make, and once made, by no means guaranteed against subsequent reconsideration.

NOTES

1. Catherine M. Kelleher, 'NATO Nuclear Operations', in Ashton Carter *et al*, *Managing Nuclear Operations*, The Brookings Institution (Washington D.C.) 1987 pp. 448-451.
2. *Defence: Outline of Future Policy* Cmnd 124, HMSO (London) 1957 para 23.
3. Walter Slocombe, 'Preplanned Operations', in Ashton Carter *et al*, op. cit. endnote 1, p. 125.
4. United States Department of Defense Annual Report, Fiscal Year 1982, p. 64.
5. Secretary of State Schlesinger, United States Department of Defense Annual Report, Fiscal Year 1976, pp. 111-2.
6. McGeorge Bundy *et al.*, 'Nuclear Weapons and the Atlantic Alliance', *Foreign Affairs* Volume 60 Number 4 (Spring 1982) pp. 753-768.
7. E. J. Feuchtwanger and R. A. Mason, *Air Power in the Next Generation*, Macmillan (London) 1979.
8. op. cit. endnote 7, pp. 25-28.
9. op. cit. endnote 7, pp. 140-2.
10. op. cit. endnote 7, p. 141.
11. *The Future United Kingdom Strategic Nuclear Deterrent Force*, Defence Open Government Document 80/23, Ministry of Defence (London) 1980, paras 5-7.
12. Lawrence Freedman, 'Britain's Nuclear Commitment to Germany' in Karl Kaiser and John Roper (eds) *British-German Defence Cooperation: Partners within the Alliance*, (forthcoming).
13. *The Economist*, April 4th 1987, pp. 21-4.
14. *Statement on the Defence Estimates 1987*, Cm 101-I, HMSO (London) 1987, p. 47.
15. op. cit. endnote 13, p. 21.

CHAPTER 8

Air Transport and Maritime Air Power

AIR TRANSPORT AND OUT OF AREA OPERATIONS
Dr Philip Towle

Fixed Wing Aircraft

The Tornado purchase should reduce the number of types of aircraft in frontline service in the Royal Air Force and lessen the maintenance problems involved in keeping them in the air. The time is surely ripe to examine our needs for larger aircraft and to see whether a similar rationalisation cannot be carried out in that area. This first of all involves assessing our requirements for the coming decades.

Requirements

The need to defend the past pieces of the Empire will, of course, be reduced in the future, thereby removing one reason for maintaining a long-range transport fleet. Hong Kong will become part of China in the 1990s and tension with Guatemala over Belize seems to be declining since Central Americans have graver worries than century-old frontier disputes. The Falkland Islands will remain a problem, pending some sort of compromise with Argentina. It is not inconceivable that such a settlement could be negotiated, though even so Britain might still have to demonstrate its ability to protect the islanders. Moreover, even if such remains of Empire are less demanding, there will still be strong reasons for wanting to project force over long distances.

As far as economics go, 51.7 per cent of our imports came from the EEC in 1986 and 48 per cent of our exports went there, almost twice as much as 20 years ago.[1] Nevertheless, we still have very important world-wide trading interests and so do our European partners. The degree of EEC dependence upon the Middle East in general (and on Saudi Arabia in particular) for oil, will increase in the mid-1990s. Our

193

investments are also world-wide and, as they earn more than five billion pounds a year, they play a vital part in bridging the gap between our imports and exports. Finally, given modern communications and the threat of local war spreading to the Superpowers, instability anywhere may affect us all. Plainly Britain's contribution to maintaining stability outside Europe must be in accordance with its resources but such a contribution can sometimes have an importance out of proportion to its size, as it did, for example, in the Dhofar War.

Forecasts about the likely degree of stability or instability in the Third World over the next decades are sharply divided. The optimists say that the immediate post-independence traumas are now past, that none of the new countries has been torn apart by its neighbours, and that few have joined the communist bloc. Some of the countries which were expected to starve in the 1960s have now managed to feed themselves and even, in the case of India, begun to export small quantities of food. Singapore, Hong Kong, Korea and Taiwan have also proved that states can move from the Third World to the First. Pessimists would stress the continued growth of the Third World population, which would bring world population to 10.2 billions, or two and a half times present levels, by the end of the next century. Population growth has led to the emergence of mega-cities, such as Mexico City with 18 million people, or São Paulo, which may have 24 million by the end of the century.[2] Years of war have drained Iran and Iraq and wreaked havoc in Chad, Ethiopia and Kampuchea.

Both the optimists and the pessimists are partly right. Some states in the Third World will continue to advance and become middle rank powers, others will continue to decay, but such deterioration will affect us all. The hijacking of aircraft to the Lebanon shows that we are all threatened when one state collapses into chaos. Both the mega-cities and the refugee camps, now housing a population as large as Australia's, are fertile breeding grounds for extremist groups. International terrorism is with us for the indefinite future and all Western states will have to protect their citizens from it and do what they can to preserve stability outside Europe.

Fortunately some of the equipment which we need to carry out our primary role on the Central Front and on the Northern and Southern flanks of Europe coincides with what we need for our secondary tasks elsewhere. After the Falklands War there was a period when the secondary role received a great deal of emphasis, hence the 1984 reforms in Fifth Brigade which now consists of four infantry battalions, a regiment of Royal Horse Artillery with 105 mm guns, the Life Guards

PLATE 8.1. Tristars such as this will fulfil tanking and transport roles for the RAF well into the 21st century. *(Crown copyright: courtesy of Air Clues Magazine.)*

with Scorpion and Fox, an Engineer Regiment and a squadron of helicopters. More recently there has been a tendency to put less weight on 'out of area' operations. They will probably always be of secondary importance but they are also more pressing: our next military operation will almost certainly 'be out of area'.

Current Equipment

What does all this mean for air transport given the continued and possibly increasing pressure on the defence budget? The purchase of nine Tristars after the Falklands War will greatly ease our strategic tanker and transport problems for the next 20 years. Three aircraft are being converted to carry 360,000 lbs of fuel and 204 passengers, whilst others will be converted to carry cargo and 300,000 lbs of fuel. What the Tristars obviously cannot do is to move the equipment and vehicles which a major military operation would involve, nor can they land on short, unprepared runways. Nevertheless, when the Tristars become obsolete, we may be advised, once again, to try to buy long-range civilian aircraft cheaply. If we can procure aircraft which have flown some 12,000 to 14,000 hours and which have an expected life of 120,000 hours then the attraction is obvious.

Leaving the Tristars to one side, currently we have about 60 Hercules transports and tankers, over 30 Nimrod maritime patrol aircraft, 13

VC-10 transports, four or five VC 10 tankers and over 15 Victor tankers.[3] We also expect to get six Boeing 707 AEW aircraft. If we could carry out some or all of the roles currently performed by these aircraft with the same airframe, servicing and other problems would be vastly reduced. Greater commonality and inter-operability with the fleets of our European allies would also be immensely helpful. This might make it possible to train aircrews jointly, as in the Tornado programme, while the longer production run which an international aircraft would produce should reduce the costs of the aircraft and of spares.

But the difficulties are obvious; the AEW is not yet in service with the RAF and it would clearly be premature even to consider its replacement. By the time it becomes obsolete, the whole technology may have moved into satellites or elsewhere. There are also difficulties in using the same airframe for the maritime patrol and transport types since maritime patrol aircraft need bomb-bays which have had to be loaded from underneath. In the past this requirement has been difficult to reconcile with the transport aircraft's need for a high wing and an aircraft floor as near to the ground as possible. British Aerospace believes that the problem can be overcome by putting the maritime patrol aircraft's weapons bay in place of the ramp and rear doors of the transport versions of the aircraft and that this will not cause centre of gravity or aerodynamic problems. If this solution is rejected, we will eventually have to join with others in replacing Nimrod, PC-3 Orion and Atlantic aircraft with a dedicated maritime patrol aircraft, though this would still substantially reduce the benefits of commonality referred to above.

This leaves the transport and tanking aircraft. The VC-10 tankers could be replaced by a tanker version of a future transport aircraft which would be cheaper than the VC-10 to operate and maintain. Such an aircraft could also operate from a greater variety of airstrips than the VC-10. This would provide it with more protection in the event of war and increase its versatility. The long-range transport of personnel is catered for by the Tristars, though their need for long runways will make them unsuitable for some operations. For the short range VIP transport we have the two BAC 146s. Some would also argue that when the VC-10 transports go out of service, and that will be well into the next century, we should not think of replacing all of them. Instead we should charter civilian aircraft when they are needed, and not maintain dedicated aircraft ourselves. It is here, if anywhere, that our large aircraft fleet may shrink. Much will depend upon economics and to some extent upon how terrorists operate. Hand-held anti-aircraft weapons, such as SAM-7, Blowpipe and Stinger, will gradually spread amongst terrorist groups. If we have a spate of attacks on airliners with such weapons, we may need dedicated transport aircraft with sufficient passive and active defensive measures to transport political and military leaders in safety.

Beyond this, the question is largely one of finding a replacement for the Hercules. The C-130 dates from 1954 and Lockheed had built some 1,800 by 1986. Hercules made possible many American operations in the Vietnam War, often flying directly into the battlefield so that the forces they carried could be used immediately, and having a major impact on the fighting in the AC-130 role.[4] Currently they are immensely useful both for operations in Europe and out of area. They can land on dirt strips, carry troops and light armoured vehicles and drop parachutists. Although no one would describe them as either fast or luxurious, their first main handicap stems from their obsolete cockpits and the absence of modern navigational aids giving all-weather day and night capabilities (even though some now have station-keeping equipment on board) and of any protective equipment. Surprise is obviously vital in many of the roles which the Hercules may have to carry out and surprise may depend upon operating at night or in poor weather. The second problem with the Hercules is size; the standard version has 4,000 cubic feet of cargo space and the stretched version has some 5,500, but an aircraft with still more space is highly desirable. In particular, the difficulty of transporting the latest types of Landrover and the 3/4 ton wide-track trailers is very serious, while the time it takes to change the aircraft from one type of load to another is considerable. Finally there is an outside possibility, as the airframes age, that we shall need to rebuild them in some major way in the mid-1990s when we would have preferred to spend the money five years later on new aircraft.

Everything we know about modern war suggests that the rate at which ammunition is used has increased. Nevertheless, logistics are sometimes ignored in arguments about NATO strategy in Europe or operations outside. Yet the value of being able to move equipment as near to the battlefront as possible was demonstrated over and over again in Vietnam. Only a specialised military transport can carry the equipment and land in the difficult circumstances required. Moreover, military transport aircraft would become even more important in a European war if normal NATO supply lines were disrupted, as they are very likely to be, by chemical, conventional or nuclear attack.

Future Prospects

Ministries of Defence and aircraft industries here and elsewhere are giving a good deal of attention to future large military aircraft (FLA). What any FLA must have is superior navigation equipment to the C-130, to enable it to operate in all conditions. It must also be equipped to know when it is under threat. Beyond these demands are the problems of size and range. The situation is complicated in the United States by the decision, after many years of hesitation, to order over 200 C-17s. McDonnell Douglas has sold the C-17 both as an inter-theatre and an intra-theatre aircraft. It is an impressive transport, able to take off with reduced loads from 3,000 feet runways and to carry some loads as effectively as the C-5.[5] But as each aircraft costs over 90 million dollars and maintenance costs are likely to be commensurate, it is difficult to see other nations having the funds to buy C-17s.

Thus several American companies are interested in making smaller, cheaper aircraft. Boeing has the YC-14 and McDonnell Douglas has plans for developing the AIMSA from the earlier YC-15 experimental assault transport. The AIMSA would have externally blown flaps to help landing and take-off on small airfields. Its smaller version would have a payload of 65,000 lbs for very dense cargoes and it would have a substantially better performance than the Hercules. Two YC-15 prototypes have already flown but the United States Air force has shown little interest in them.[6] Lockheed has developed its own 'high technology testbed' based on the C-130. This uses very advanced equipment to enable it to take off and land within 1,500 feet. However, the HTTB is not a prototype and Lockheed has been working for the last four years with British Aerospace, Aerospatiale and MBB on a Future International Military/Civil Airlifter (FIMA). In normal circumstances one would have expected the United States to satisfy its transport requirements by buying C-17s and a smaller, advanced STOL aircraft to replace the Hercules but the American defence budget is likely to be under ever-increasing pressure and so FIMA could well satisfy many of its requirements.

The German, French, British and American companies have co-operated to meet their national requirements. Despite their gradually extending horizons, the Germans currently foresee little need to procure aircraft for operations outside the NATO theatre, although they do see a requirement to move troops to the flanks. The French are committed to operations in Africa and we have the commitments which I referred to above. The British and Americans have generally wanted larger and longer-range aircraft than the continentals. The companies involved have also been keen to produce an aircraft with sales potential and see the largest market outside Europe and the United States at around 44,000 lb payload. Nevertheless the Future International Military/Civil Airlifter programme (FIMA) has progressed as compromises have been reached. Currently, the four companies propose that FIMA should use tried technology wherever possible to avoid risks and should take up to 55,000 lbs in payload for the most common types of cargo or 65,000 lbs of high density cargo over a shorter range. FIMA could be ferried over 5000 nautical miles but would have an unrefuelled range for operations of about 2,000 miles. Former Hercules passengers may also be pleased to note that FIMA should be 100 knots faster and more comfortable.

Meanwhile the Independent European Programme Group has been working on an Outline European Staff Target for a joint programme to replace transport aircraft. Spain, Italy, Portugal, Belgium, Denmark, Germany, France and the United Kingdom have all seen the need for (FLA) successors to the Hercules and Transall. Since they may all want new aircraft around the year 2000, the moment is ripe for this sort of co-operation and the European Defence ministers meetings in 1984 and 1985 suggested that it should continue. The danger is that all will consider the issue so remote that little movement is made at this stage. Given lead times for design, development and production, the Europeans will have to work together now in order to commit themselves to the project in 1992 and to obtain the aircraft within the required period. We have talked for a long time about how much more effectively NATO could spend its resources if we co-operated and this is an excellent opportunity to get both the European and American nations involved. But it would be only too easy for the Europeans to let the opportunity slip and for the Americans, with their greater needs — perhaps 600 aircraft as against 400 for the Europeans, to go their own way, taking some of the Europeans with them, as they did over the F-16, rather than achieving a genuinely co-operative effort. Our publics will become less forgiving over failures to co-operate as the years pass, and compromises with requirements are essential now if agreement is to be reached.

Operations

What would we expect to do with the new aircraft? Tankers are needed both to increase the range of transport, AEW and maritime patrol aircraft and to ferry fighters in peacetime to North America for training and to the Middle East and elsewhere on exercises of the 'Swift Sword' pattern. In that exercise six Tornados were flown directly from the United Kingdom to the Middle East with tanker assistance and were in operation within 35 minutes of arriving in the area. Similarly, whatever the political advantages and disadvantages of the United States action against Tripoli, it clearly demonstrated how force could be projected in long-range strikes.

Tankers are also vital to keep Tornado ADVs on station over the North Sea and to extend the range of United Kingdom based Tornados operating on the Central Front. There is also a possibility that we might want to arm some of our large aircraft with missiles for anti-ship, anti-air or anti-land target roles or to use these to lay defensive mines. In particular, a large aircraft might take over some of the maritime strike roles of the 60 or so Buccaneers.

As far as transports are concerned, they would:

Rush troops, vehicles, stores and ammunition from Britain to the Central Front or to the European flanks should they be needed. These forces and the Royal Air Force squadrons deployed forward would need to be kept supplied with vital stores, possibly in the face of enemy air activity.

Allow us to carry say 1,500 men and associated equipment quickly to some part of Asia of Africa where a friendly country has asked for our assistance and where airfields may be small or in poor repair.

Enable us to seize an airfield either by a parachute assault or by an air-land assault, though these are clearly far more difficult operations.

Carry small parties of highly trained special forces to rescue British citizens seized by terrorists in operations similar to those carried out by the Israelis at Entebbe or the Germans at Mogadishu.

Take emergency relief equipment and supplies to disaster zones, as Royal Air Force aircraft did after the San Salvador earthquake or in support of famine relief in Ethiopia.

Enable us to participate quickly and effectively in international peace keeping operations wherever a British contingent might be needed.

Some might argue that several of these roles could be carried out by civilian aircraft. Certainly we should never forget the ability of civilian airlines to assist the military in some circumstances. This capability is likely to grow rather than diminish as the years go by. Even if we accept that there will be another oil crisis in the mid 1990s, as various fields begin to dry up, the growth in the number of people travelling by air is likely to pause only momentarily, as it did in the 1970s. According to the IISS, in 1985–6[7] the United States already had 133 Boeing 747s used for passenger services and 31 used for cargo, 152 DC-10s, and 103 Tristars, not to speak of smaller aircraft. Similarly the Europeans had 99 Airbuses, 91 Boeing 747 passenger aircraft, 62 DC-10 and 46 Tristars, together with a great number of shorter-range aircraft. These are potential assets of immense significance.

In a full-scale war in Europe, no doubt these aircraft and some of those of our European allies could be taken over and used for ferrying troops, though they would be dependent on civilian pilots and maintenance staff. The advantage of dedicated, specialised aircraft, even in those circumstances, is that they can fly into smaller airfields, carry military vehicles and generally be more readily available and versatile than civilian planes. Much the same holds good for secondary operations in Africa or Asia, with the added problem that civilian aircraft would have to be chartered and it would be uncertain whether they would be available. As far as carrying specialist anti-terrorist troops is concerned, some would point out the *advantages* in taking troops by civilian airline, since the arrival of such a civilian aircraft on an airfield where a hijacked airliner was located would be less conspicuous than the arrival of a Royal Air Force transport. On the other hand, speed is of the essence on these occasions and the ready availability of military aircraft, their communication systems, their ability to take any necessary appliances and, in the future, their ability to operate in all conditions, give them advantages which it may be useful to have in other circumstances. Because of the likely frequency of operations of this type and the great importance placed upon them by the public in general, it is desirable to have a number of options available.

Helicopters

Recent Campaigns

The importance of transport helicopters has been underlined in *every* recent campaign in which we have been involved. The historians of the Malayan insurgency, of Confrontation and of the Aden operations are unanimous on this point. As two of them put it, 'the helicopter was the real battle-winner of Confrontation; without it, it would have been impossible for the security forces to control such a vast area against the guerrillas.'[8] Similarly, after the Radfan operations, one commented, 'the helicopters were the key to the mobility and speed of the campaign.

They could reduce the time it took a picquet to get into position on a mountain top from three hours to three minutes. Tactical mobility depended directly on the numbers of helicopters available.'[9] None of us need reminding of the effect which the loss of all but one of the Chinooks in Atlantic Conveyor had on the Falklands campaign in 1982 or indeed of the vital importance of the rotary wing and transport aircraft in making Operation Corporate possible.

These experiences suggest that, whatever else happens in our next campaign in Europe or elsewhere, there will be a shortage of helicopters to move troops around, together with their arms and supplies, as commanders would wish. They also suggest that helicopters should be able to operate as much as possible away from their main bases which in any case, in a European conflict, would be desperately vulnerable to attack by chemical and other weapons. Despite our knowledge of the requirements of war, we seem to have put less emphasis on helicopters in Britain than the Russians, the Americans or even some of the continental nations such as Germany or France. After all, the IISS attributes 65 SA-316, 130 Puma, 162 SA-341 and 128 Gazelles to the French Army alone. [10] On the other hand, the British Army has 155 Gazelle and 110 Lynx helicopters and the Royal Air Force has some 56 Wessex, 31 Puma and 30 Chinook for transport purposes. In the past, the Royal Air Force tended to feel that helicopters were too vulnerable on the battlefield and contributed little to the command of the air. Rebutting army demands for large helicopters, a member of the Air Ministry commented on 5 April 1951, 'I do not feel that we should fritter our resources away on this sort of aircraft which cannot make useful contributions to the outcome of the air battle.'[11] This attitude may help to explain some of the inter-service friction over the use of the Belvedere helicopter during the Radfan operations[12] and between the United States Air Force and Army over helicopter operations in Vietnam[13]. On the Army's side there has perhaps been too much reluctance to spell out exactly the tasks for which they wanted helicopters. As a result of all these factors, we have procured too few aircraft, leading the late General von Senger und Etterlin to complain about 'the British shortfall in attack and transport helicopters'.[14]

Future Equipment

Our helicopter force does not offer the scope for 'rationalisation' which can be found in the FLA field. Helicopters are roughly divided for convenience into very heavy types, such as the Soviet Mi-26,

PLATE 8.2. The EH-101 helicopter will replace the Royal Navy's Sea Kings and Lynxes and the Royal Air Force's Puma transports. *(Photo: courtesy of Westland Helicopters.)*

medium support helicopters (MSH) of about 13 tons, such as Chinook, light support helicopters (LSH) of about 9 tons, and light battlefield helicopters. Looking at these categories, a strong case could be made for having a small number of heavy helicopters but we are unlikely to procure them and the problem devolves into the correct mix of the other types. The Chinook and Lynx will remain into the next century and some naval Lynxes may become available to the army to supplement the EH-101, which we have now decided to produce for troop transport. In its utility version, the EH-101 should be able to carry a 6,000 lb payload and either between 20 and 30 fully- equipped troops or two Landrovers.[15] It will have a cruise speed of some 160 knots and endurance of more than four hours. The EH-101 will replace the Puma in its current roles and the Puma will take over the functions of the older Wessex.

As far as future helicopter equipment is concerned, clearly, in an ideal world, even transport helicopters should be armed, otherwise they will be regarded as easy targets for enemy aircraft or for ground fire. Whenever possible, they should be protected by fixed wing aircraft in the combat zone but this is not always feasible; there are occasions when helicopters can fly and fixed wing aircraft cannot or when the fighters will have other roles to attend to. In its 'out of area' operations in Malaysia and Aden, Britain was fortunate that its support helicopters did not have to face hand-held anti-aircraft missiles. In future operations of this sort we could expect much more sophisticated opposition from the ground, if not from the air. Some 4,500 helicopters were destroyed during the Vietnam War, though by no means all the damage was the result of enemy fire.[16] Nevertheless, the war showed that support helicopters cannot keep out of the way of enemy ground fire if they are to evacuate casualties or to resupply troops.[17] Similarly, press reports suggest that the Soviets are losing many Hinds and other helicopters to Stinger missiles in Afghanistan, even though most of their helicopters, including the Hound and Hook types, are armed.[18] Already they have modified both their tactics and their equipment to meet the threat and it will be extremely interesting to see how their future helicopter operations are influenced by their experience in Central Asia.[19] What one *can* say is that, apart from some armament, at the very least helicopters need a comprehensive warning system to show them when they are under threat from radar guided weapons and should take evasive action.

There has been some uncertainty about whether transport helicopters would need to carry underslung loads. Such loads would make them far more vulnerable, because they would have to fly higher, and perhaps jettison the loads, if threatened. Yet it is surely wise to give them the capability. Nobody expected the Belvedere to take 105 mm guns up into the Radfan mountains but that is what they had to do. Conversely, worrying too much about designing helicopters to carry stretchers may be too great a luxury. It is most important to rush the casualties from the battlefield as quickly as possible; how they are carried is less important. After all, many lives were saved in Malaya by carrying stretchers on the outside of the Dragonfly.

For operations out of area one would ideally have helicopters that could be carried in Hercules or at least FIMA-sized aircraft. Currently the Puma can be carried in a C-130 and the Chinook in a Belfast — though with some difficulty. The EH-101 will not be so readily transportable as the Puma, or as the Blackhawk would have been, had we ordered it. Of course it is possible for helicopters to ferry themselves over long distances with extra tanks or even refuelling from aircraft. Nevertheless on many occasions when we have to respond quickly out of area in the future we may find ourselves relying on Lynx or Puma helicopters transported by aircraft.

Conclusion

It would be extremely unwise to undervalue the importance of fixed and rotary wing transport aircraft. Our next military operations will almost certainly be outside Europe, as we can expect order to deteriorate in parts of the Third World over the next 20 years. Our ability to use military tankers and transports in order to rush troops rapidly to friendly countries outside Europe, to evacuate British citizens or to encourage stability by sending supplies to stricken areas is certainly of great value. It does not detract from the more vital but less immediate requirements within Europe. NATO as a whole needs to co-operate in order to produce a Transall-Hercules replacement for the year 2000. As far as support helicopters are concerned, every war underlines their importance for mobility, their vulnerability and thus the need for greater numbers.

NOTES

1. 'Growing trade with partners in Europe', *The Times*, 4 February 1987 and 'Invisibles close Britain's £835 million trade gap', *Daily Telegraph*, 26 November 1986.
2. 'Slowdown in world population,' *The Times*, 13 June 1984; 'Population crisis unites nations', *The Times*, 17 August 1984. See also Robert Fisk, 'Rise of the insatiable mega-city', *The Times*, 4 July 1986.
3. 'World's air forces', *Flight International*, 29 November 1986, p. 55
4. J. S. Ballard. *Development and Employment of Fixed Wing Gunships, 1962–1972.* Office of United States Air Force History, Washington, 1982.
5. *The case for the C 17: The Operators' View,* Military Airlift Command, undated. See also *C17: the Modern Multipurpose Airlifter that makes the difference*, McDonnell Douglas, undated.
6. *Advanced International military STOL Airlifter (AIMSA) Based on the YC-15 with C-17 Developed improvements*, McDonnell Douglas, undated. See also Colonel N. Dodds, 'Transport aircraft for tactical airlift' *Asian Defence Journal*, 5/1985. 'Still humping and heaving — tactical air transport today', *Defence* February, 1987.
7. IISS *Military Balance, 1985–6*, p. 192 passim.
8. H. James and D. Sheil-Small, *The Undeclared War; The Story of Indonesian Confrontation. 1962–6,* Leo Cooper, London, 1971, p. 86.
9. Julian Paget, *Last Post: Aden 1964–1967*, Faber and Faber, London, 1969, p. 103.
10. IISS *Military Balance 1986–1987*, p. 63 passim.
11. Public Record Office, London, AIR/20/7357, minute of 5 April 1951.
12. Paget p. 48.
13. R. F. Futrell and M. Blumenson, *The Advisory Years to 1965*, Office of United States Air Force history, Washington, 1981, p. 155. M. W. Browne, *The New Face of War*, Cassell, London, 1965, pp. 48–58.
14. General Von Senger und Etterlin, 'The Air-Mobile Divisions: operational reserves for NATO', *RUSI Journal*, 1 March 1987.
15. F. G. McGwire, 'NATO transport helicopters', *NATOs Sixteen Nations*, June-July 1983. See also Lt Colonel R. Canning, 'Independence in Action: The Supply Helicopter', loc. cit. October-November 1983; A. W. Hall, 'Battlefield mobility',

Aviation News, 19 October–1 November 1984. For the British decision to buy EH 101 utility aircraft see 'Younger bails out Westland', *The Times*, 10 April 1987, 'EH-101 helicopter rolled out', *Aviation Week and Space Technology*, 13 April 1987 and 'EH-101', *Defence*, June 1987. For the history of the EH-101 decision see L. Freedman's article in *International Affairs, Winter 1986–7*.

16. M. J. Armitage and R. A. Mason, *Air Power in the Nuclear Age, 1945–1984*, Macmillan, London, 1985, pp. 92 and 113.
17. For a vivid account of helicopter operations in Vietnam see Robert Mason, *Chickenhawk*, Penguin, New York, 1984.
18. 'Thirty die as Afghans down plane', *The Times* 10 February 1987.
19. Lieutenant Colonel D. R. Nelson, 'Soviet air power; tactics and weapons used in Afghanistan *Air University Review*, January–February 1985, p. 34. See also John Gunston, 'Special Report: Afghan War', *Aviation Week and Space Technology*, 29 October 1984.

MARITIME AIR POWER AFTER THE YEAR 2000
Air Marshal Sir Barry Duxbury, KCB, CBE, RAF

In discussing maritime air power, I will focus on shore-based air power since Admiral Ben Bathurst will be discussing organic aircraft and systems. I will also exclude out of area operations and concentrate upon the NATO Scene — but let me say that if we can cope with that, it is my belief that we should be able to cope anywhere — with two caveats: firstly, we would need sound intelligence, and secondly we must not become too dependent on main base facilities.

In order to develop my theme, I would like to recall some current maritime concepts in a NATO/WP setting. Let me concentrate on the Kola Peninsula and the Barents Sea, which are the home of the Soviet Northern Fleet. What threats do the Soviets fear in these northern waters? Setting aside the threat from the ICBMs, they see themselves faced with submarine and air-launched cruise missiles and by manned bombers which can strike the Soviet homeland from over the Pole. There is also the NATO Striking Fleet Atlantic (STRIKFLTLANT) poised to frustrate their offensive in North Norway.

These northern waters are also more and more the area where Soviet ballistic-missile-firing submarines (SSBNs) are deployed. The Soviets must see an overriding need to control the Barents Sea. It is my belief that the future Soviet fixed-wing aircraft carriers and nuclear powered cruisers will be designed and used to extend air defences to counter the perceived threat and to provide an umbrella to protect their SSBN fleet: the so-called bastion defence concept. In addition, they see the need to deny the North Norwegian Sea to NATO's Striking Fleet, and would also wish to maintain an ability to threaten NATO's sea lines of communication in the Atlantic, which are absolutely vital to the United States reinforcement of Europe, since 90 per cent of all the reinforcement equipment and stores must come by sea.

What then of NATO's maritime strategy, to which the United Kingdom forces contribute? As a defensive alliance, our foremost concern must be to provide adequate deterrence. It is in NATO's interest to ensure that our military strategy continues to pose potential threats in the far North, so that the Soviets are forced to continue with bastion defence. We *must* keep Soviet submarine effort concentrated as far north as possible, not least because NATO may not have enough anti-submarine effort available to cover both northern waters and the Atlantic concurrently. In this respect, protection of our sea lines of communication should start far forward and east of the North Cape. We must retain the capability to deploy our forces forward and, in particular, aim to get our anti-submarine forces and the United States Striking Fleet and its supporting units into the Norwegian Sea as early as we can. Should the carriers be delayed (and United States Navy Secretary Lehman has reminded us of American commitments outside the NATO area) then the in-theatre forces would initially need to hold the fort. The SSGNs, SSNs and SSBNs must be detected, marked and attacked in the North.

With that background, I will now address some of the factors which will affect maritime air power of the future. I cannot stress too much the importance of Information Technology (IT) which should spawn the future generations of C^3I systems. Here, fusion of the surveillance product from satellite and other strategic systems with that from tactical sensors should be possible. We can expect to have to cope with the impact of stealth technology, not only on aircraft, but on ships and submarines as well. We must not forget that many of today's platforms will still be in use in the year 2000, although I hope my current fleet of Nimrods and Buccaneers will not be around much beyond then. As for the Nimrod replacement, I see the prospect of more collaboration in procurement and better, more cohesive, Alliance force planning as an influence on our selection. We should not go it alone.

I have already mentioned the importance of the Norwegian Sea to both NATO and the Warsaw Pact. Both will appreciate the vital importance of securing a favourable air situation. Soon, big improvements will have been completed to the air defences of Iceland and the United Kingdom. AEW will, of course, be further augmented by the British and French buys of E-3 aircraft and — suitably updated — they should operate effectively well into the next century. The punch will be provided by tanker-supported Tornado F-3s from Britain, by F-15s from Iceland and — to a certain extent — by F-16s based in Norway. From a Royal Air Force perspective, I do not believe CINCUKAIR would mind me saying that he seldom differentiates between the air defence of the Fleet and that of the United Kingdom itself; indeed we have come a long way in integrated air defence. Naval units with an AD capability are regularly integrated into the UKADR, and procedures exist to use Striking Fleet aircraft or to provide shore based Air Defence of the Striking Fleet, for example, in adverse deck weather conditions. I see this integration and co-ordination being carried further. Even so, there will still be areas in the North Norwegian and Barents Seas where our forces — surface ships especially — will find it more and more difficult to operate.

I will now turn to anti-submarine warfare (ASW). First, I am an advocate of the need for quality in our ASW systems; at the end of the day, I believe this to be more important than quantity. It would be false economy for us to abandon our hard won technical edge in favour of more numerous but less capable platforms. Secondly, it is clear that there will be a wide range of future options for both active and passive detection systems. I have no doubt that submarines will continue to reduce their noise levels and we will need continuously to improve our acoustic systems. Personally, I am convinced that passive acoustic detection systems will still be viable well beyond 2000, despite the current view that we must move increasingly to active and non-acoustic systems. My third point concerns Research and Development. All our vital passive acoustic systems depend on advanced digital signal processing techniques. Put another way, there is a very large customer base. The need for us to continue to make the best use of our pool of knowledge and R&D between Services and nations is obvious. This is especially important in the face of the extensive Soviet effort and investment in quietening and in mastering the ocean environment.

Although the Soviet Navy is primarily a land-based air and submarine force, the Russians are expected to continue to build impressive surface combatants. Overall, the numbers can be expected to have declined by the turn of the century as the older, smaller destroyers and frigates are replaced by the newer, larger and more capable cruisers and destroyers. However, we can expect them to be operating perhaps two large aircraft carriers by then. As I suggested earlier, I expect the Soviet surface fleet, despite its peacetime blue water role, to be used primarily in defence of the homeland in time of war and particularly in support of their submarines. Soviet writings have frequently criticised the German failure to support their submarines as a major reason for the U-boat defeat in World War Two. I anticipate that the Soviet surface fleet is most likely to operate in large, mutually supportive groups, and predominantly in the far North. In any conflict, we must retain the capability quickly to dispose of this surface threat.

Our submarines will continue to be the only platforms which are able to operate continuously under hostile air defence — and I certainly expect them to be deployed well forward. However, only aircraft can be sure of bringing sufficient weight of near-simultaneous attack against large Surface Action Groups to clinch success. Ideally, the Soviet units should be faced with a multiple threat from both below and above the surface but we should not be obsessed by the need to *kill* the high value units.

What maritime force mix, then, can we foresee? We should remember that distances are huge in maritime warfare. The battle will have to be fought above, on and below the waves and there will be no clear cut demarcation between friendly or enemy territory — no Forward Edge of the Battle Area. The arguments for submarines, both nuclear and conventionally propelled, are powerful and persuasive. Their long patrol times, their covertness and their ability to operate against both ships and other submarines, and in concert with aircraft, do not need much restatement here. Ships contribute to command and control and, with towed arrays, perform as area search platforms, and provide local anti-ship missile defence. They can give continuity to ASW patrols and act as mother to ASW and AEW helicopters. Regrettably, they and their logistic tail are vulnerable to both submarine and air attacks. Neither ships nor submarines can necessarily prosecute their own long-range submarine detections, and both will need the support of maritime patrol aircraft (MPA) to localise and attack many of their contacts. Of course, MPA also have an important autonomous search capability in their own right, a role which will continue to be just as important in peacetime as well as in transition to war for surveillance and intelligence gathering. We will continue to need shore-based aircraft for air defence, as well as aircraft capable of delivering high numbers of sophisticated anti-ship missiles.

At this point, let me draw attention to the significance of air-to-air refuelling in maritime warfare. The Falklands conflict and the American raid on Libya demonstrated the reach, flexibility and staying power that air to air refuelling confers. It allows enormous operational diversity and, in offensive operations, the ability to surprise an enemy. The considerable investment in the United Kingdom tanker force will enable us to increase the on-patrol time of our Nimrods significantly. Similarly, a single Tristar tanker could support six attack aircraft, out and back, for a low-level attack near North Cape from their United Kingdom base. Should circumstances demand, that same force could be tasked to the south into the Mediterranean or to the Atlantic approaches to Gibraltar within a matter of hours. True versatility — true flexibility. In my view, in any conflict, the contribution of tanker aircraft could well be decisive. I would like to see them being used flexibly by many users

— AD, AEW, Strike/Attack and MPA types alike as a theatre reserve — and not necessarily tied to a particular mission.

Next, I should make mention of the potential use of tactical ballistic missiles (TBM) in maritime warfare. I believe that targeting TBMs against moving ships will remain very difficult for some time and the terminal guidance problems, although surmountable, will be very expensive to overcome. It seems to me that it would make more sense to use such weapons against static targets of more immediate and direct relevance to the land battle. I envisage that the Soviets could well use TBMs with chemical or conventional warheads but, because of their range, their use against maritime targets, even beyond 2000, may only be possible following a significant loss of NATO or neutral territory. My own view of TBMs is that they will not be cost-effective weapons for some time and that it would be more productive for both NATO and the Warsaw Pact to place greater reliance on cruise missiles where launch could be from ship, submarine, aircraft or even from shore. They would, of course, be available for use 'out of area.'

So what do I see as the future aircraft requirements for both ASW and ASUW? Indeed, will it be possible to combine both roles in a new maritime patrol aircraft (which might still be in service in 2050!)? There are good arguments to retain a semi-agile aircraft of the Buccaneer/ Tornado type whose speed, profile and performance would give it an excellent chance of weapon delivery and survival for re-attack as well as greater flexibility as the scene changes in its long life. Such aircraft would certainly be less vulnerable than the relatively slow MPA. On the other hand, fighter-type aircraft would carry fewer missiles and will probably continue to need attack direction or targeting information from the MPA or AEW aircraft anyway. It is my view that increasingly, we must train and equip our crews and aircraft for more than one task. I would be inclined to keep my options open by retaining MPA which can deliver anti-ship missiles but would also wish to have a call on fast jets.

The Buccaneer airframes are unlikely to last, even with good luck, beyond the turn of the century and the debate about a successor will be a keen one. My feeling, strongly influenced by cost but also because weapons will, increasingly, be delivered from well beyond horizon range, is that we might make do without a dedicated force of maritime strike/attack aircraft. Rather we might have to consider using the same aircraft for overland and maritime targets, or for strike/attack and maritime air defence. Clearly, there are risks with such policies, not least in choosing between the competing claims for the services of those aircraft.

Deciding on a replacement for Nimrod will be no easy matter either. I have already indicated that I believe in MPA having at least a limited ASUW and self defence capability but, of course, the aircraft should be optimised for ASW. The airframe might be an offshoot of the European search for a single large aircraft type or could be an aircraft developed in collaboration with the USN who are also seeking a new MPA to replace their ageing P-3 Fleet. I confess to preferring the latter option out of a wish to ease maritime interoperability, particularly in respect of the sensors and weapons — for in these areas we must certainly not let national whims and prejudices rule. My successor, several generations on, really ought to be able to call upon any NATO MPA and turn it around without limitation at any of the designated maritime airfields.

If the features of the shore-based aircraft which will be involved on the maritime scene in the year 2000 are apparent, the overall force mix of all assets which will be required is not so clear. However, while our strategy is one of forward defence, maritime forces will themselves need to operate well up-threat. Given such a setting, only MPA would be available in sufficient strength to begin comprehensive forward operations in the early stages of TTW. Their speed of reaction is also unique. I foresee a growing dependence on shore-based AD, AEW and tanker support for *all* maritime operations and a continuing dependence on the United States for much of the intelligence upon which we deploy our forces. I understand wishes to decrease that dependence — but the maritime scene is not one in which we could go it alone.

MARITIME AIR POWER: A NAVAL PERSPECTIVE
Vice Admiral Sir Benjamin Bathurst, KCB

I do not intend to seize the 50th anniversary of the Inskip award, which handed back control of naval aviation to the Admiralty, to score a few inter-service points. The most encouraging feature of my career as a naval aviator has been the increasing recognition both of each other's aviation professionalism, and of the interdependence and interaction between sea and air power. I am a paid up member of both fan clubs. Nor — for the most part — am I going to make revolutionary suggestions or claims for the future which, however intellectually stimulating, radical, and ingenious are likely to require such fundamental shifts of resources or changes in our defence policy that in my judgement they are unlikely to be realised.

Why am I being so dull and so unimaginative? Principally because 2005 is not far away in defence procurement terms and, to a large extent, the set of moulds in which the naval aviator will operate are already formed; indeed some of the costings have already been made. In the United Kingdom it takes us on average some 12–15 years from the birth of any major aircraft project to the time that it enters service. Thus we will be stuck with essentially what we have now on the drawing boards as we enter the 21st century. Some of our equipment will be new but some will be coming to the end of its effective life. It is only in this band that we have real room for manoeuvre. Furthermore I have to start from somewhere — the blank piece of paper approach is not a sensible starting point — and so I am going to have to make some assumptions which reflect the present projections of our defence policy.

So, from this rather dull and perhaps optimistically stable platform, I am assuming that the basic size and shape of the Royal Navy is much as we see it today. In other words, we shall have a submarine force and a surface fleet and aircraft that fly above the fleet. The United Kingdom will still provide the backbone of the forces in maritime Eastlant. There will still be armies in Europe, and going slightly further afield, the balance between what we do within the NATO area or 'in area' will be in roughly the same proportion as at present to what we do 'out of area'. We will still be a part of the NATO Alliance and therefore will still be looking at developments in Alliance terms. All this adds up to a steady progression or development between now and 2005: there will not be any sudden, dramatic change in the balance of forces.

In maritime terms we will still have our aircraft carriers, the three CVSAs, brought into service in the early 1980s and with a life currently planned to last beyond the end of the first decade of the next century. To fly off these we shall have the EH-101 helicopter, in development now and coming into service during the 1990s. This entirely new collaborative development with Italy will provide the backbone of the anti-submarine defence of the Fleet and will last through until the end of the planned life of the CVSAs. They will, of course, fly off the smaller ships as well, and, for that matter, off any other platform that we can provide. There is thus no blank sheet of paper here.

Also flying off the CVSAs in the early 2000s we will have the updated version of the Sea Harrier, with a pulse doppler look-down shoot-down radar and AMRAAM — a different and much punchier version of that which achieved sufficient air superiority to enable the Falklands to be regained in 1982 and which will embody many of the air combat lessons learnt from that conflict. Plans are already in hand, however, to replace this with an advanced version which will provide a much improved capability.

Against this background, I want to examine the technological developments that may be available and which can be exploited to improve the reach and capability of air power deployed from sea. Many, if not all, are equally applicable in other contexts but I make no apology for repeating them, though I hope to add a naval bias.

Advancing technology will bring helicopters with improved aerodynamic performance. The British experimental rotor programme (BERP) has yielded dramatic improvements, as we have seen from the recent establishment of a new world helicopter airspeed record by a Lynx using BERP blades. Using this technology, the EH-101, an aircraft 50 per cent heavier and 50 per cent faster than the Sea King, is being built with the same rotor diameter and configuration. Aircraft weight can be reduced by use of composite materials and by using improved designs, such as advanced gear profiles and skeletal gear-box castings. Power-to-weight ratios of aircraft engines are increasing at a steady rate, leading to greater payload capacity and endurance. Advances in engine control systems, for both fixed and rotary wing aircraft, will enable engines to operate closer to the surge limits and thus exact more power at any given point in the operating spectrum. This will make a significant difference for instance to the combat thrust available in any fixed-wing aircraft at high level over the thrust achievable with the older hydro-mechanical systems in use up to the present day.

Active control technology, ACT, is currently transforming the way that aircraft are manoeuvred. The advantages are well known but, in particular, the amalgamation of engine controls with the aerodynamic control systems will enable finer control of the aircraft and this will be most beneficial during recovery at sea when precise control is essential. The reliability of modern avionics has dramatically improved, despite an increase of two or three orders in complexity over the past 20 years. This trend will no doubt continue and will allow more and more routine functions to be carried out by computer. For instance, the pilot, instead of having to monitor a large number of gauges to know the state of his engine, will have a computer doing it, only presenting him with vital clues. This approach is leading us to an ASW helicopter driven by one pilot and, in the future, may lead to aircraft with no pilots.

Computer prediction of ship movement may enable recoveries to take place when, in the past, flying operations would have been impossible. Ship stability itself may be improved; this same computer prediction of ship movement in a seaway, perhaps coupled with a developed microwave recovery aid, such as MADGE, and even linked directly into the aircraft's own flight control system, could well extend the deck movement envelope significantly for both fixed and rotary wing operators. Totally automatic recoveries may well be the norm by 2005. An alternative approach is to use a ship-mounted stabilised landing platform. This might be more expensive but would certainly be an easier way to extend our ability to operate in bad weather.

But going on from here, what improvements may take place in the carrier itself? As I have said earlier, I see the general size and shape of the Fleet being about the same as at present in overall terms. Thus we will continue to operate the three CVSAs with their highly sophisticated command and control facilities and ability to direct and co-ordinate the activities of the Fleet. Looking beyond the present generation of CVSAs, further improvements in communication techniques may allow us to separate the actual aircraft operations from the ship controlling the operation. In the past it has been essential to have the aircraft at the same physical location as the C^3 assets in order to make the best use of all resources. Perhaps we shall find it preferable to keep our aircraft in an alternative location — a 'garage' ship concept for instance.

The materials with which we construct our ships and aircraft are also

PLATE 8.3. The improved FRS2 version of the Sea Harrier will enhance the air defence capability of the Royal Navy in the next decade. *(Artist's impression: by courtesy of British Aerospace and Air Clues Magazine.)*

changing. The Buccaneer, for instance, needed a massive undercarriage to enable it literally to bounce off aircraft carriers with almost total impunity. Technology will work here for us in two ways — first it will enable the same strength to be built into considerably less mass, and secondly, through the clever control and prediction capabilities that I have already discussed we shall be able to make do with less in-built strength anyway. Less mass means more range or endurance both for the aircraft and for its mobile airfield.

I have already referred to the concept of unmanned aircraft, and I see significant strides being made to develop the idea. There are tasks which could be effectively done without a crew, for instance, airborne early warning and over the horizon targeting. The advantage of such a vehicle would be that the payload requirement would be much less than a manned vehicle and thus we could have a much more cost-effective aircraft, which might mean we could afford more. Ship attack is much better carried out from afar. Indeed, we are already using stand-off weapons such as Sea Eagle and it is a logical progression to make the weapon go all the way from launch platform to target, so long as you can predict adequately where the target is going to be when the weapon gets there. Aircraft are expensive but, more importantly, are exceedingly scarce assets when you actually come to conflict. Any war will be fought with only those assets that we actually have in place at the time that it starts. The days of lengthy and protracted build-ups for action are very much behind us and here I believe that we can take a clear message from the Falkland Islands campaign where we had a considerable period of consolidation between the departure of the Fleet from the United Kingdom and the first action off the Falklands — some four weeks to be precise. Yet there was very little in the way of new equipment that was used in anger that had not been procured beforehand. A future war will not allow even this period.

So far I have stuck to my self-imposed remit to remain within the art of the likely, but let me conclude by unshackling myself a little from conventional thinking and spending some time outside 'controlled airspace'.

First of all, is the military case for the aircraft carrier or something very much like it going to be tenable in the 21st century for those who wish to control the air above the sea or in the context of their countries' maritime strategy? As a commander at sea, I will still want my air power, I will need it to react and I need economy of effort. I know from experience that I can only depend on those assets I actually have under command at the time. All this points to having a proportion of this air with me on the spot. I must balance the ability to deploy and distribute that air on to a variety of platforms — penny packet operations — with the economy of scale achieved by putting the bulk of my air assets on a larger hull.

As a great believer in the flexibility of air power, I must consider not only the future opportunities for its use but also its limitations. Here I would take an example from recent history — the Libyan raid. I accept the attack criteria limitation on the aircraft embarked in the carriers which led the United States to use F-111s, but also I remember the high political and diplomatic profile and the extensive tanking effort. The American action in the Gulf is an apt and more recent example. Here, with the help of Saudi-based AWACS, a Carrier Battle Group is ensuring 'sea use' by providing air superiority in the area. Diplomatically, it seems to be the only feasible option.

Now if you want to project power, do you believe international sensibilities over such things as overflying rights are going to get less or greater? The freedom of the seas and of the air above, the principle of which was not an issue raised even by the Americans' sternest critics, seems to me to offer an easier domain in which to conduct military business than that over land. So, unless one is going to spend a quite disproportionate amount of time and effort in circumventing such restrictions, I would suggest organic air will be an attractive option. But my point really is that one needs both; it is only the question of the ratio of the mix which presents us with a problem, and that issue I suggest is more a question of resources than of military judgement.

Now I realise that resources are likely to limit my naval air ambition. I've got to produce effective organic air power at reasonable cost. Notwithstanding the exciting possibilities of the ASTOVL programme, vectored thrust is always going to have to trade away some performance and so should we not be asking if we could not, with technology's help, get CTOL or STOL back to the deck in a more cost-effective way? First the aircraft. If I can control that aircraft down to the deck to a more precise degree, at slower speed, in all weathers, then much of the mass hitherto built in to cope with the margins of error of carrier operations can be dispensed with. The technologies to do this are, I suggest, here now — they will certainly be here by the 21st century. Now the platform. An aircraft carrier is steel and fresh air and that's cheap, until one straps oneself down with the C^3, hard kill, soft kill, and all the paraphenalia of our conventional thinking. Technology will allow us to separate the airfield function from the rest. Could our future carrier be to less conventional standards? A combination of soft kill, PDMS, and electronic deception devices might afford satisfactory survivability. Have we really thought out the possibilities that the use of modern materials and new technology could give to both catapults and arrester gear — one wire plus a spare?

But let me get back to controlled airspace; such is the way ahead for air power in the year 2000. In the Fleet we need the reach that air power affords but we need it where and when it is required, not on call at a distance. Helicopter development will produce for us the EH-101 and in the fixed-wing arena Advanced STOVL looks the most promising at present. Those aspects of shipborne aircraft design that some would argue put us at a disadvantage in the past will no longer apply in the future, but then this has not really been a disadvantage anyway: the Phantom, the Buccaneer, the Sea Harrier, the Sea King and the Lynx are hardly second rate aircraft.

I hope I have managed to convey some of the concerns and problems that I feel are important and also to give some idea of how I see maritime air power developing over the next few years. There is inevitably a huge difference between the art of the possible and that of the practicable. What I do know for sure is that producing any new system seems to take longer than intended, particularly where international collaboration is concerned. The seeds of what we will have in the early part of the year 2000 are already firmly planted in most cases and there may, therefore, be only limited room for change.

SOME FURTHER THOUGHTS
Dr Philip Sabin

The papers by Philip Towle, Admiral Bathurst and Air Marshal Duxbury provide a comprehensive coverage of the air transport and maritime air debates. Here, I shall merely tease out some of the issues which they raise, make some linkages between the different areas, and contribute a few further thoughts of my own.

Rationalisation and Multi-Role Systems

Philip Towle rightly points out the manifold benefits of rationalising aircraft procurement to reduce the current wasteful diversity of types in service. However, it is not just narrow-mindedness and bureaucratic inertia which stand in the way of such rationalisation; there are real drawbacks which must be set against the advantages to be gained. Openly spelling out such trade-offs may defuse the scepticism aroused by more one-sided presentations, hence allowing a more objective assessment of where and when rationalisation is appropriate.

Using one basic airframe to fill several roles raises the obvious problem that it will not be optimised for every single one. The EH-101, for example, offers a great improvement over the Lynx in maritime air capabilities, but falls between the Puma and the Chinook in terms of tactical transport, forfeiting the smaller size and greater numbers of the former without gaining the load-bearing ability of the latter. The airmobility trials involving 6 Brigade are said to have shown the need for a helicopter which can carry a whole platoon, but it is far from clear that the EH-101 will be able to carry so many men with all their equipment, particularly if fitted with the self-defence capabilities to protect such a valuable load. The EH-101 may nevertheless be more cost-effective than a tailor-made transport helicopter because of the savings achieved from a longer production run, but efforts must be made to increase its suitability for the transport role without introducing so many modifications as to wipe out the savings involved.[1]

A logical extension of using the same design to fulfil different roles is to have individual aircraft able to switch roles according to the needs of the moment. Such multi-role capability offers welcome flexibility, but imposes severe costs in terms of multiple equipment or avionics fits which may not be worthwhile for more than a small fraction of the fleet. Is it, for example, worth equipping *all* future transport aircraft for possible conversion to tankers, or will some invariably have to fulfil a transport role? Similar considerations apply to Air Marshal Duxbury's suggestion for a force of dual-capable overland/maritime strike aircraft. One *design* may be capable of fulfilling both roles, as experience with the Buccaneer and Tornado clearly indicates, but providing dual avionics and training for these two rather different missions could be a costly undertaking. The peak demand for maritime strike aircraft is likely to coincide precisely with that for overland strike aircraft, particularly given the new emphasis on follow-on forces attack (FOFA) and the possible need to hold more strike aircraft back as a nuclear reserve in the wake of a 'double zero' arms control deal. A case could certainly be made against dedicated maritime strike aircraft waiting idle for Soviet surface targets to come into range, but if a dual-capable strike force were mauled in the land battle, would it really be satisfactory to be thrown back on a maritime patrol version of the FIMA transport aircraft, whatever its potential in the anti-submarine role? Rationalisation through multi-roling may, perhaps, be taken too far.

An alternative means of rationalisation is equipment commonality among different NATO nations. The problems here is that sharing out the work among the various national aircraft industries can be extremely difficult, and that different nations have different requirements even within the same broad tactical role. A further difficulty is often that different nations undertake modernisation programmes at different times, but this problem is alleviated in the field of fixed-wing air transport by the co-incident obsolescence of the Hercules fleets within NATO. As Philip Towle notes, most European NATO members and potential Third World customers favour a somewhat less capable replacement than does the United Kingdom, while the United States will probably wish to make greater use of new technology to avoid difficult trade-offs between payload, short-field capability and the like. Britain should do its best to ensure that a common transatlantic programme is nevertheless set in train, not only because of the obvious financial and operational benefits, but also because such a compromise solution is more likely to accord with Britain's own mid-range requirements than either a wholly American or wholly European programme.

Inter-Service Co-operation

The close inter-service co-operation to which Admiral Bathurst refers at the start of his paper was amply demonstrated during the Falklands conflict, and was one of the major factors making for victory over the much less well co-ordinated Argentine forces. However, the fact that British transport helicopters and most land-based maritime aircraft are controlled by the Air Force rather than the Army or Navy does represent a clear difference from the practice in certain other nations. There are obvious benefits in terms of the co-ordination of aerial operations as a whole, but there are also penalties, which need to be identified and as far as possible overcome.

Land or naval commanders whose air support does not arrive on time will often be tempted to blame this on inadequate inter-service co-operation, but more often than not the real problem lies elsewhere. Helicopter transport operations are planned through a joint Army and Air Force command structure, and if one land commander fails to receive support, it is usually because the very limited resources are being used by another land commander elsewhere on the front. Similar considerations apply to maritime air support, with the added proviso that bad weather may 'sock in' an airfield whether it is run by the Air Force or the Navy. The relationship between land-based and organic maritime air power raises many other questions besides inter-service co-operation, and will be discussed in more detail below.

One area of operations where there is still a need for improvement in inter-service co-ordination is that of IFF. The tragic loss of an Army Gazelle helicopter to a missile from HMS Cardiff during the Falklands war illustrates the continuing problems of relying on automatic IFF equipment to prevent 'blue-on-blue' engagements.[2] As high intensity aerial operations become more and more frenetic and confused, every effort must be made to transcend the separate command structures so that Army or Navy air defence personnel are informed of friendly aircraft movements by something other than their own fire control radars.

Another area deserving of attention is that of joint-service procurement decisions. Such questions as the proper balance between airlift and sealift or between helicopter and ground transport resources must not be neglected because they transcend the boundaries of a single service. Nor must one-off studies be regarded as sufficient, given the changes in operational parameters over time; improvements in Soviet air defences and in the precision-guidance capability of Western artillery and MLRS rounds may one day, for example, make it worthwhile to spend less on close support aircraft and more on helicopters used for the rapid resupply of artillery batteries. There must also be closer consultation between different services in their respective procurement decisions, to avoid situations like that whereby the latest Land Rovers cannot quite fit side-by-side in a Hercules. It is to be hoped that the new Central Staffs organisation within the Ministry of Defence will facilitate such co-ordinated procurement, and will be able to avoid the log-rolling compromises which characterise American inter-service politics.

Maritime Air: Land-based or Sea-based?

Both Admiral Bathurst and Air Marshal Duxbury rightly state that there must be a balanced mix of land-based and sea-based maritime aircraft, but a question remains as to where this balance should be struck. Helicopters must naturally fly from ships themselves, and long-range maritime patrol aircraft from airfields on land, but in the realm of fighters and strike aircraft both solutions are possible and one must decide whether the current mix is the optimal one.

In the Falklands War, sea-based aircraft defeated a land-based air threat despite the added vulnerabilities which flowed from conducting an amphibious landing, but it is far from clear that the Royal Navy could see off the much more sophisticated Soviet air threat, despite the added capability gained from airborne early warning helicopters. The Falklands experience itself obviously highlights the need for organic maritime air power, but if force planning is instead to be driven by European contingencies, then few areas of ocean lie outside the range of land-based fighters and strike aircraft, provided that Allied bases are available and air-to-air refuelling is employed. Would greater investment in land-based aircraft be a better bet than the extremely expensive option of basing more aircraft (of necessarily limited capability) at sea?

The important distinction seems to lie between offence and defence. Land-based aircraft cannot provide continuous, reliable fighter cover over a convoy or task group against a threat which might materialise at any time, whereas, with adequate warning, improved Sea Harriers can perform such a role even from 'deck alert'. On the other hand, when land-based aircraft hold the initiative, they may conduct strikes against surface targets or escort maritime patrol aircraft in a considerably more cost-effective way than sea-based units. Thus, since what matters is whether friendly naval units need continuous protection, the question of the correct balance between land-based and sea-based air assets depends on the larger issue of whether all the roles played by surface warships and transports are so vital that it is worth spending large resources to defend them. Whatever one's conclusion, there is more of a case for Britain to base fighters than to base strike aircraft on carriers, but the irony is that the maritime strike role is becoming less demanding thanks to stand-off weapons, and so can be tacked on to Sea Harrier capabilities, whereas the primary interceptor role involves 'big league' contests like that between the Backfire and Tomcat, in which Britain's small carriers may find it harder and harder to maintain a meaningful stake.

Out of Area Operations

British force planning now depends almost exclusively on European contingencies, but (partly because of the successful maintenance of deterrence in Europe) Philip Towle is probably right when he says that our next actual military operation will almost certainly be 'out of area'. Many have argued that this possibility should be taken more into account in procurement decisions, but even if this were desirable, the question is how to do so. Not only is the *number* of aircraft required entirely scenario-dependent, but so also is the *type* of aircraft needed. There are contingencies in which the Tristar transports would be invaluable, and others in which they would be hopelessly cost-ineffective compared to sealift, or of little use except as tankers, thanks to the lack of suitable airfields. Similarly, there may be crises like the Falklands in which carrier-based air power is indispensable, and others in which it would arrive far too late and the only useful response is to stage land-based aircraft to friendly airbases. It is true to say that the less capabilities Britain has, the less crises in which she will be able to offer a satisfactory response, but this is hardly a useful guide as to priorities.

The problem with 'out-of-area' operations is akin to that of Brer Rabbit facing the Tar Baby — interventions and commitments around the world may be much harder to disengage from than to begin, and can be an alarming drain on defence resources. We have been fortunate so far that 'out of area' crises have not coincided with East-West tensions in Europe; if the two were to occur together (and there are obvious reasons for Moscow to encourage this to divert Western efforts) then Britain would be faced with the terrible dilemma of whether to send forces to the local flashpoint at the risk of weakening NATO defences. It is here that air power may be of most help, because of the speed with which forces may be switched from one area to another as circumstances dictate. The advantage of the air bridge to the Falklands is not only that a smaller garrison is required in peacetime, but also that the garrison (and the associated aircraft) may be brought swiftly home if Britain herself faces a serious threat. Land-based aircraft and air-portable forces undoubtedly have severe limitations compared to slower-moving naval forces in the out of area role, but it would be tragic if agonising deployment decisions had to be faced in some regional East-West confrontation less because of the inherent unsuitability of air power than because of the lack of appropriate air assets.

The Falklands conflict showed the inestimable value of helicopter transport in 'out of area' operations, and the loss of such resources aboard Atlantic Conveyor was a serious setback to the land commanders.[3] It is therefore a matter for considerable regret that the EH-101 will not be air-transportable for possible 'out of area' deployment, even by the Hercules replacement. Acquisition of EH-101s by the Royal Navy and of a new light attack helicopter by the Army will make several dozen Lynx helicopters available for use as utility transports, but their limited payload reduces the cost-effectiveness of shipping them by air. Contingency plans should therefore be made for tasking the remaining Pumas (which will be sent to Northern Ireland) as the primary air-transportable helicopters for 'out of area' operations, especially since a FIMA-size aircraft should be able to carry them without the lengthy delays associated with dismantling the rotor head for carriage in the Hercules.

Peacetime and Wartime

Most RAF aircraft are (apart from their deterrent function) of limited utility except in time of war, but transport aircraft perform many essential tasks even in peacetime. The Tristar fleet, for example, has to fulfil its primary role in nearby airspace and is also busily engaged in such tasks as servicing the Falklands garrison and conveying fighter squadrons to North America for training. This is one reason why the notion of 'civilianising' air transport is highly dubious — second-hand Royal Air Force aircraft fetch little if sold off, and the cost of chartering civilian services risks making the whole venture uneconomic, even if civilian aircraft of the right type are available when required. It may be better to follow the Tristar precedent and buy second-hand civilian aircraft for Royal Air Force service, especially since the lower usage

PLATE 8.4. One candidate to replace the Hercules in the tactical transport role is the Future International Military/Civil Airlifter. *(Artist's impression: by courtesy of British Aerospace.)*

rates of military transports would allow such aircraft to be kept in service longer than in civilian life.

However, this does not mean that the civilian air transport fleet should be overlooked in wartime as a possible *supplement* to dedicated military air transport. Britain already plans to make extensive use of civilian shipping for NATO reinforcement, and the value of ships 'taken up from trade' was amply demonstrated during the Falklands conflict. Military air transports are invaluable for carrying cargo and for operating into rough forward airstrips, but short-haul civilian airliners offer a very useful way of bringing military personnel quickly to one of the many local airports dotted around Europe, thus freeing dedicated transport assets to concentrate on the tasks they alone can perform. The lack of military aircrew for civilian aircraft is a problem, but surely not an insurmountable one — after all, Britain might not have avoided defeat at Dunkirk if she had relied solely upon military personnel to rescue the BEF!

Given the shortage of helicopters which Philip Towle rightly laments, particular attention should be paid to the potential wartime utility of the civilian helicopter fleet. There are over five hundred civilian helicopters in Britain, although most of them are light passenger transports and such heavier machines as there are might still be required to service the North Sea oil rigs.[4] Plans are currently being discussed for some civilian helicopters to be used in home defence, and although there are grave training and communications problems in using civilian helicopters on the continent, it may be possible to send them to Northern Ireland, thereby allowing the Pumas to return to the Central Front. The proportion of military helicopters based in Britain in peacetime will increase in 1988 when 6 Brigade is re-mechanised and the airmobile role is transferred to 24 Brigade at Catterick; there must be adequate preparations to transfer these aircraft and their associated units swiftly to Germany should a crisis occur.

Self-Defence Capabilities

Philip Towle argues that some form of self-defence capability is likely to become essential in future for both fixed-wing and rotary-wing transport aircraft. Such capabilities were fitted quickly to many aircraft during the Falklands campaign, and seem to have been proved worthwhile in action.[5] The problem is that self-defence equipment imposes costs, not only in financial terms but also by reducing the payload which the aircraft can carry. Choices must therefore be made, and since there are so many different types of self-defence capability available, one must consider what threats aircraft are likely to face and hence which particular defences they require.

As regards air-to-air threats, the main development is likely to centre around long-range radar-guided missiles fired from beyond the protective umbrella provided by escort fighters, and with an increasingly efficient look-down shoot-down capability. Helicopters should be able to outmanoeuvre such large missiles provided they have a radar-warning receiver to let them know they are under attack, but large aircraft may need decoys or jammers as well as RWR if they are to escape. Helicopters operating near the front line face an added peril from armed Soviet helicopters and from roaming fixed-wing aircraft; perhaps the best counter here is not to aim at passive protection from all the possible threats, but to hang one or two air-to-air missiles in unobtrusive locations on *some* friendly helicopters, such that the enemy will never know whether it is safe to press home an attack.

More important than protection from other aircraft is defence against ground fire, given the increasing availability of sophisticated anti-aircraft weapons to terrorists and guerrilla forces, and given the tendency towards fluid land battles in which temporarily isolated ground forces will be particularly dependent on air resupply across enemy-occupied areas. One threat comes from infra-red homing missiles, and future transport aircraft should have a minimal IR signature and be equipped to carry flares, as are Soviet aircraft in Afghanistan.

Another threat stems from cannon and machine-gun fire, and this should be tackled where possible by component redundancy rather than heavy armour, so as to avoid undue payload and manoeuvre penalties. Self-defence capabilities should ideally be fitted for each individual mission rather than being integral to the airframe, to reduce the financial and performance costs which such capabilities would impose if carried by all aircraft, whether necessary or not.

New Technology

Admiral Bathurst is right to point out that most of the equipment for the year 2000 and beyond is already on the drawing-board, and that more speculative technologies will have to wait a long time before they see the light of day. However, different technologies progress at different rates, and it is possible for new components to be incorporated into an existing system considerably faster than a whole new system may be developed. Furthermore, since systems such as ships or transport aircraft which enter service around the year 2000 may continue in use for several decades, possible friendly or enemy technological developments which may affect their successful operation must be considered over this much longer time span. It is therefore worthwhile to look somewhat beyond present horizons, if only to make sure that radical technological upheavals are *not* likely to transpire.

Air Marshal Duxbury is probably right to be sceptical about the prospect of maritime strike aircraft being superseded by conventionally-armed ballistic missiles. Such missiles would be spotted easily on radar and would have to search and perhaps slow down to find their targets in their terminal phase, thus laying themselves open to jamming, deception and interception just like cruise missiles. The suggestion that satellites may ultimately replace maritime patrol or airborne early warning aircraft is similarly worthy of scepticism, since all the electronic improvements in the world will not remove the predictability and inflexibility of reconnaissance vehicles in low earth orbit, and since advances in jamming technology are just as likely as those in satellite electronics. The area to watch as regards satellites is that of target designation, since the arrival of a missile attack may be timed to coincide with the point when the satellite is overhead and can correct the missiles' course.

In thinking about future large aircraft, European nations tend to shy away from the technological frontiers which the United States is willing to explore, and to concentrate on 'proven technology' which does not include the same risks of failure or cost escalation. However, what will be 'proven technology' in the year 2000 when Hercules replacement begins is not necessarily so today, and the FIMA companies need to maintain flexibility in this regard so as not to be undercut by a more advanced design put forward by later entrants into the competition. One interesting possibility is that the wing-in-ground-effect principle, with which the Soviet Union has been experimenting, will prove practical as a means of lengthening the endurance of maritime patrol aircraft, and that this will reduce the chances of FIMA being chosen to replace the Nimrod and Atlantic.[6] Another possibility is that the tilt-rotor principle of the American Osprey programme will catch on as an intermediate step between the helicopter and the fixed-wing transport. However, such radical technological leaps remain unlikely in European forces, and it is more probable that Britain's air transport and maritime air fleets in the early 21st century will look not all that dissimilar from those of today.

NOTES

1. Cost-effectiveness was not, of course, the only reason for the EH-101 decision. There was also the politically sensitive issue of the well-being of the Westland helicopter company. See Lawrence Freedman, 'The case of Westland and the bias to Europe', *International Affairs*, Winter 1986/87.
2. See 'Falklands errors led to aircraft loss', *The Times*, February 3 1987.
3. See Valerie Adams, 'Logistic Support for the Falklands Campaign', *RUSI Journal*, September 1984.
4. For a listing by type, see the *International Register of Civil Aircraft, 1987, Volume I* (London: Civil Aviation Authority, 1987).
5. See Ray Braybrook, *Battle for the Falklands (3), Air Forces* (London: Osprey, 1982) pp. 14–15.
6. See *Soviet Military Power, 1986* (Washington DC: US Department of Defense, 1986) p. 93.

CHAPTER 9

Conclusions

AIR CHIEF MARSHAL SIR DAVID HARCOURT-SMITH,
KCB, DFC, FRAeS, RAF

As has been pointed out on several occasions in the preceding chapters, we have now seen some 42 years without open warfare between the nations in Europe, and we must not underestimate the significance of that achievement in a world that has been otherwise notably unstable. It is difficult to conclude that we would have seen such peace in Europe without the sustained demonstration by the free nations of an adequate defence capability matched by a believable resolve to make full use of it if necessary — and air power is very much a part of that.

Paradoxically, however, we are becoming victims of our own success; the ever fainter memories of the enemy at the gate call into question in many minds the need for continuing expenditure on defence. Moreover, air power is a difficult subject to debate in this context. The land and the sea are familiar territory to most people; the roles of armies and navies are easy to conceptualise and the history books are full of their exploits. The position of air power is not so self-evident, and its short history and the unprecedented rate at which its capabilities have developed have not helped to generate any wide understanding of its characteristics or of the vital part it plays in defence. Forty-two years of peace also mean that we are pretty short of practical experience, and this, together with the unpredictable nature of war, makes it even more important that we study the lessons of history and retain a flexibility of mind for the way ahead.

Rather than attempting to summarise the earlier discussions, I will instead take three threads that I believe are central to any debate on this subject: the capabilities of air power, technology, and resources.

Earlier chapters have rehearsed the arguments for the continuing commitment of air power to all its traditional roles, and for the continuing dedication of resources to them. The division of finite resources between a number of capabilities has been the basis of Staff College exercises and the subject of operational analysis over many years and I would not want to question the outcome of this work. I would recall two points made by Sir David Craig: the first is that our aircraft can be used in a number of roles; the second, and I believe more important point, is that air power is a single entity. It is not divisible into well defined compartments each with its own dedicated resources and with no interest in anyone else's problems.

These points are fundamental to air power. The use of air defence squadrons for close air support and interdiction in 1918 and 1944/45, the use of the Lancaster force for tactical operations in Normandy in 1944, and the use of B-52s for tactical operations in support of the ground operations in Vietnam, while the tactical air was making strategic attacks on Hanoi, are examples of air power's inherent flexibility that spring readily to mind. But the argument can only be stretched so far, and a force will only be effective in a role in war in which it has invested some thought, some time, and most important of all, considerable practice before the shooting starts. Multi-role aircraft are easier to make than multi-role crews.

But the ultimate constraint of finite resources does raise the fundamental question of whether we can — and indeed whether we should — continue in the long term to maintain all our current capabilities or whether we would be better at some stage in the future to get out of one or more of them and concentrate our efforts and our resources on the remainder. Let me say here that we should not assume at this point that we are already covering all the ground — space is certainly an area where we are not well represented and where we have little ability to use our current assets against a developing threat, and as an airman I find that profoundly worrying. But to return to the main point — that of role shedding: we would have to be very sure of our facts before we started to cut capabilities. Roles are like one's reputation; easy to lose but remarkably difficult to regain, and I would offer the history of the United Kingdom's air defence capability since 1957 as proof positive of that truism.

A pre-occupation with missiles was at the root of the troubles of 1957, of course, and missiles continue to be offered as the cost-effective solution to so many of our requirements. The facts are, however, that missiles are not cheap, they only fly once, they are in a number of ways inherently less flexible than manned aircraft, and they are only as accurate as their targeting and guidance systems will allow them to be. Nevertheless, there are, within these fundamental constraints, particular applications for which missiles can undoubtedly prove to be the best option; the final point defence layer of air defence is one, and the provision of an adequate stand-off weapon for the attack of ground targets in a concentrated air defence environment is another. But missiles are not a panacea, and we would rely too heavily upon them at our peril; too many studies have shown that really smart, if not brilliant, weapons are all too often sensitive to the electronic warfare environment, to target disposition, decoys, camouflage and to enemy tactics. And it will not have escaped notice that the two examples I quoted just now are in effect measure and counter-measure; an effective point defence system begets an effective stand-off weapon and vice versa. Neither reduces the need for manned aircraft or makes them unacceptably vulnerable.

The history of warfare is full of technological thrust and parry with only the occasional major step function such as the stirrup, the longbow, gunpowder, wireless, the aircraft, the jet engine, nuclear weapons and digital electronic data processing which changes the rules overnight. But although most advances are evolutionary rather than revolutionary and many of the steps are quite small, technology continues to play the part of the Siren, and it lures us towards the rocks with promises of quantum jumps in capability in short time-scales and, of course, at modest cost.

King Lear had obviously just attended a presentation in the early days of such a project when he said: 'I will do such things, what they are I know not, but they shall be the terrors of the Earth'. Shakespeare does not record what Lear subsequently offered to the Public Accounts Committee of the day by way of explanation of the cost and time-scale overruns, but he has left a graphic description of Lear's ultimate fate, and that should be a lesson to us all, and not one that I would wish upon any Chief of Defence Procurement or Controller Aircraft for that matter.

The problem is that technology routinely offers us two quite different ways of enhancing our performance. On the one hand it offers ways of doing existing things better, and on the other it offers ways of doing existing things more economically; only very rarely does it offer ways of doing completely new things.

Stealth is one obvious area where technology is evolving and providing either more capable ways of reducing signatures or improved sensors to detect the resulting, less observable, targets. Technology has also evolved ways of allowing us to see in the dark, and it is the synergy of night vision goggles and forward looking infra-red that will soon allow our aircraft to operate passively at night with much the same freedom that they currently enjoy during the day and to deny the enemy the protection of darkness to rest, recuperate and continue his advance. The new Harrier GR5 will carry these systems and it is a topical example of a project where technology has not only improved the range/ payload characteristics and the weapon delivery accuracy of the basic system but has also at the same time significantly reduced support costs. It is, of course, much easier and much more economical to build the technology of repair and maintenance improvements into a system during development than it is to modify it in later. However, despite the constraints on the retrospective introduction of changes to reduce support costs, we must continue to be alive to the potential of some of the improvements in this area and exploit them to the full, for they will free resources that can be more profitably employed elsewhere.

Resources and affordability are crucial issues and the life-cycle costs of our systems must be fundamental factors in all our considerations. It is a fact that the initial unit procurement costs of aircraft have risen remorselessly and faster than inflation since 1945. As a consequence, each decade has seen a steady decline in the number of front line aircraft available to the Royal Air Force. The individual aircraft are ever more capable, of course, as weapon delivery accuracies have improved, weapon effectiveness has increased and, in some cases, the number of weapons carried has been greater. But sheer numbers have declined, and arithmetically undeniable projections of the trend have been produced showing various air forces around the world at some point in the next century having only one aircraft. It would undoubtedly be a very capable aircraft, but the quantity versus quality argument would, I suggest, have been carried too far.

As Sir Ronald Mason recalled, it was Lenin who said that 'quantity has a quality all of its own', and all our experience of air power in war is that it is fundamentally unwise to trade too much quantity for quality. So what can be done about this trend of ever diminishing numbers? A lot no doubt, but let me point out two things that *have been done:* better Requirements — with a capital 'R' — are being produced, and much more commercial procurement practices are being adopted, as was explained in detail by Mr Levene. We have already seen significant cost savings as a result, allied to much tauter contracts on a number of projects, and we have seen funds released for use in other areas. But these improvements can only slow the trend down; better procurement cannot stop it on its own. I am very much inclined to the view that a defence review should be accepted as a regular and necessary event and not driven merely by financial expediency.

Future generations of aircraft will have to be more capable if they are to exploit to the full the fundamental characteristics of air power in an increasingly hostile environment. We will also have to look to technology to provide more *capability* — reliably and economically — and we will have to look critically at our overall defence system as it evolves, to ensure that it is not duplicating or overlapping capabilities and that it does not have any weak links. Command and control is always a potential weak link, but it is an essential element of air power. We under-resource or under-protect our command and control system in the future at our peril. Let me repeat that the essence of air power is its flexibility, its speed of response, its reach and its punch. Adequate and survivable command and control facilities are vital to its ability to exploit these fundamental characteristics.

Air power can be deployed over great distances at short notice and can operate when it gets there in roles appropriate to the circumstances. It is central to all modern land warfare and to all modern sea warfare, and it does not recognise any barriers between them. In its very short history, air power has demonstrated on many occasions the ability to respond to the unexpected at very short notice, to operate at very great range and then to conduct those integrated and joint operations over land and sea that are so often a key factor in bringing the campaign to a successful conclusion. I would emphasise the words 'integrated' and 'joint', for they are as fundamental to an understanding of air power as are the words 'interactive' and 'interdependent'. Here, in these words, is the nature of air power, and if this volume has crystallised that in our minds, then it has served its purpose well.

Index